JOE DiMAGGIO
A BIOGRAPHY

DAVID JONES

BASEBALL'S ALL-TIME GREATEST HITTERS

GREENWOOD PRESS
WESTPORT, CONNECTICUT • LONDON

Library of Congress Cataloging-in-Publication Data

Jones, David, 1977–
    Joe DiMaggio : a biography / David Jones.
        p. cm.—(Baseball's all-time greatest hitters)
    Includes bibliographical references and index.
    ISBN 0–313–33022–0 (alk. paper)
    1. DiMaggio, Joe, 1914–1999.   2. Baseball players—United States—Biography.   I. Title.
    II. Series.
    GV865.D5J615 2004
    796.357'092—dc22   2004053049
[B]

British Library Cataloguing in Publication Data is available.

Library of Congress Catalog Card Number: 2004053049
ISBN:0–313–33022–0

First published in 2004

Greenwood Press, 88 Post Road West, Westport, CT 06881
An imprint of Greenwood Publishing Group, Inc.
www.greenwood.com

Printed in the United States of America

The paper used in this book complies with the
Permanent Paper Standard issued by the National
Information Standards Organization (Z39.48–1984).

10 9 8 7 6 5 4 3 2 1

To Carl Scheeler—for Kansas City, Cooperstown,
and the places yet to come.

CONTENTS

Series Foreword   ix

Acknowledgments   xiii

Chronology   xv

Introduction   xix

CHAPTER 1 ◆ Origins   1

CHAPTER 2 ◆ With the Seals   11

CHAPTER 3 ◆ The Promise Fulfilled   21

CHAPTER 4 ◆ Triumphs and Tribulations   33

CHAPTER 5 ◆ The Best Player in Baseball   45

CHAPTER 6 ◆ We Want Him on Our Side   59

CHAPTER 7 ◆ Out at Home   79

CHAPTER 8 ◆ Coming Back   89

CHAPTER 9 ◆ "His Bat Spells Bingo"   101

CHAPTER 10 ◆ End of the Line   115

CHAPTER 11 ◆ Marilyn   127

Contents

CHAPTER 12 ♦ Legacies   139

Epilogue: Making of a Legend   153

Appendix: Joe DiMaggio's Career and World Series Statistics   157

Selected Bibliography   159

Index   163

SERIES FOREWORD

The volumes in Greenwood's "Baseball's All-Time Greatest Hitters" series present the life stories of the players who, through their abilities to hit for average, for power, or for both, most helped their teams at the plate. Much thought was given to the players selected for inclusion in this series. In some cases, the selection of certain players was a given. **Ty Cobb**, **Rogers Hornsby**, and **Joe Jackson** hold the three highest career averages in baseball history: .367, .358, and .356, respectively. **Babe Ruth**, who single-handedly brought the sport out of its "dead ball" era and transformed baseball into a home-run hitters game, hit 714 home runs (a record that stood until 1974) while also hitting .342 over his career. **Lou Gehrig**, now known primarily as the man whose consecutive-games record Cal Ripken Jr. broke in 1995, hit .340 and knocked in more than 100 runs eleven seasons in a row, totaling 1,995 before his career was cut short by ALS. **Ted Williams**, the last man in either league to hit .400 or better in a season (.406 in 1941), is widely regarded as possibly the best hitter ever, a man whose fanatical dedication raised hitting to the level of both science and art.

Two players set career records that, for many, define the art of hitting. **Hank Aaron** set career records for home runs (755) and RBIs (2,297). He also maintained a .305 career average over twenty-three seasons, a remarkable feat for someone primarily known as a home-run hitter. **Pete Rose** had ten seasons with 200 or more hits and won three batting titles on his way to establishing his famous record of 4,256 career hits. Some critics have claimed that both players' records rest more on longevity than excellence. To that I would say there is something to be said about longevity and, in both cases, the player's excellence was the reason why he had the opportunity to keep playing, to keep tallying hits for his team. A base hit is the mark of a successful plate appearance; a home run is the apex of an at-bat. Accordingly, we could hardly have a series titled "Baseball's All-Time Greatest Hitters" without including the two men who set the career records in these categories.

Joe DiMaggio holds another famous mark: fifty-six consecutive games in which he obtained a base hit. Many have called this baseball's most unbreakable record. (The player who most closely approached that mark was Pete Rose, who hit safely in forty-four consecutive games in 1978.) In his thirteen seasons, DiMaggio hit .325 with 361 home runs and 1,537 RBIs. This means he *averaged* 28 home runs and 118 RBIs per season. MVPs have been awarded to sluggers in various years with lesser stats than what DiMaggio achieved in an "average" season.

Because **Stan Musial** played his entire career with the Cardinals in St. Louis—once considered the western frontier of the baseball world in the days before baseball came to California—he did not receive the press of a DiMaggio. But Musial compiled a career average of .331, with 3,630 hits (ranking fourth all time) and 1,951 RBIs (fifth all time). His hitting prowess was so respected around the league that Brooklyn Dodgers fans once dubbed him "The Man," a nickname he still carries today.

Willie Mays was a player who made his fame in New York City and then helped usher baseball into the modern era when he moved with the Giants to San Francisco. Mays did everything well and with flair. His over-the-shoulder catch in the 1954 World Series was perhaps his most famous moment, but his hitting was how Mays most tormented his opponents. Over twenty-two seasons the "Say Hey Kid" hit .302 and belted 660 home runs.

Only four players have reached the 600-home-run milestone: Mays, Aaron, Ruth, and **Barry Bonds**, who achieved that feat in 2002. Bonds, the only active player included in this series, broke the single-season home-run record when he smashed 73 for the San Francisco Giants in 2001. In the 2002 National League Championship Series, St. Louis Cardinals pitchers were so leery of pitching to him that they walked him ten times in twenty-one plate appearances. In the World Series, the Anaheim Angels walked him thirteen times in thirty appearances. He finished the Series with a .471 batting average, an on-base percentage of .700, and a slugging percentage of 1.294.

As with most rankings, this series omits some great names. Jimmie Foxx, Tris Speaker, and Tony Gwynn would have battled for a hypothetical thirteenth volume. And it should be noted that this series focuses on players and their performance within Major League Baseball; otherwise, sluggers such as Josh Gibson from the Negro Leagues and Japan's Sadaharu Oh would have merited consideration.

There are names such as Cap Anson, Ed Delahanty, and Billy Hamilton who appear high up on the list of career batting average. However, a number of these players played during the late 1800s, when the rules of baseball were drastically different. For example, pitchers were not allowed to throw overhand until 1883, and foul balls weren't counted as strikes until 1901 (1903 in the American League). Such players as Anson and company undeniably were the stars of their day, but baseball has evolved greatly since then, into a game in which hitters must now cope with night games, relief pitchers, and split-fingered fastballs.

Ultimately, a list of the "greatest" anything is somewhat subjective, but Greenwood offers these players as twelve of the finest examples of hitters throughout history. Each volume focuses primarily on the playing career of the subject: his early years in school, his years in semi-pro and/or minor league baseball, his entrance into the majors, and his ascension to the status of a legendary hitter. But even with the greatest of players, baseball is only part of the story, so the player's life before and after baseball is given significant consideration. And because no one can exist in a vacuum, the authors often take care to recreate the cultural and historical contexts of the time—an approach that is especially relevant to the multidisciplinary ways in which sports are studied today.

Batter up.

ROB KIRKPATRICK
GREENWOOD PUBLISHING

Acknowledgments

First, I would like to thank all the DiMaggio biographers and scholars whose work has helped to frame the discussion of DiMaggio's unique place in the American story, particularly Richard Ben Cramer, Maury Allen, David Cataneo, Roger Kahn, and Michael Seidel.

Special thanks also go to Tim Wiles, the Director of Research at the A. Bartlett Giamatti Research Center at the National Baseball Hall of Fame, and his wonderful staff, particularly Reference Librarian Claudette Burke and Researcher Gabriel Schechter, who provided me with voluminous amounts of material on DiMaggio in a prompt and professional manner. Bill Burdick, head of the Hall of Fame's tremendous photo department, came through in the clutch and provided most of the images that appear in this volume.

I am also grateful to Eric Enders and his fantastic staff at EEE Productions, who provided me with additional material under a very tight deadline, and offered valuable feedback on the manuscript while it was in progress.

My colleagues and friends at the Sage Colleges Libraries have been extremely supportive of all my efforts on this and other projects during the past year. For that, I am eternally in their debt. Special thanks go to Mary Dirolf, Margaret Lanoue, and Lynne King, and the interlibrary loan staff, especially Andy Krzystyniak, Joyce Cockerham, Rosedelia Redwood, and Carrie Will.

I would like to thank my dear friend, Jennet Jones, for her tireless support and encouragement, and for her helpful advice on the selection of photographs included in this volume.

A special thank you also goes out to Edith Lundquist and Maureen Sullivan, who provided me with much needed support and advice while I was working on the manuscript.

David Smith (www.retrosheet.org) and Sean Forman (www.baseball-refer ence.com) maintain the two best baseball resources on the Internet, free of charge, and their invaluable Web sites made my work much easier.

Carl Scheeler, Jim Moore, Christopher Jones, and Steve Treder all shared their knowledge and insights on DiMaggio, and Rebecca Jones offered constructive criticism of portions of the manuscript. Many thanks to each of them.

I would also like to thank my editors at Greenwood Press, John Wagner and Rob Kirkpatrick, for their patience and encouragement while I was working on the manuscript, and Diane Cipollone, whose keen editorial eye caught many er rors and passed balls. Whatever mistakes remain are my responsibility alone.

Finally, and most importantly, I would like to thank my wife, Tracy Jones, for her continued understanding, love, and support, and my infant daughter, Anna Elizabeth, for behaving like a true princess while her Daddy was busy with baseball books and box scores. Someday I promise to explain all of it to you.

CHRONOLOGY

1914   November 25: Joseph Paul DiMaggio is born in Martinez, California.

1932   October 1: A 17-year-old DiMaggio appears in a professional game for the first time, playing shortstop for the San Francisco Seals; he was 1-for-3 with a triple.

1933   July 25: DiMaggio's sixty-one-game hitting streak, a record for the Pacific Coast League that stands to this day, comes to an end. It remains the second longest streak in professional baseball history.

1934   November 24: The New York Yankees acquire DiMaggio from the Seals for $25,000 and five players. DiMaggio will play the 1935 season with San Francisco, batting .398 and leading the league with 154 RBIs.

1936   May 3: Batting third and playing left field, DiMaggio makes his major league debut for the New York Yankees, going 3-for-6 with three runs scored. By season's end, DiMaggio will become the Yankees everyday center fielder, and will finish his rookie season with a .323 batting average, 29 home runs and 125 RBIs, as the Yankees win their first of four consecutive World Series titles.

1937   June 13: DiMaggio connects for three home runs in a game against the St. Louis Browns. DiMaggio will go on to hit a career-high 46 four-baggers for the season.

1938   April 20: Two days into the regular season, DiMaggio ends his controversial salary holdout and signs a contract paying him $25,000 for the year.

1939 October: DiMaggio wins his first batting title, and his first of three Most Valuable Player Awards, as the Yankees win a record-setting fourth consecutive world championship.

November 19: DiMaggio marries movie actress Dorothy Arnold.

1941 May 15: DiMaggio collects a single off the White Sox Edgar Smith, launching his record-setting fifty-six-game hitting streak.

June 29: DiMaggio extends his hitting streak to forty-two games, establishing a new American League record.

July 2: DiMaggio homers off Boston Red Sox pitcher Dick Newsome, extending the streak to a major league record forty-five games.

July 17: DiMaggio's hitting streak ends at fifty-six games, as he goes 0-for-3, with Cleveland third baseman Ken Keltner robbing him of two potential base hits.

October 23: DiMaggio's only child, Joe DiMaggio Jr., is born.

November 11: In a close vote, DiMaggio beats out his longtime rival, Red Sox slugger Ted Williams for the American League MVP. DiMaggio's storybook season is capped by another World Series title, as the Yankees defeat the Brooklyn Dodgers in five games.

1943 February 17: DiMaggio enlists in the United States Army. He will spend the war years playing baseball for the Seventh U.S. Army Air Force Fliers.

1944 May 12: A Los Angeles court grants Dorothy Arnold a divorce from DiMaggio. In the ruling, Dorothy wins custody of the couple's only child.

August 17: DiMaggio is hospitalized for treatment of ulcers. He will remain under hospital care for the next nine weeks.

1945 September 14: DiMaggio is discharged from the Army. He will rejoin the Yankees in time for spring training in 1946.

1947 In a highly controversial vote, Joe DiMaggio wins his third and final Most Valuable Player award, receiving one point more than Ted Williams. Led by DiMaggio, the Yankees advance to the World Series, where they defeat the Brooklyn Dodgers in seven games.

1949 February: DiMaggio signs a $100,000 contract for the 1949 season, becoming the highest paid player in baseball history.

June 28–30: After missing the first sixty-five games of the season with a heel injury, DiMaggio returns in time for a pivotal series against the Boston Red Sox at Fenway Park. In one of the greatest comebacks in baseball history, DiMaggio goes 5-for-11 in the 3 games, including 4 home runs, 9 RBIs, and 5 runs scored. The Yankees will go on to win the pennant and the World Series.

1951   December 11: After the Yankees win another world championship, DiMaggio announces his retirement from baseball.

1954   January 14: In a civil ceremony at San Francisco's City Hall, DiMaggio marries the film actress Marilyn Monroe.

October 27: After a violent argument over her part in the film *The Seven Year Itch*, Monroe and DiMaggio are divorced.

1955   January 26: DiMaggio is elected to the National Baseball Hall of Fame in Cooperstown, New York. He is inducted in a ceremony on July 25.

1962   August 5: Monroe dies after taking an overdose of sleeping pills.

1968–   DiMaggio serves as coach and executive vice president for the Oakland
1969   Athletics.

1969   July 21: In a special vote of the baseball writers, DiMaggio is named the game's "Greatest Living Player."

1975   DiMaggio begins appearing in commercials for "Mr. Coffee."

1977   DiMaggio receives the Presidential Medal of Freedom.

1992   The pediatric wing of Memorial Regional Hospital in Hollywood, Florida, is renamed the Joe DiMaggio Children's Hospital.

1998   October: DiMaggio undergoes surgery to remove a cancerous tumor from his right lung.

1999   March 8: At the age of 84, DiMaggio passes away in his sleep.

INTRODUCTION

I have no doubt that when future generations look back at the best of America in the twentieth century, they will think of the Yankee Clipper and all that he achieved.

—Bill Clinton

Joe DiMaggio was dead. In the early morning hours of March 8, 1999, the news arrived via fax machine at the offices of the Associated Press, which relayed the announcement of DiMaggio's passing, at 84 years of age, to radio, television, print, and online news media throughout the United States and around the world. By the time Americans on the East Coast were getting up for work on this Monday morning in late winter, twenty-four-hour cable news channels were already airing old black and white film of DiMaggio in Yankee pinstripes, while commentators waxed nostalgic about the Yankee Clipper and all that he meant to America. They talked about Ernest Hemingway and his story *The Old Man and the Sea*, in which the main character says: "I would like to fish with the Great DiMaggio. They say his father was a fisherman. . . ." They talked about singer-songwriter Paul Simon, too, and his bittersweet ode to lost innocence, "Mrs. Robinson."

The news of DiMaggio's death arrived too late to make that morning's newspapers, but obituaries and appreciations that had been filed away for years were quickly displayed on the Internet. In their reminiscing, the print media wrote about Hemingway and Simon, too. They also described DiMaggio's graceful, effortless style of play—how, they said, he never had to dive for a fly ball, never made a mistake on the base paths or in the field. They talked about his hitting, about his beautiful swing, and about how his fifty-six-game hitting streak in 1941 captivated an entire nation during the summer before Pearl Harbor. They wrote about the pride he took in his profession, about his insistence that he always play hard because "There is always some kid who may be seeing me for the first or last time. I owe him my best." They talked about his long retirement, his brief marriage to Marilyn Monroe, and the steadfast way he protected her memory, and his privacy, as he aged. They talked about how he aged—gracefully, with dignity and class.

Those words, "dignity and class," were used often to eulogize Joe DiMaggio, and hovering above those praiseworthy attributes was another word that only a few intrepid souls dared to utter: "perfect." For some, DiMaggio represented the very embodiment of perfection. Phil Rizzuto said as much when he explained to writer David Cataneo, "[DiMaggio] shaved with such distinction. It was beautiful to watch. Now it might be flaky to say that, but he was perfect in everything he did."[1]

In the long history of baseball, DiMaggio was one of the few star players (Jackie Robinson and Cal Ripken Jr. also come to mind) who were honored more for who they were than what they did. From the statistical record, we know that what DiMaggio did was considerable, to say the least. Aside from the fifty-six-game hitting streak, DiMaggio won three Most Valuable Player Awards, helped his Yankees to ten American League pennants and nine world championships, batted .325 over the course of his thirteen-year career, and collected 361 career home runs while striking out only 369 times, all while amassing a reputation for stellar defensive play in center field equaled by few in the history of the sport.

Yet because of the graceful way he scaled the game's summits, the way he glided after fly balls and charged around the basepaths, observers detected equal parts art and science in his game, and it was this abundant aestheticism that first brought out the poetry and the flowering prose from his legions of admirers. When DiMaggio conducted himself in his retirement as the reluctant celebrity—reserved, prideful, and careful about how he appeared before his adoring public—those attributes, dignity and class, were extended from his playing ability to his personhood and his very name. As a result, the mere mention of his name in a Hemingway story or a Paul Simon song added a mythic quality whose cultural currency required no further explanation. As George Will wrote upon the great ballplayer's passing, "DiMaggio, one of Jefferson's 'natural aristocrats,' proved that a healthy democracy knows and honors nobility when it sees it."[2] Emerging from a poor childhood as the son of Sicilian immigrants, DiMaggio became something like an American saint.

This portrayal of DiMaggio, both as player and as human being, was a distortion, an oversimplification, and, as such, was ripe for dismantling. As it turned out, the halo was ripped away forever less than two years after DiMaggio's passing with the publication of *Joe DiMaggio: A Hero's Life*, by Pulitzer Prize–winning author Richard Ben Cramer. The book rocketed to the top of the bestseller lists with its sordid portrayal of DiMaggio as a greedy, self-absorbed man who verbally and physically abused his two wives, ignored his only son, and surrounded himself with only those souls servile enough to do whatever he asked of them, expecting nothing in return. Beyond the platitudes about grace, dignity, and class, DiMaggio had really accomplished little in his private life, certainly nothing to warrant the effusive and hyperbolic praise that was heaped upon him in his later years. Ironically, considering the public's celebration of DiMaggio as a man apart from the superficial materialism of the late twentieth century, his life now seemed a testament to the contemporary gospel of style over substance.

In examining the life of any celebrity, there is always the urge to simplify a complex individual into a few words that can serve as an object lesson in how we as mere mortals ought to live our own insignificant lives. One could argue that is why we celebrate athletes in the first place, not because hitting a baseball is such a miraculous thing but because the celebration of that act is cathartic for us. And when the athlete's private flaws are exposed, we can also simplify that, just as we might boo him for striking out or making an error. The hero's world has no room for moderation. One slip-up, one revealed flaw, and "Camelot" becomes "The Dark Side of Camelot."

Joe DiMaggio was never perfect. Not as a baseball player, and not as a human being. In the latter category, DiMaggio could, at times, seem like a contradictory figure: loving but jealous, confident yet fearful, arrogant but modest. In this respect, DiMaggio was just like the rest of us, "containing multitudes," in Whitman's phrase. Or, as the French writer Marcel Proust once observed in his novel *In Search of Lost Time*, "we present . . . to the spectacle of life only a dubious vision, destroyed afresh every moment by oblivion, the former reality fading before that which follows it as one projection of a magic lantern fades before the next as we change the slide."

In the steady progression of images that form the life of Joe DiMaggio, we see a shy, introverted son of Sicilian immigrants, struggling for acceptance. We see a young, prodigiously talented baseball player, confident in his athletic skills yet uncertain in the social arena. We see a maturing young man growing into his role as sports hero, team leader, and national icon, while pursuing the pleasures of celebrity life. We also see an aging human being, lonely, burdened with grief, and determined to protect his unique place in the American cultural memory. By the 1980s, the man who had once held the nation's media capital in the palm of his hand, the man who had climbed the Mt. Everest of male adolescent sexual fantasy by bedding Marilyn Monroe, struck at least one observer as "a very angry man. A bitter man."[3]

More than five years after his death, DiMaggio now appears to us as a tragic, yet mysterious figure. To begin to understand the mystery, we must first examine the soil from which the DiMaggio clan emerged: the tiny, ancient island of Sicily, stationed in the waters of the Mediterranean Sea, some 4,468 miles, as the crow flies, from the heart of downtown Manhattan.

NOTES

1. David Cataneo, *I Remember Joe DiMaggio: Personal Memories of the Yankee Clipper by the People Who Knew Him Best* (Nashville, TN: Cumberland House, 2001), 1.

2. *Albany Times-Union*, March 10, 1999.

3. Cataneo, *I Remember*, 133.

ORIGINS

The Negro is not the farthest man down. The condition of the coloured farmer in the most backward parts of the Southern States in America, even where he has the least education and the least encouragement, is incomparably better than the condition and opportunities of the agricultural population in Sicily.
—Booker T. Washington in 1913, after a visit to Italy

Between 1880 and 1920, over twenty-three million immigrants arrived in the United States, an influx of human cargo utterly unprecedented in the history of the world. More than four million of the new arrivals came from Italy, making that nation the single largest contributor to the so-called "Second Wave" of immigration. Of those four million, most came from the Mezzogiorno, the southern part of the country, and in particular, from the island of Sicily, an expanse of land approximately the size of the state of Maryland, nestled between the Tyrrhenian Sea to the North, the Ionian Sea to the East, and the Mediterranean Sea to the South and West.

Located at the nexus of three continents, Sicily became a prized possession in the geographic tug and pull for world hegemony. Beginning with the Roman conquest in 241 B.C., the island fell under the control of a series of foreign powers utterly indifferent to the fortunes of Sicily's fishermen and farmers, from the despotic rule of Frederick II to the corrupt reign of the Spanish Bourbons. Though King Victor Emmanuel united Sicily with the Italian mainland in 1861, bitter parochialism divided the fledgling nation. United in name only, North-

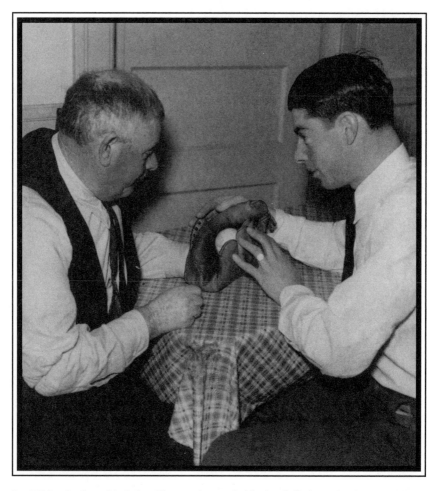

Joe DiMaggio shows his father Giuseppe how to hold a baseball glove. *San Francisco History Center, San Francisco public library.*

ern Italians tended to view the Mezzogiorno, and Sicily in particular, with its mixture of Spanish, Arabian, Italian, Carthaginian, and African bloods, as a sort of bastard child of Italy, "a ball of lead at our feet," as one government official observed, alluding to Sicily's geographic relationship to the boot-shaped mainland. With most of Sicily's population denied the right to vote, the more affluent, property-owning North dominated parliament, and subjected the Mezzogiorno to a tax burden disproportionate to its limited financial resources, while mandating that all its young men serve in the armed forces. Ruthlessly exploited, Sicily descended into the state of abject poverty that would so shock Booker T. Washington in the twentieth century. As historians Jerre Mangione and Ben Morreale describe it, most Sicilians lived in single-story huts, with entire families crowded together with mules, chickens, and pigs. Because there was no plumbing, "children defecated and urinated in the streets. At night, urinals and pots were emptied into those same streets."[1] Epidemics of cholera, malaria, and other infectious diseases were rampant.

Making matters even worse for the average Sicilian was the emergence of the infamous Mafioso. Though instrumental in ousting the Spaniards from the island, in the decades after the revolution the mafia established an extensive network of corruption that monopolized the island's scant resources, enforcing its dictates with an iron fist and establishing a reign of terror. As historian Raleigh Trevelyan has noted, at this time in Sicily "smuggling was everywhere, often with the connivance of custom officials. Prisons were a scandal. The very way the tax system was administered bred graft, corruption and terrorism. Life became cheaper than ever; in two years there were 1,500 murders in Palermo alone."[2] Exploited by wealthy Northerners and terrorized by their corrupt neighbors, the average Sicilian developed a profound, deep-seated mistrust of government and authority, which they would carry with them wherever they settled.

Increasingly, "wherever they settled" meant "anywhere but Sicily," and in particular, the United States. By the last decade of the nineteenth century, "emigration fever" swept the island, as hundreds of thousands of Sicilians, enticed by the lure of ample work and better pay across the Atlantic, decided to undertake the hazardous journey. One of those who left was Giuseppe DiMaggio, a fisherman living on Isola Delle Femmine, a tiny island located just off Sicily's northern shore, in the Golfo di Carini near the city of Palermo. As Richard Ben Cramer notes in his biography of Giuseppe's son, the seclusion of the little island bred into its inhabitants a heritage "of stillness and isolation."[3] If Sicilians were known for their mistrust of all outside authority, then the men and women of the Isola Delle Femmine would nurse that hostility in silence.

Other than fishing the waters of the Tyrrhenian Sea, little is known of Giuseppe's life in Sicily. At some point, he met and married fellow islander Rosalie Mercurio, and was drafted into the Italian Army in 1896, where he served in Italy's losing adventure in Abyssinia. This experience, coupled with his daily struggle for survival on the impoverished and corrupt island, convinced him to make the journey to America. In emigrating from Sicily in 1898, Giuseppe left behind Rosalie, then pregnant with the couple's first child, promising to send for her and the baby once he was settled in his new country.

Unlike most of his fellow Sicilians, whose journey to America would end in a crowded tenement slum in Manhattan, Giuseppe journeyed 3,000 miles further west, to California, where many of his relatives had already settled. An Italian immigrant once described California as "like the best parts of Italy—but without the poverty."4 Indeed, many of Giuseppe's relatives had found in the waters of San Francisco Bay the ideal setting for taking up their ancient and timeless vocation, fishing. After working for a time on the Union Pacific railroad, Giuseppe earned enough money for materials to build a boat and establish himself in Martinez, a village located on the eastern shore of San Francisco Bay, a few miles north of the city. He named his skiff *The Rosalie*, after his wife, and in 1902 he sent word for her and the daughter he had never seen, Nellie, to join him in Martinez. They did, and over the next decade the family grew rapidly as Rosalie gave birth to Mamie, Thomas, Marie, Michael, Frances, and Vincent DiMaggio. Joseph DiMaggio was the couple's eighth child, born on November 25, 1914. A little over two years later the couple's last offspring, Dominic, was born.

During Joe's infancy, the family still lived in their Martinez apartment, which Joe would later describe as "[nothing] more than a cabin." With his large family having outgrown this modest living arrangement, Giuseppe uprooted his family and moved again, this time into a four-room apartment on Taylor Street in San Francisco's North Beach section, a crowded Italian neighborhood located at the base of Telegraph Hill, a few blocks from Fisherman's Wharf.

During the great San Francisco earthquake of 1906, much of Telegraph Hill had been saved from the devastating fires that ravaged the city when residents successfully fended off the flames with blankets soaked in wine. Yet the neighborhood that the DiMaggios moved into was not without its own internal divisions. The first Italian immigrants to settle in Telegraph Hill had come from the northern province of Genoa, and they were not happy when waves of Sicilians began to crowd onto their turf. A fierce battle for control of San Francisco Bay's fisheries ensued, and was still ongoing when the DiMaggio family arrived at Taylor Street. To the outsider, the Genovesi and the Sicilian were both Italian, but even in this new land old animosities and prejudices flourished between the Northern Italians, who still formed a solid majority of the Italian community in San Francisco, and Sicilians, who were regarded by Northern Italians as dirty, ignorant, and possessing few marketable skills—in short, an embarrassment to Italians everywhere.

As a Sicilian, Giuseppe understood the divided world his family inhabited, and it bred in him, as with many other Sicilians, an outlook on life that bordered on the fatalistic. In honor of his favorite saint, Giuseppe, a Roman Catholic, had given each of his sons the middle name Paul, though it is unlikely that this uneducated fisherman was inspired by, or even familiar with, Paul's canonical epistles extolling the virtue of charity. The Paul that Giuseppe knew more likely came from the popular legends that had circulated on the island for centuries. According to one story, during the persecution of the Christians, while Paul was living in Rome, the Roman emperor, believing that Christians could be identified by their distinctive beards, began massacring all men with facial hair. A group of bearded men, fearful of the fate that stalked them, came to Paul and implored him to shave off their beards. Paul responded by calmly honing his razor, lathering his face, and shaving himself. The men, now in a panic, cried out to the sainted man, "We'll be torn to pieces! Shave us, for Christ's sake!" Unmoved, Paul responded, "If there is time and your throats are not cut, I'll shave you also. Eeh, true charity begins at home."[5] For a people who had been exploited and betrayed for centuries, the moral of the story was clear: to survive, a man must look out for his own interests above all else.

For ordinary Sicilians like Giuseppe DiMaggio, earthly redemption, if it ever arrived, could only be earned through hard labor. Rising every morning at 4 A.M. to head out into the waters of San Francisco Bay, Giuseppe caught mostly small fish, earning only a modest income from his sales. "He kept that boat sailing for a long time, fishing every day . . . making his living from the sea," Tom DiMaggio later told Maury Allen. "When it couldn't sail any more he sold that boat and got another." The family's strained financial resources meant that most of life's luxuries were sacrificed. "Everybody's clothes fit everybody else," Joe later remembered, "which meant that only Nellie, the oldest girl, and Tom, the oldest boy, ever got a chance to wear new clothes. Hand-me-downs outfitted the rest of us."[6]

Giuseppe expected his sons to follow him into the fishing business, and his two oldest, Tom and Mike, did take to the boats with their father. But the youngest three, Vincent, Joe, and Dominic, resisted. Joe proved particularly stubborn. For one thing, as he later admitted to sportswriter Jimmy Cannon, he "never liked the smell of the boats or of the fish."[7] Nor did he relish the daily ritual of washing out the boat and cleaning the nets, a task that required the use of an oak-bark solution stored in large vats in the warehouse where the DiMaggio's boat docked, and the pungent smells of fresh rock cod, sardine, crab, salmon and seawater wafted in the stagnant air. It was hard, physically demanding work, and the indolent DiMaggio wanted no part of it. As DiMaggio later recalled in *Lucky to Be a Yankee*, "I was always giving him [Giuseppe] excuses, principally that I had a weak stomach, but he insisted I was merely lazy."[8]

Giuseppe might have been more accepting of his son's aversion to manual labor had Joe not proved to be such an indifferent student. The North Beach section housed a Catholic school run by the Salesian friars, but that order was headquartered in northwest Italy, leading San Francisco's Sicilian community to regard with much suspicion the education it dispensed. The Salesians steered many of their young charges into the priesthood, hardly the most honored occupation in a Sicilian community increasingly charged with anticlerical sentiment. Though DiMaggio did frequent the Salesian Boys' Club at times during his youth, playing football, baseball, and tennis, it was to the local public grammar school that his parents sent him to study the three "Rs." How much actual learning DiMaggio accomplished during his days as a schoolboy is debatable (childhood friend Frank Venezia later attested that neither of them ever opened a textbook), but young Joe did learn to read, write, and speak English. In this respect, he distinguished himself from his parents, who remained set in their Old World ways, unable to comprehend the native tongue of their adopted land.

After he became a success with the New York Yankees, friends remembered the young DiMaggio as shy, aloof, and awkward around girls. According to Venezia, DiMaggio's shyness reflected a latent embarrassment over his family's reclusive lifestyle and persistent Sicilian ways. "Joe's parents only spoke Italian" Venezia told Maury Allen. "Most of the other families around learned English. I think that had something to do with his shyness. I really can't tell you if Joe spoke Italian to his parents or what they spoke to him. Nobody around there could tell you. Nobody ever got invited inside their house."[9]

But if DiMaggio felt embarrassed by his parents' solitary ways, then it was a shame that was projected as much on himself and his own seclusion. As Venezia later remembered, "I was the only friend Joe had. He was really shy then, even more shy than me, and a real loner. If his brothers weren't around, he would sit in the playground and not talk to anybody."[10]

Yet despite all his difficulties at school and in forming friendships, Venezia later insisted that Joe possessed a "keen mind. He would have been good at anything he did. He just wasn't interested in school."[11] So what was he interested in? For much of his childhood, it was hard to tell. By the age of ten, DiMaggio had begun to show an interest in baseball, in all its quirky urban manifestations. Former schoolmates later remembered him excelling at the schoolyard game of piggy-on-a-bounce, played with a stick and rubber ball. As a young child, DiMaggio had worn braces on his legs to correct a deformity, and the clunky devices had briefly left him with weak ankles. But as he grew older and taller, his legs, arms, and wrists all grew stronger, and he soon began to dominate the softball games played at nearby North Beach playgrounds. With a bat in his hands, the very qualities that hindered DiMaggio in social settings were transformed into powerful and unique assets, as the shy, reclusive youngster assumed a relaxed focus at the plate that allowed him to patiently wait out each pitch before uncoiling his long arms and sending terrific drives to the deepest parts of the asphalt grounds.

By the late 1920s, just when DiMaggio was first discovering the game, San Francisco began producing a steady crop of major league baseball players, even though the closest big league city was still half a continent away in St. Louis. Like DiMaggio, Ping Bodie, an outfielder who spent nine seasons with the White Sox, Athletics, and Yankees, and Tony Lazzeri, a Hall-of-Fame second baseman for the Yankees, were second-generation Italian Americans. For them, as for many other sons of European immigrants, baseball offered an accessible route to assimilation in a culture that still regarded Italians with much suspicion. (This was also the decade when two Italian anarchists, Nicola Sacco and Bartolomeo Vanzetti, were executed in New York for murders they most likely did not commit.)

In *Blood of My Blood: The Dilemma of the Italian-Americans*, Richard Gambino writes of the conflicts that often arose between Italian immigrants and their children over the American obsession with baseball. "The pragmatic men of the old country judged this interest of their sons and grandsons by the old standards," Gambino writes. "Could this mania be productive in terms of the welfare of . . . their families?" Before Joe had fully developed a genuine interest in playing baseball, the clash of old and new cultures was already playing itself out in his Taylor Street home. His older brother Vince rebelled against his father first by refusing to help with the fishing, preferring to sell newspapers or work in a fruit market instead. Even more serious, he began devoting much of his time to baseball, becoming something of a legend on the North Beach sandlots. At the age of seventeen, Vince received a professional offer to play baseball in the lumber leagues of Northern California. Because he was still a minor, he required his father's approval, but Giuseppe refused. "Baseball, what is that?" Giuseppe would shout. "A bum's game! A no good game! Whoever makes a living at baseball?"[12] So Vince, in the ultimate act of rebellion, faked his age, signed the contract, and left home. Banished from his parents' house, Vince was able to return to the good graces of his father only after he was signed by the San Francisco Seals of the Pacific Coast League (PCL). When he did return home, with $1,500 in tow, Giuseppe saw for the first time the earning potential of this strange American game. Vince's financial windfall was a shocking revelation for a man who had stared into the abyss of poverty his entire life, keeping his head above water only through constant, grinding labor. And just like that, Giuseppe's reservations about his sons' playing baseball disappeared altogether.

Vince's gamble had paved the way for his younger brother to follow him into professional baseball, but for two years Joe had shown little interest in the game. Indeed, from the ages of 14 to 16 he seems to have nearly stopped playing ball altogether. Perhaps more troubling, he had also stopped going to school. Joe struggled to fit in at Galileo High School, where, as Venezia later recalled, "there were a lot of kids from the better sections, and they were better dressed than us and had better schooling and seemed to adjust more easily to high school."[13] DiMaggio and his friend started playing hooky, hanging out on the docks of Fisherman's Wharf, smoking cigarettes. One day, when an unprepared DiMaggio received a dressing-down from his teacher in front of the entire class, Joe bolted from the classroom in shame. In the end, he lasted only one year in high school.

To help support his family, Joe took a job hawking newspapers on North Beach street corners, faithfully handing his weekly earnings over to his mother. He also briefly worked as an orange peeler in an orange juice bottling plant, and as a common laborer on the docks, but nothing stuck. Giuseppe tried to make Joe a fisherman, but the boy continued to resist. Here, he received some help from his mother, who, fearful of watching her husband drive off another son, sternly told Giuseppe: "He's a good boy, leave him alone."[14] Nonetheless, by the age of sixteen, Joe DiMaggio was seemingly going nowhere. Having already rejected the livelihood of his father and the intellectual refinements of the American education system, DiMaggio seemed destined for a life spent drifting between menial jobs at low wages. It was a hard route to take, particularly in the early 1930s, when the Great Depression threatened the livelihoods of millions of Americans. But for Joe DiMaggio there would be a reprieve from this future of suffering and hardship, in the unlikely form of an olive oil dealer named John Rossi.

In the fall of 1931, Rossi fronted the money necessary for some of the North Beach kids to put together a sandlot team, called the Jolly Knights, that would play in a semipro league. Despite Joe's absence from the sandlots over the previous two years, everybody in the neighborhood knew he could play. They remembered his earlier exploits in softball and piggy-on-a-bounce, and they had seen him grow into a well-muscled six-footer. It didn't take long for Venezia to ask Joe to join the team. He did, becoming the club's shortstop and cleanup hitter. Rossi provided his players with the equipment (bats, gloves, real uniforms) that they had never had playing on the sandlots, and trained them on the fundamentals of the game. Soon, the Jolly Knights became a powerhouse, and DiMaggio a hero when he smacked two home runs to win a playoff game, earning two gold baseballs as his reward.

Over the next year, DiMaggio became, in Cramer's words, a "hitter for hire," selling his services to the highest bidder, and in the process playing for numerous sandlot teams. In eighteen games with Sunset Produce, Joe batted an astonishing .632, earning for his efforts a pair of spikes. With a powerful bat, excellent foot speed, and an exceedingly strong arm, DiMaggio quickly made a name for himself, earning a reputation as perhaps San Francisco's finest sandlot player. By late summer, 1932, DiMaggio was still only 17 years old, but already, the San Francisco Missions, one of the city's two minor league teams, were interested, offering him $150 a month to play.

While Joe pondered that offer, another, more promising one, opened up. The San Francisco Seals, who played at the highest minor league classification as part of the Pacific Coast League, found themselves lacking a shortstop at the end of the 1932 season. Their regular shortstop, Augie Galan (who himself would go on to have a fine major league career) left the team a week before the end of the season to play in a barnstorming tour in Hawaii. Vince, then an outfielder for the Seals, informed manager Ike Caveney that his younger brother could play a good shortstop, and just like that, Joe DiMaggio was in the Seals line-up for the last three games of the season.

By his own admission, his play at shortstop was awful. Though Joe possessed great range and a prodigiously strong arm, he had no idea where the ball was going. "I was wild high," he later recalled. "Most of my throws hit about five rows up in the box seats."[15] But he instantly impressed with his bat. In his first trip to the plate, he lined a pitch to the left-field wall for a triple. The next game he collected his second extra-base hit for the series, a double. Ultimately, those were the only two hits that DiMaggio would collect in his three-game tryout, ending the season with a less-than-gaudy .222 batting average. Ironically, in donning the Seals uniform DiMaggio had forfeited the $150 a month pay day offered by the Missions, as the Seals did not pay him any salary for his three games of work. But the club had seen enough power in Joe's bat, enough strength in his arm, and enough range in his fielding to be intrigued. The following spring, DiMaggio received an invitation to the Seals training camp. He was only 18 years old, but already Joe DiMaggio was on his way to stardom.

NOTES

1. Jerre Mangione and Ben Morreale, *La Storia: Five Centuries of the Italian American Experience* (New York: HarperPerennial, 1992), 37.

2. Ibid., 62.

3. Richard Ben Cramer, *Joe DiMaggio: The Hero's Life* (New York: Simon & Schuster, 2000), 17.

4. Mangione and Morreale, *La Storia*, 193.

5. Ibid., 42.

6. Joe DiMaggio, *Lucky to Be a Yankee* (New York: Grosset and Dunlap, 1951), 45.

7. Maury Allen, *Where Have You Gone, Joe DiMaggio?: The Story of America's Last Hero* (New York: E. P. Dutton and Co., 1975), 22.

8. DiMaggio, *Lucky to Be a Yankee*, 45.

9. Allen, *Where Have You Gone*, 24.

10. Ibid., 22.

11. Ibid., 24.

12. Roger Kahn, *Joe and Marilyn: A Memory of Love* (New York: William Morrow and Company, 1986), 54.

13. Allen, *Where Have You Gone*, 25.

14. Cramer, *Joe DiMaggio*, 22.

15. Bucky Walter, "Down Memory Lane with Joe DiMaggio," *San Francisco Sunday Examiner and Chronicle*, December 21, 1980.

WITH THE SEALS

I soon shall be in Frisco,
And then I'll look around;
And when I see the gold lumps there,
I'll pick them off the ground.
—Edwin Markham

During the winter and spring of 1933, while Joe DiMaggio contemplated his future in professional baseball, millions of Americans fell out of work and into bread lines as the Great Depression entered its most exacting, terrible phase. With fully one-quarter of the working population unemployed, and dust storms suffocating the states of the Great Plains, destroying entire harvests, hundreds of thousands of families packed up their belongings and headed to California, with hopes of finding work and starting a new life.

But the Golden State was having problems of its own. Like most other states in the Union, California saw its once-bustling economy implode in the wake of the 1929 stock market crash. By 1932, ramshackle encampments occupied by unemployed men and their families were sprouting up like flowers after a rainstorm in San Francisco, Oakland, and Los Angeles. With thousands of Dust Bowl refugees pouring into the state, a veritable humanitarian crisis ensued, as thousands of California families fought a daily struggle for basic necessities. "I have seen, with my own eyes, children being fed 'milk' made by stirring flour and water together," one reporter observed. "I have seen families living for a week on mushrooms."[1]

But if times were hard throughout the state, life was remarkably good on Taylor Street. In the spring of 1933, the San Francisco Seals, impressed by Joe DiMaggio's performance at the end of the 1932 campaign, offered him a plum contract: $225 a month, almost twice the standard rookie deal. In a year when the average American earned just $678, DiMaggio would pull in over $1,500 in just seven months, simply for his remarkable ability to hit a baseball.

In offering DiMaggio a better contract than he might otherwise have received, San Francisco Seals owner Charlie Graham gambled that he would be able to auction off DiMaggio to a major league club down the road, and thus receive ample compensation for his investment. It was a strategy that had worked in the past. In 1929, Graham sold the club's best pitcher, future Hall-of-Famer Vernon "Lefty" Gomez, to the New York Yankees for $35,000. Two years later, Graham did even better, grabbing $72,000 from the Bronx Bombers for his shortstop, Frank Crosetti. Emboldened by such lucrative deals, in 1931 Graham tore down the Seals old wooden ballpark and replaced it with Seals Stadium, a magnificent steel-and-concrete structure that featured, in the words of baseball historian Eric Enders, "an emerald-green façade and an architecture evocative of the California mission style."[2] The new palace cost Graham a cool $1 million, but the owner gambled that the economic slump was just a bump in the road. By 1933, however, Seals Stadium remained heavily mortgaged, and, with few San Franciscans able to spare even the twenty-five cents needed for a ticket, the park's 20,700 seats were increasingly unoccupied.

Those empty seats, intermingled with the few fans capable of paying the price of admission, would witness Joe DiMaggio's coming of age. In one of the greatest performances by an 18-year-old in baseball history, DiMaggio batted .340 with 28 home runs, 129 runs scored, 259 hits, and a league-leading 169 RBIs in 187 games. Despite that performance, the Seals could only manage a disappointing sixth place finish, with an 81–106 record, a distant thirty-three games out of first place.

Lacking the high drama of a pennant race, the season's significant developments were relegated to baseball's traditional domain of the day-to-day, assuming forms that were both typical and historic. Entering spring training in 1933, DiMaggio possessed obvious potential and a hefty—for a minor leaguer in 1933—contract, but no clear position. Back from his Hawaii barnstorming, Augie Galan reclaimed his role as the club's shortstop, and with Joe still battering the seats behind first base with his erratic throws, Galan's everyday position was secure. With his excellent range and cannon for an arm, DiMaggio was tailor-made for the outfield, and in the season's third game, he played right field for the first time.

He would remain there the rest of the season, while the Seals released his older brother, then suffering from an arm injury. Later that year, Vince would land a job with the Hollywood Stars of the PCL. For years, imaginative yet lazy sportswriters would claim that Joe had taken Vince's job, but as Joe himself would later point out, Vince's injury virtually assured his eventual release. Either way, no one was going to block Joe DiMaggio from a position in the everyday line-up, not in 1933. Though his unfamiliarity with playing the outfield led the youngster to commit 17 errors that summer, (including one embarrassing incident when a fly ball bounced off the top of his head), he also showcased his rocket throwing arm with a league-leading 32 outfield assists.

But it was with a bat, not a ball, in his hands that Joe DiMaggio was most dangerous, and most memorable. At the plate, he assumed a stance reminiscent of Joe Jackson, who had batted .356 over 13 major league seasons. Aside from minor alterations, it would remain his batting pose for his entire career. "Statuesque" is the word sportswriters most often used to portray DiMaggio's relaxed posture at the plate, and the description fits. Standing nearly erect and utterly motionless, with his bat held shoulder-high and his feet approximately twenty-four inches apart (though later in his career he would widen his stance somewhat), DiMaggio took only the slightest of strides as the pitcher released the ball, moving his front foot perhaps one or two inches, then smoothly pivoting his hips and, with his strong wrists and long arms, whipping the bat through the hitting zone. A pronounced pull hitter, though he possessed the capacity to hit the ball to all fields, DiMaggio's bat produced line drive bullets rather than soaring fly balls, and over the course of his baseball career he would find many of his hits in the left-center alleyways. "DiMaggio reminds you of Joe Jackson," one reporter commented in 1936. "But in his application of power at the very last fraction of a second Joe is more reminiscent of Tris Speaker. . . . How DiMaggio gets so much power on the ball when it is right on top of him is amazing."[3] Such comparisons do nothing to convey the remarkable grace of his swing: though he initially used a heavy bat (38 inches long, 40 ounces), DiMaggio made hitting seem effortless, simply a matter, as Joe once described it, of "good vision" and a "level swing." Unlike Ted Williams, the contemporary with whom he would be endlessly compared, DiMaggio was primarily a contact hitter, albeit one with considerable power. For a hitter of his stature, he seldom walked; he even more rarely struck out. Judging the aesthetic quality of a hitter's swing is inevitably a subjective matter, but DiMaggio's is perhaps the most beautiful right-handed swing in baseball history. That it was so often compared to the swings of great left-handed hitters (such as Jackson and Speaker) speaks volumes for its marvelous simplicity and natural fluidity. Though finished in a fraction of a second, DiMaggio's stroke nonetheless seemed to unfold as if in slow motion—a precise, inexorable rendezvous between bat and ball.

Still just 18 years old in 1933, DiMaggio had yet to fully grow into his six-foot, two-inch frame (a San Francisco reporter described him that spring as "a gawky, awkward kid, all arms and legs like a colt"),[4] but that magnificent swing was already there, and its potency soon manifested itself in historic fashion, as DiMaggio embarked on the longest hitting streak of his professional career. It began modestly, on May 28, with a single in four at-bats against Portland, and ended in equally unspectacular fashion, sixty games later, with a lone infield hit in five trips to the plate against Oakland. In between, DiMaggio pasted PCL pitching to the tune of a .411 batting average. In the process, he demolished the old PCL hitting-streak record of forty-nine games, established by Jack Ness in 1915, and briefly energized the struggling circuit, as fans throughout the league came to the ballpark to see if DiMaggio could extend his streak. "There were people who would go to the ballpark, and when Joe got a hit, they'd leave," remembered Dario Lodigiani, a San Francisco native who would one day play for the Seals himself. "I went out there as a kid a number of times to watch him."[5] Some fans went out to the ballpark specifically to bet against the precocious DiMaggio and his improbable streak. When Steve George, an official scorer for Sacramento, awarded DiMaggio a base hit on a questionable infield groundball that extended the streak to sixty games, a mob of angry gamblers tried to break into the press box. George managed to escape "without a pummeling," thanks only to the presence of armed police guards who escorted him from the park.

The sixty-one-game hitting streak finally came to an end on July 26, in front of a large Seals Stadium crowd that watched with disappointment as Ed Walsh, the son of the great Hall of Fame pitcher of the same name, held DiMaggio hitless in four at bats. DiMaggio's streak fell just eight games shy of the all-time professional record, established by Joe Wilhoit of the Wichita Jobbers of the Western League in 1919. To this day the streak remains the second-longest in professional baseball history, and it helped gain for DiMaggio his first national audience, as the *Sporting News* ran a profile of "Joe De Maggio" in its July 7 issue, noting that "San Francisco fans are acclaiming him as the find of the season."

By mid-summer, all sixteen major league clubs had at least one scout following him, and Charlie Graham began having visions of the $75,000 windfall that would surely be his when he eventually sold DiMaggio's services to the highest bidder. Though such a price seemed extravagant in the midst of the Great Depression, the increasingly flattering tone of DiMaggio's press notices highlighted the youngster's status as a rare—indeed, historically rare—commodity. "Funny, isn't it, that many of our great ball players come from the hidden places," New York sportswriter Jack Kofoed observed in 1933. "Babe Ruth was found in a Baltimore protectory. Jackson was brought up in the misery of a Southern mill town. And now DiMaggio thrusts his head from a fisherman's shack." Kofoed then went on to boldly predict that "you'll be hearing of [DiMaggio] under the big top next season, and he'll be a great star before he's 21."[6] Even old Giuseppe caught the DiMaggio fever. Though he still couldn't read English, the senior DiMaggio became literate in the specialized language of the baseball box score, and eagerly gathered up the newspaper every morning to find out if "his boy" had gotten another hit.

Within this swirling vortex of media hype and fan interest, DiMaggio remained the same: quiet, aloof, and uncomfortable around outsiders. When his streak began to fizzle out, one reporter suggested that he was "weakening under the strain" of all the attention, and that it was only "a question of how soon he would crack."[7] But all streaks must come to an end, and for his part, DiMaggio displayed no outward signs of stress, or any other noticeable emotion, for that matter. As San Francisco newsman Ed R. Hughes succinctly put it, DiMaggio "either has nerves of steel, or he has no nerves at all."[8]

To frustrated reporters, whose postgame questions were answered only with monosyllabic grunts or shrugs, DiMaggio came to be known as "Dead Pan Joe," the homegrown superstar who swatted his home runs and chased down fly balls while cloaking himself in a vaporous, inscrutable silence. In time, this quality of DiMaggio's, undoubtedly an inheritance of his immigrant roots and awkward adolescence, would be romanticized into a stoic, imperturbable professionalism, but at the time it was simply perplexing. When Graham confronted him about the correct spelling of his name, after many newspapers persisted in the incorrect spelling of "DeMaggio," Joe gruffly replied, "Aw, spell it any old way you like."[9] And when the Seals organized a ceremony to celebrate his great hitting streak, DiMaggio's acceptance speech consisted of two words: "Thank you." According to a teammate, he had been practicing the speech in front of a mirror for days.

For his part, DiMaggio later conceded that, during that first year, "I still had plenty to learn, not only about baseball but about life. Few kids at eighteen have the ability to mix with older people and my case was complicated by an inordinate shyness."[10] One roommate's testimony confirms DiMaggio's appraisal of his social skills. "He was just backward," teammate Steve Barath recalled. "He'd just sit in the hotel with the *Sporting News* from St. Louis, checking a lot of guys' averages. I lived with him for weeks and we never even had a conversation."[11]

But during the winter of 1934, DiMaggio began to revel in his new celebrity status, gaining more confidence in himself, as he started dating girls and developing new friendships with neighborhood kids eager to play second fiddle to San Francisco's rising star. Rumor had it that DiMaggio would be in the big leagues by 1935, with the Chicago Cubs of the National League said to be among the top suitors for his services. His prolific hitting had also helped Graham boost attendance during the Depression's worst year, and so when it came time for salary negotiations the following spring, Tom DiMaggio, acting as Joe's agent, worked out a special deal for his younger brother: a $6,500 cut of the payout Graham would receive when he sold DiMaggio's services to a big league club. In acceding to such an unusual request, Graham expressed confidence in the market for DiMaggio. He intended to set a $75,000 price tag on the young outfielder's services, and then let the bidding war begin.

But early into the 1934 season, Graham's dreams of a sizeable payout were dashed, and Joe's hopes for a cut of the final sale were scuttled, when DiMaggio suffered the first of what would be many perplexing injuries throughout his baseball career. Some seventy years later, the details of how DiMaggio came to injure his left knee remain in dispute. According to his autobiography, *Lucky to Be a Yankee*, on the evening of May 21 DiMaggio went to his sister's house for dinner, and then afterwards, decided to board a jitney cab for the ride home. During the ride, DiMaggio claimed, his left foot fell asleep, so that when he tried to disembark from the vehicle, his left leg crumpled against the pavement, and down he went, as though he "had been shot." DiMaggio would remember: "There was no twisting, just four sharp cracks at the knee, and I couldn't straighten the leg. The pain was terrific, like a whole set of aching teeth in my knee, and I don't know yet why I didn't pass out."[12]

According to DiMaggio, he then hobbled over to a nearby movie house, where the manager agreed to drive him to the hospital. But as Richard Ben Cramer notes in his biography of DiMaggio, Joe's story does not conform with the *San Francisco Examiner*'s report the following day, which stated that DiMaggio had injured his knee well after midnight, on Market Street in downtown San Francisco, as he attempted to board a parked car. According to the report, DiMaggio "suddenly lost his footing on the running board, grasped desperately to save himself, and fell."[13] Given the timing and circumstances of the injury, the newspaper story raises questions about DiMaggio's sobriety at the time of the injury, but in any event, the paper did not follow up on the incident. Regardless of how the injury occurred, it succeeded in transforming DiMaggio, almost overnight, from a can't-miss super-prospect just biding his time in the minors, into damaged goods, a promising 19-year-old kid with a bum knee.

Doctors told DiMaggio that he had badly sprained the tendons in his left knee, and after Joe gamely attempted to play through the injury for a couple of days, club doctors packed his injured leg in an aluminum splint. Three weeks later, the splint came off, and DiMaggio returned to the line-up. Though his excellent hitting continued (he would finish the 1934 season with a .341 batting average), his shaky left knee prevented him from firmly planting his front foot, and as a result his power numbers were severely curtailed. In 1933, a healthy DiMaggio had, in addition to his 28 home runs, collected 45 doubles and 13 triples on his way to a robust .543 slugging percentage. In 1934, his slugging percentage dipped twenty-six points, with most of his 36 extra-base hits coming before the injury. With his foot speed and outfield range also drastically reduced by the injury, DiMaggio's ill-starred sophomore season finally ended on August 10 when he slipped in the dugout and his knee popped out for a second time.

With that, the once robust market for DiMaggio's services evaporated, as financially-strapped major league clubs backed away from paying top dollar for such a risky investment. Indeed, the only major league team that continued to show an interest in DiMaggio was the New York Yankees. From 1921 to 1932, the Babe Ruth–led Bronx Bombers had captured seven American League pennants and four World Championships. But by 1934 the Babe was approaching age 40 and in his last season with the Yankees, while another future Hall-of-Famer, outfielder Earle Combs, was also nearing the end of the line. The Yankees still had their power-hitting first baseman, Lou Gehrig, but even with Lou leading the American League in just about every hitting category in 1934, the Yankees still finished seven games behind the Detroit Tigers. Clearly, the Yankees needed an infusion of young blood in their outfield if they hoped to remain competitive with the insurgent Tigers. Though attendance at Yankees games had slackened with the onset of the Great Depression, the deep coffers of New York's big-spending owner, Jacob Ruppert, ensured that the Yankees could afford to gamble on the sort of high-risk/high-reward acquisition that DiMaggio offered.

Besides, DiMaggio still had at least one believer in Yankees scout Bill Essick, who had been following Joe closely throughout his first two seasons with the Seals. Unlike most of the scouts on DiMaggio's trail, Essick had confidence that a youngster like DiMaggio could overcome a knee injury. "Don't give up on DiMaggio," he reportedly told Yankees General Manager Ed Barrow. "I think you can get him cheap."[14] Essick urged Charlie Graham to have DiMaggio inspected by a Los Angeles doctor, who determined that, despite the injured tendons, DiMaggio's knee was otherwise sound. With that medical green light in hand, Essick convinced Barrow and the Yankees to make Graham an offer for DiMaggio: $25,000 plus five players: pitchers Floyd Newkirk and James Densmore, infielders Eddie Farrell and Leslie Powers, and outfielder Ted Norbert. With attendance having bottomed out at 1,058 per game, and with Seals Stadium still heavily mortgaged, Graham had little choice but to accept the offer. The deal officially went through on November 24, 1934.

DiMaggio would later credit Essick as the man most responsible for his success in baseball. "That I got to the Yankees at all or even stayed in baseball," DiMaggio later insisted, "was due to the persistence of Bill Essick."[15] At the time of the sale, however, Joe was disappointed that he would not receive the $6,500 payday that he had been promised prior to the season. But in his disappointment he was hardly alone. With the injury to DiMaggio's knee, Charlie Graham had watched his star player's market value plummet, to the point where he received only one-third of his anticipated reward for DiMaggio's services. All was not doom and gloom, however. To ensure that DiMaggio would indeed recover from his knee injury, the Yankees loaned Joe to the Seals for the 1935 season. Though he would be wearing a San Francisco uniform, DiMaggio was in fact the property of the New York Yankees, who would dictate to the Seals how and where DiMaggio could be used.

DiMaggio's performance in 1935 would vindicate Essick and the Yankees, as Joe demonstrated beyond all doubt that he had fully recovered from his knee injury. That season, DiMaggio batted an astounding .398, with 34 home runs and a league-leading 154 RBIs. He also paced the league in runs (173), triples (18), and outfield assists (32). Though his 21 errors that summer indicated that he still had considerable room for improvement in his fielding skills, Joe had an excuse for his shaky glove: on the specific order of the New York Yankees, the Seals began playing DiMaggio in center field, where it was believed his superior foot speed would enable him, with practice, to develop into one of the game's finest outfielders.

As his tutor, DiMaggio had the Seals new manager, Lefty O'Doul. A San Francisco native himself, O'Doul knew the game inside and out, and would one day earn his greatest fame as baseball's chief ambassador to Japan. First arriving in the big leagues in 1919 as a pitcher for the New York Giants, O'Doul injured his arm, and out of necessity, transformed himself into an outfielder and very dangerous hitter. From 1928 to 1932, O'Doul batted over .300 every season, with a high mark of .398 for the Philadelphia Phillies in 1929. With DiMaggio, the affable O'Doul succeeded where others had failed, reaching out to the youngster with instructive sessions on how to pull the ball down the left-field line. (This lesson was in anticipation of DiMaggio's arrival at Yankee Stadium, where the left-field fence stood just 301 feet from home plate at the foul pole, before quickly jutting out to 460 feet in deep left center field.)

Generous with fans and well-wishers, O'Doul also taught DiMaggio how to act like a big-leaguer: how to carry himself off the field, how to dress, how to graciously accept the adulation of an adoring public. Though in later years O'Doul would always downplay the significance of the advice he imparted to DiMaggio in 1935, Joe rarely failed to credit O'Doul for his helpful advice, noting simply in his autobiography, "He helped me a lot."

As he elevated his hitting to new levels, DiMaggio's fielding also began to draw significant praise around the Pacific Coast League. "You've seldom seen a more accomplished flychaser," gushed Cliff Harrison of the *Seattle Star*. Bob Cronin of the *Los Angeles Illustrated Daily News* thought that "DiMaggio has the strongest and most accurate throwing arm since [former Yankee outfielder] Long Bob Meusel."[16] Graham was no less effusive in his praise for his soon-to-be-departed young star: "DiMaggio gets balls in almost every game that no other right fielder could reach," he noted. "I believe it has been definitely established that he has the strongest and most accurate throwing arm in baseball."[17]

With the Seals capturing their first PCL championship since 1931, DiMaggio was the near-consensus choice for league MVP. There was no doubt now about where he would be playing in 1936. Abe Kemp, baseball reporter for the *San Francisco Examiner*, proclaimed DiMaggio as "the greatest ballplayer I have ever seen graduate from the Pacific Coast League. And I have seen all of them since 1907." During the off-season, the Yankees mailed DiMaggio an initial salary offer of $5,625, only $1,125 more than his 1935 salary with the Seals. Joe rejected the offer, on the advice of baseball legend Ty Cobb, who was friends with Graham and then living out his retirement near San Francisco. When Ed Barrow sent a second offer, this time for $6,500, Cobb, a shrewd businessman who was well versed in the art of baseball salary negotiations, told Joe to stand his ground, bluntly stating "That's not enough," then dictating to DiMaggio a letter in response to Barrow's offer. Finally, Barrow sent DiMaggio a third contract, for $8,500, along with an attached note: "This is the limit. Don't waste another three-cent stamp. Just sign it. And tell Cobb to stop writing me letters."[18]

Joe signed the contract, and was ordered to report to the Yankees spring training camp in St. Petersburg, Florida, by March 1, 1936. To make sure that their prized rookie made the cross-country trip in one piece, the Yankees instructed second baseman Tony Lazzeri and shortstop Frank Crosetti, both San Francisco natives, to escort DiMaggio across the country in Lazzeri's brand-new Ford sedan. It would be an arduous, seventy-two-hour journey, as Lazzeri and Crosetti took turns behind the wheel. DiMaggio, who didn't know how to drive, sat in the back seat, and silently stared out the window. It was the first time he had ever been anywhere east of the Rocky Mountains, and the land he saw through his back seat window was a land that had witnessed the wholesale devastation wrought by the Great Depression, the same land whose once-fertile soil had been choked by the decade's great dust storms.

The week of DiMaggio's cross-country journey was a week filled with ominous signs. In Japan, a group of militarists briefly seized control of Tokyo, assassinating four government ministers. In Europe, France and Russia fretted over how to contain the imperialist aims of Adolf Hitler's Nazi Germany, while the British government announced that it was now preparing for war within the next four years. As Benito Mussolini's armies mounted another campaign in Ethiopia, U.S. President Franklin Delano Roosevelt signed yet another in a series of neutrality pacts. The situation was every bit as bleak on the domestic front, as Roosevelt signed into law the Farm Aid bill, providing needy farmers with $500 million in annual government benefits. At the same time, Roosevelt asked Congress to raise another $786 million in new taxes, and the financially strained Works Progress Administration (WPA) moved to drop 320,000 jobs. In New Jersey, 2,000 hungry and desperate out-of-work men stormed the State Assembly in Trenton, demanding relief funds. Yet during this winter of discontent, there were also reminders that the daily struggle for food extended beyond the human family. In Madison, New Jersey, a pack of starving, emaciated deer descended upon the residencies of Central and Ridgedale Avenues, scrounging through garbage cans and nibbling on bread crumbs from bird feeders. When game wardens arrived on the scene with more suitable food, the frightened deer fled the town, disappearing into nearby woods.

NOTES

1. *Riverdale Free Press*, January 14, 1932.

2. Eric Enders, *Ballparks: Then and Now* (San Diego: Thunder Bay Press, 2002), 141.

3. Dan Daniel, "Joe DiMaggio Gets Two Hits," *New York World-Telegram*, March 11, 1936.

4. Cramer, *Joe DiMaggio*, 45.

5. Cataneo, *I Remember*, 31.

6. Newspaper clipping reprinted in Richard Wittingham, ed., *The DiMaggio Albums: Selections From Public and Private Collections Celebrating the Baseball Career of Joe DiMaggio* (New York: G. P. Putnam's Sons, 1989), 28.

7. Newspaper clipping reprinted in Wittingham, *The DiMaggio Albums*, 25.

8. Cramer, *Joe DiMaggio*, 51.

9. Newspaper clipping reprinted in Wittingham, *The DiMaggio Albums*, 23.

10. DiMaggio, *Lucky to Be a Yankee*, 52.

11. Cramer, *Joe DiMaggio*, 59.

12. DiMaggio, *Lucky to Be a Yankee*, 58–59.

13. Cramer, *Joe DiMaggio*, 63.

14. Ibid., 69.

15. Joe Durso, *DiMaggio: The Last American Knight* (New York: Little, Brown, and Company, 1995), 41.

16. Cramer, *Joe DiMaggio*, 72.

17. Newspaper clipping reprinted in Wittingham, *The DiMaggio Albums*, 31.

18. Cramer, *Joe DiMaggio*, 72–73.

THE PROMISE FULFILLED

Here is the replacement for Babe Ruth.
        —Dan Daniel, *New York World-Telegram*, March 1936

More than any other city, New York had come to symbolize the optimism and decadence that defined the "Roaring Twenties." From Babe Ruth's majestic home runs and Rabelaisian appetites for food, liquor, and sex, to the numerous jazz joints and Prohibition speakeasies that prospered in Harlem and downtown Manhattan, the Big Apple was, as the French historian Bernard Fay noted in 1929, both "wretched and opulent, with its countless tiny brick houses squatting beneath marble palaces which house banks and industrial offices."[1]

That delicate balance between a prosperous elite and a struggling populace, which for Fay had been symbolized by the metropolis' incongruous architecture, would be shaken by the 1929 stock market crash and subsequent economic catastrophe. By 1936, the Citizens' Family Welfare Committee estimated that approximately 22 percent of the city's eligible working population was either unemployed or on the city's massive relief rolls. With the end of Prohibition in 1933, a New Yorker could legally buy himself a drink, the only question was whether he could afford it.

As hard times descended upon the city, so too did the New York Yankees experience their own, albeit far less humbling, fall from grace. As the decade advanced, Babe Ruth the superhuman slugger gradually gave way to Babe Ruth the overweight malcontent, and after the 1934 season Ruth left to join the woe-

A young Joe DiMaggio poses for photographers during his first spring training with the Yankees. *National Baseball Hall of Fame Library, Cooperstown, N.Y.*

begone Boston Braves of the National League. During his decline and subsequent absence, the Yankees still managed to field a very good team, as they continued to boast of having the game's greatest player in their stoic slugging first baseman Lou Gehrig. But Gehrig possessed neither the box office appeal of the Babe, nor the ability to single-handedly lift the Bombers to their accustomed station atop the American League. For three successive seasons, from 1933 to 1935, the Yankees finished in second place.

All things considered, it was an admirable performance, but in New York City, especially during the Great Depression, it was not sufficient. In 1935, the Yankees finished just three games off the pacesetting Detroit Tigers, but still managed to draw just 657,000 fans, an average of 8,885 per game, the franchise's poorest showing in the thirteen-year history of Yankee Stadium.

As gate receipts diminished and pennants became more scarce, pressure increasingly mounted on the Yankees skipper, Joe McCarthy, to right the ship. McCarthy had taken over the New York managerial reins in 1931, after earning his stripes by guiding the Chicago Cubs to five consecutive winning seasons and one National League pennant. McCarthy brought to the Yankee clubhouse a no-nonsense style that rankled the free-spirited Ruth, but that also established a level of professionalism and decorum that would remain a Yankee trademark for decades to come. Under Joe McCarthy, or, as he was known to some in the press, "Marse Joe," players were forbidden to play cards or smoke pipes in the clubhouse. They were also discouraged from drinking beer, because, according to McCarthy, it "went to the legs." (McCarthy's preferred beverage was whiskey, the consumption of which he regarded as more manly, honorable, and conducive to athletic achievement.) During road trips, players were also required to report for breakfast every morning at 8:30 A.M., wearing a coat and tie. A man of few words, McCarthy expected his players to obey orders, stay focused, and maintain a winning attitude. Otherwise, they would be on the first train out of town. Once, when McCarthy stormed into the clubhouse in a surly mood following a loss to Detroit, reserve outfielder Roy Johnson muttered, "What does McCarthy want? Does he want us to win every day?" McCarthy overheard the remark, and the next day Johnson was sold to the Boston Braves for the waiver price.

DiMaggio quickly proved himself to be McCarthy's kind of player. Keeping his head down and his mouth shut, DiMaggio impressed McCarthy with his hustle in the outfield and on the base paths. Two weeks into spring training, the normally reserved McCarthy was effusive in his praise for the Yankees' new recruit. "DiMaggio has everything it takes for success," he told the *New York World-Telegram*. "He has the eye, the arm, the legs. In all sincerity, there is nothing about the young man which suggests any misgivings or doubts."[2] In another article, McCarthy declared that "In the field he ranges well. The other day he made three catches which no outfielder this club has had in the last three years would have accomplished." As for DiMaggio's hitting stroke, all McCarthy could do was sit back and admire. "It would be dangerous, and an injustice to the boy, to attempt to change him in any particular," he noted.[3]

But if McCarthy was somewhat indulgent in his characterization of DiMaggio's abilities, the Yankee beat writers were positively ecstatic. Weeks before DiMaggio ever faced major league pitching in a regular season game, reporters such as Dan Daniel of the *New York World-Telegram*, and James Kahn and Frank Graham of the *New York Sun* were already favorably comparing DiMaggio to Babe Ruth, and pinning the hopes for the rejuvenation of the franchise on his young shoulders. "The excitement created by Joe's arrival here is still present, but is being repressed," Kahn reported from Florida on March 17. "Every one is a little afraid to go overboard on him, because he has not had a real test. Still, he continues to look every inch a ball player and a young man who can do everything. If he has a weakness, it has not been discovered." If observers such as Kahn were afraid of "going overboard," they tossed aside such fears after DiMaggio's spring training debut, when he collected ten hits in his first fifteen trips to the plate. On March 20, Kahn was ready to declare DiMaggio the Yankees top star, better even than Gehrig, who was just one season removed from winning the Triple Crown. In an article headlined "Rookie May Don Ruth Mantle," Kahn wrote that "Now that the Babe has gone, leaving an opportunity for Lou to step out boldly on his own, a new figure, rookie Joe DiMaggio, is swinging up over the baseball horizon and threatening to obscure him again."[4]

Just two weeks into his first spring training, DiMaggio was being compared to famous sluggers such as Joe Jackson, Tris Speaker, Ed Delahanty, and Babe Ruth. His throwing arm was said to rank "with the best ever seen in baseball," while his fielding was also judged to be flawless. In the long history of baseball, few, if any, rookies have had so much praise heaped upon them so suddenly. Yet, to outsiders, DiMaggio seemed unconcerned with the high expectations incumbent upon his role as the franchise's savior. Dan Daniel, who had taken to calling DiMaggio the "Little Bambino," conceded that he "looks like a youngster who rarely gets excited. . . . Certainly DiMaggio is no 'holler guy.' His feats may make him colorful, but his makeup promises no fanfare."[5] In an interview with Frank Graham, DiMaggio was characteristically nonresponsive. When Graham asked, "How do you like Joe McCarthy and the rest of the Yankees?" DiMaggio answered, "Fine." "What did [McCarthy] say to you when you reported?" "Nothing much," was Joe's response.[6]

DiMaggio's shyness got him into trouble in late March, when his left foot swelled up following an accidental spiking at second base. In order to treat the injury, Yankee trainer Doc Painter placed the foot in a diathermy machine, which would apply electric heat to the swollen area. But the foot was accidentally left in the machine for twenty minutes, far longer than needed. As the machine's baking mechanism seared his foot, DiMaggio remained silent, either afraid or unwilling to admit that he was in pain. When the foot was finally removed from the machine, it was covered with burns. Doctors ordered him to remain in bed for forty-eight hours, and not to return to action for ten days. But even after the ten days had elapsed, the injured foot still had not healed itself. Joe attempted to take the field with the foot heavily bandaged, but after a few exercises blood began to seep through his bandages and woolen sock, and DiMaggio was taken to the hospital. He would not return to action for another month, thus missing the first two weeks of the regular season. It was just the beginning of a disturbing trend: over the course of his thirteen-year career, DiMaggio would miss six Opening Days due to contract disputes and various injuries.

But when DiMaggio finally appeared in a Yankee line-up, on May 3, 1936 against the St. Louis Browns at Yankee Stadium, he delivered on his promise, connecting for three hits, including a triple, and scoring three runs in the Yankees' 14–5 pasting of the Browns. For his first game, and for the rest of the season, DiMaggio batted in the third spot in the batting order, Ruth's old position, a convergence not lost upon the legions of New York scribes who eagerly covered the rookie's major league debut. "Unless every baseball man of any experience who has had a chance to see DiMaggio in action is a lunatic," Kahn opined in his account of the game, "young Joe is destined to move right along in the same manner in which he has started."[7] Because the Yankees already had Ben Chapman, a highly-regarded fielder to play center, DiMaggio initially alternated between playing in left field at home and right field on the road. DiMaggio's old manager Lefty O'Doul criticized McCarthy for this maneuver, which he regarded as a "terrible mistake. . . . With DiMaggio in left, or even center, field one of his great abilities will be lost. I mean his throwing arm, which I consider the best in baseball."[8] But McCarthy defended the decision, noting that DiMaggio's superior range made him an asset in Yankee Stadium's left field, dubbed "Death Valley" because the fence in left center field stood some 460 feet from home plate.

By the end of the home stand, the Yankees stood in first place, and DiMaggio was sitting pretty with a .323 batting average. Among the ten hits he collected in his first seven games was a home run, his first in the major leagues, off the Athletics George Turbeville on May 10. By then, word of DiMaggio's exploits had filtered out West, where newspapers announced the imminent arrival of "the flawless one, about whom the most reticent baseball men have become downright maudlin."[9] Out West, DiMaggio continued his hot hitting, pushing his batting average up to .375 by May 28, and dispelling the myth that he couldn't hit a curveball. "Somebody has written, without foundation of fact, that DiMaggio pulls away from a curve ball," McCarthy snorted. "Well, you saw him handle curves. He can hit those as well as fast balls." Detroit's catcher-manager, Mickey Cochrane, confirmed McCarthy's assessment. "He's a real good hitter," Cochrane declared. "I've never seen a hitter with a nicer free swing than that kid has."[10]

All the praise soon translated into extra gate receipts for the Yankees, who would better their 1935 attendance by more than 300,000 fans in 1936. Undoubtedly, some of that increase was due to the Bombers all-around improved play, but the frequent sight of waving Italian flags at the Stadium that summer also testified to DiMaggio's strong appeal with New York's sizeable Italian American population. "Coming uptown in the Eighth Avenue subway," a reporter observed, "one saw Italians, young and old, scanning the maps and asking directions to the Yankee arena. In the Stadium there was a constant round of vivas for the son of an Italian fisherman from Sicily who somehow has intrigued the 600,000 Italians of New York."[11] As one-time New York governor and Italian American Mario Cuomo would later say, "[DiMaggio] looked like an American. He was a symbol of what Italian-American kids like me could accomplish."[12] Such identification was of immeasurable value to an Italian immigrant community still often stereotyped and subjected to racial slurs whenever they displayed their ancestry in a public setting. "Dear Joe," went one fan letter to the Yankee slugger, "I want to stop here and congratulate you for the great name you have made for yourself. You hold a very important place in the heart of every true Italian."[13]

A cursory scan of DiMaggio's press notices reveals the undercurrent of cultural stereotyping that was still considered acceptable in the pre–World War II era. One story praising DiMaggio noted with astonishment that he used water, not olive oil, to slick back his hair, and that his breath "did not reek of garlic." Another feature, printed in the national publication *Life* magazine, noted that Italians, though "bad at war, are well-suited for milder competitions, and the number of top-notch Italian prizefighters, golfers and baseball players is all out of proportion to the population."[14]

If DiMaggio was indeed drawing more fans to the Stadium that summer, it was certainly not because of his personality, which by any measure was far from magnetic. Though he uncharacteristically engaged in some boastfulness in May, when he confidently declared that "I think I can hit .350 in this league, and maybe in a couple of years lead it," for the most part DiMaggio avoided reporters, afraid of saying something to embarrass himself. Early in the season, when one reporter asked, "Hey Joe, how about a quote?" DiMaggio replied, "Sorry, I don't have any." Though DiMaggio would later be known for his active pursuit of the nightlife, in 1936 he spent most of his time away from the ballpark in hotel lobbies, hanging out with fellow Italians Crosetti and Lazzeri. The trio did not exactly make for the most exciting of companions, as one reporter discovered that summer. Spying the threesome sitting together in a hotel lobby, the scribe decided to eavesdrop on their conversation. After a few minutes, the eavesdropping turned into clock-watching, as the reporter began to time how long it would take for one of the three to say something. Finally, after an hour passed by in silence, DiMaggio cleared his throat, prompting Crosetti to ask, "What did you say?" "He didn't say a damn thing," Lazzeri responded. "Shut up."[15]

DiMaggio found a more stimulating companion in Vernon "Lefty" Gomez, the Yankees veteran pitcher with whom he formed a lasting friendship. Like DiMaggio, Gomez would one day enter the Hall of Fame, thanks to a lifetime .649 winning percentage forged over fourteen years with the Yankees. But there, the similarities between the two ended. If DiMaggio could be quiet, aloof, and surly, Gomez was loud, talkative, and funny. Yet, he instantly took to the shy outfielder, or as Gomez put it, "adopted him," and his acceptance of DiMaggio helped to signal to the rest of the team that the rookie belonged. "You had to know Joe to really understand his personality," Gomez later said. "He's quiet but he could be a very funny fellow. I liked to needle him . . . and he could take it. He would never get mad, just look at me and say 'Aw, Lefty.' A lot of people who didn't know Joe thought he was conceited. He wouldn't talk much to the other guys or to the writers or to the fans. It wasn't that. It was just that he was shy; he wasn't comfortable talking to strangers."[16] According to Gomez, DiMaggio sometimes went weeks without saying a word to anyone, occupying his down time during road trips by listening to radio quiz shows and reading *Superman* comic books.

Even as Gomez helped protect the young DiMaggio from an unfamiliar world, he gradually introduced him to that world. At first rooming with him on the road, the pair eventually started living together during the season. Gomez also accompanied DiMaggio to the numerous banquets and receptions given in his honor. Joe accepted the awards, leaving Gomez to regale the audience with selections from his extensive repertory of humorous baseball anecdotes.

DiMaggio was also introduced that summer to another important benefactor, Toots Shor, whose exclusive restaurant on Fifty-first Street in Manhattan served as the informal meeting grounds for New York's elite, from politicians and actors to journalists and sports stars. Over the years, Shor's restaurant would become something of a second home for DiMaggio, a refuge where he could unwind after a game without the fear of being bothered by autograph seekers, a breed that Shor made sure to keep at bay in his establishment. "He would come into the place and sit at his regular table and I'd eat with him," Shor later remembered. "Nobody bothered him. Everybody would look at him, but nobody would bother him."[17] Although Shor loved to tease his patrons (he liked to refer to DiMaggio as "that crumb bum"), he could also be a loyal friend, often going to great lengths to satiate the egos of the stars who frequented his joint. For DiMaggio, he often served as host at his Monmouth, New Jersey, home, or as his personal chauffeur, driving Joe to the Stadium before games. On days when DiMaggio was in a bad mood, usually following a Yankees loss, Shor would deliver his meal to his hotel room. All of these services were free of charge—Shor's payment came with the satisfaction of catering to New York's rapidly rising star.

As the 1936 season progressed, DiMaggio demonstrated beyond all doubt that he was indeed a star of the first magnitude. By the All Star break, with the Yankees holding a comfortable ten-game lead in the standings, his batting average stood at .354, and with 27 doubles, 7 triples, and 11 home runs, his slugging percentage was .637. He was an easy selection for that year's All Star Game, played at Boston's Braves Field, but his play in the fourth annual Midsummer Classic would mark the one sour note in an otherwise outstanding rookie campaign. Indeed, his performance in the game ranks among the worst in All Star Game history. Going hitless in five at bats, DiMaggio ruined a potential first inning rally by grounding into a double play, and then popped out to second base to end the game in the ninth inning with the tying run on second base. But his play in the field was even more atrocious. In the second inning, DiMaggio misplayed a Gabby Hartnett flyball into a triple which led to two runs for the National League. Then in the fifth inning, he committed an error on a Billy Herman single that led to the decisive run in the National League's 4–3 victory.

Though it was only an exhibition game, DiMaggio's brutal performance, both at bat and in the field, had virtually single-handedly provided the National League with its first ever All Star Game victory. And though only 25,000 fans had attended the game, the larger sporting public paid close attention to the newspaper accounts of the contest, most of which prominently featured DiMaggio's failures. "DiMaggio was the goat, with something to spare," Dan Daniel wrote in his account of the game. "He did nothing to help, and something to hurt. He got one error. He might have been charged with a second one."[18] Though the humiliation he endured rankled him for many years (in his autobiography he admitted that he would "never forget it, much as I'd like to"), in the immediate aftermath of the All Star fiasco DiMaggio took his lumps quietly, displaying a reserve that impressed the veteran Gehrig. "Nothing. . . . He never says anything," Gehrig remarked a few days after the game. "He is always the same no matter whether he goes four for four or four for 0. . . . He has a marvelous disposition for a ballplayer. He is the only young player I ever went overboard on. You mark my words. He is going to be the greatest righthanded hitter in baseball."[19]

In his estimation of his teammate's character, Gehrig had hit upon one of DiMaggio's greatest competitive strengths. Beneath the awkward veneer of shyness lay a quiet yet unshakable confidence in himself and his ability to hit, catch, and throw a baseball. Certainly, many players throughout the game's long history have possessed this gift of self-mastery; indeed, such a psychological tool is necessary to withstand the day-in, day-out, up and down rigors of the long baseball season. But few, if any, players in the history of the game can claim such an overabundance of even-temperedness on the baseball diamond. Baseball's extensive lore is saturated with tales of DiMaggio's coolness under pressure, and undoubtedly this characteristic has been exaggerated by some who have sought to lionize a player they perceived as without parallel when it came to matters of grace, beauty, and style. Nonetheless, DiMaggio did possess a remarkable aptitude for maintaining his composure (at least on the baseball field), and this attribute, which first manifested itself on the sandlots of San Francisco, had sustained him during his first long hitting streak in 1933, and would do so again in 1941. Likewise, it would help him to rebound from the public embarrassment of his performance in the 1936 All Star Game.

By the end of August, DiMaggio was still batting a robust .343, and with a barrage of 14 home runs over a span of seven weeks, had elevated his RBIs total to 110. In a more significant development, DiMaggio began playing more frequently in center field. Lefty O'Doul was undoubtedly on to something when he noted DiMaggio's particular aptitude for playing either of the corner positions. In his rookie year, DiMaggio led the league in outfield assists with 22, a clear indication of his throwing prowess. But DiMaggio's most valuable defensive skill was not his arm, but his superior range. His adept handling of Yankee Stadium's cavernous left field had convinced McCarthy and the rest of the organization that DiMaggio belonged in center field. Accordingly, on June 14, New York traded Chapman to the Washington Senators for outfielder Jake Powell. Powell could also play center field, but unlike the veteran Chapman, he was inexperienced and not noted for his defensive play. For the remainder of the 1936 season, Powell and DiMaggio split the playing time in center field, with DiMaggio gradually moving into the position on a daily basis by season's end. He would not relinquish his hold on the everyday center field job for the remainder of his career.

In the last month of the season DiMaggio slumped badly at the plate, batting just .240 with 8 extra-base hits in his last 26 regular season games. The late season swoon somewhat dampened DiMaggio's final numbers, as he finished his rookie year with a .323 batting average, 29 home runs, and 125 RBIs. Still, by any standard DiMaggio's 1936 campaign ranks among the finest ever had by a rookie. In addition to leading the league with 15 triples, DiMaggio also established the all-time American League rookie record with 132 runs scored, despite missing seventeen games due to injury. That record was a reflection not just of DiMaggio's abilities, but also of the Yankees powerhouse line-up, which scored 1,065 runs, 144 more than any other team in the league. Every position featured an above average hitter. In addition to DiMaggio, catcher Bill Dickey batted .362 with 107 RBIs, and first baseman Lou Gehrig batted .354 while slugging 49 home runs, driving in 152 runs, and leading the league in on-base percentage (.478) and slugging percentage (.696). Second baseman Tony Lazzeri drove in 109 runs, third baseman Red Rolfe batted .319, shortstop Frank Crosetti posted a .387 OBP, and outfielders George Selkirk and Jake Powell each batted better than .300, with Selkirk posting an impressive .420 OBP and driving in 107 runs. But the 1936 New York Yankees were not just a great offensive team. Their pitching staff, anchored by Red Ruffing (20–12) and Monte Pearson (19–7) also allowed the fewest runs in the league. It all added up to a final record of 102–51, an astonishing 19½ games better than the second place Detroit Tigers.

Facing the cross-town New York Giants in the World Series, the Yankees continued to slug their way to victory. After dropping Game 1 at the Polo Grounds, the Bombers responded in Game 2 with a World Series–record 18 runs scored, including two by DiMaggio, who went 3 for 5 with 2 RBIs. From there, the Yankees proceeded to win two of the next three games, before closing out the Series with a 13–5 shellacking in Game 6, in which DiMaggio once again connected for three hits. In his first World Series, DiMaggio batted .346 with three doubles, while recording 17 put-outs in center field. Giants manager and star first baseman Bill Terry was duly impressed. "DiMaggio is a marvel," he gushed to reporters following the Series. "Without him they wouldn't be the Yankees. He can do everything."[20]

Measured against the extravagant hype heaped upon him in spring training, DiMaggio's rookie year must be judged an unqualified success, even if he didn't measure up to Babe Ruth. "No one is going to be another Babe Ruth, because there was only one like him," James Kahn observed. "Instead of being the second Babe Ruth, here is a young man who is going to be the first Joe DiMaggio."[21] For his part, DiMaggio had few regrets about his performance in his first season, noting only that "I made one mistake for which I could kick myself: not talking to anybody. I dunno. I'm sorry about that."[22] Following the Series, DiMaggio collected his winner's share, $6,431, nearly as much as his regular season salary, and boarded a train for the long ride back to San Francisco, where he received a conquering hero's welcome, complete with a ticker-tape parade and key to the city. It would be an enjoyable off-season for DiMaggio, who eschewed rigorous workouts in favor of a little partying with old friends, long naps, and hearty, home-cooked meals.

Perhaps DiMaggio also took a little time to reflect on how far he had come. Just five years earlier he had been a high school dropout, playing baseball for nickels and dimes on the sandlots of San Francisco. Now, at 22 years of age, he suddenly found himself a World Series hero, Italian American icon, and nationally recognized superstar, featured on the cover of *Time* magazine. The transformation was complete. When Ruppert mailed Joe his contract for the 1937 season, DiMaggio promptly sent it back, unsigned.

NOTES

1. Quoted by Robert R. McDonald. "Director's Introduction" to *Berenice Abbott: Changing New York*, an exhibition at the Museum of the City of New York, September, 2003.

2. Dan Daniel, "DiMaggio Flashes Power," *New York World-Telegram,* March 18, 1936.

3. Dan Daniel, "DiMaggio Impresses Yanks," *New York World-Telegram,* March 9, 1936.

4. James Kahn, "Rookie May Don Ruth Mantle," *New York Sun,* March 20, 1936.

5. Daniel, "Joe DiMaggio Gets Two Hits."

6. Newspaper clipping reprinted in Wittingham, *The DiMaggio Albums,* 67.

7. James Kahn, "Rookie Joe Comes Through," *New York Sun,* May 4, 1936.

8. "O'Doul Says DiMaggio Is Better in Right Field," Associated Press, January 24, 1936.

9. Gerald Holland, " 'Perfect Ballplayer' Coming to St. Louis," DiMaggio Clippings File, National Baseball Hall of Fame Library.

10. James Kahn, "Tour Triumph for DiMaggio," *New York Sun,* May 22, 1936.

11. DiMaggio Clippings File, National Baseball Hall of Fame.

12. Morris Engelberg and Marv Schneider, *DiMaggio: Setting the Record Straight* (St. Paul, MN: MBI, 2003), 16.

13. James Kahn, "DiMaggio Deluged by Letters," *New York Sun,* June 6, 1936.

14. Noel Busch, "Joe DiMaggio," *Life,* April 30, 1939, 64.

15. Tommy Henrich, *Five O'Clock Lightning: Ruth, Gehrig, DiMaggio, Mantle, and the Glory Years of the NY Yankees* (New York: Carol Publishing Group, 1992), 27–28.

16. Allen, *Where Have You Gone,* 45.
17. Ibid., 61.
18. Dan Daniel, *New York World-Telegram,* July 7, 1936.
19. *New York World-Telegram,* July 9, 1936.
20. *New York World-Telegram,* October 8, 1936.
21. Kahn, "Tour Triumph for DiMaggio."
22. *New York Herald-Tribune,* October 10, 1936.

TRIUMPHS AND TRIBULATIONS

Mr. Roosevelt covered a lot of territory in his brisk workout on the economic field . . . but he didn't get around to saying anything about the downtrodden slaves of baseball, and this was an unfortunate omission.
                                                                    —Joe Williams

When DiMaggio rejected the Yankees 1937 salary offer of $8,500, the same as his 1936 pay, he once again engaged Ruppert in baseball's age-old salary negotiations game. Every winter, the game's owners mailed contracts to their players that usually reflected their previous year's pay. And every winter, most players mailed the contracts back, unsigned, and demanded raises ranging anywhere from a few hundred to tens of thousands of dollars. From there, the two sides gradually inched closer until they reached an agreed upon figure, which usually ended up being closer to the owner's original offer than the player's "extravagant" demands.

That was because, in this particular game, the owners held an important trump card, the infamous "reserve clause," which bound a player to his club for the rest of his career, or until the club traded him away or released him outright. Instituted by the owners in the nineteenth century to artificially suppress salaries, the clause, which one disgruntled player had once likened to a "fugitive slave law," had withstood several attempts by the players to overthrow it until the United States Supreme Court declared it valid in a curious 1922 decision, in which Chief Justice Oliver Wendell Holmes declared that baseball was

Joe shares a happier moment with Yankees owner Col. Jacob Ruppert. DiMaggio's contro-versial holdout during the spring of 1938 angered the autocratic Ruppert. *National Baseball Hall of Fame Library, Cooperstown, N.Y.*

exempt from the nation's antitrust laws because the sport was somehow not en-gaged in interstate commerce. Thus sanctioned by the highest court in the land, the reserve clause essentially gave the player two options: agree to ownership's demands, or find another profession. Free agency and salary arbitration would not exist for another forty years, and players were forbidden to have agents.

After rejecting the owner's initial offer, DiMaggio asked Ruppert for $17,500, more than double his 1936 pay. From DiMaggio's perspective, the request seemed eminently reasonable: his performance in 1936 had helped to restore the Yankees to the pinnacle of the sport, while helping Ruppert boost atten-dance to pre-Depression levels. Indeed, that winter the Yankees drafted plans to expand the Stadium's seating in anticipation of the larger crowds DiMaggio would bring in. In terms of real value, DiMaggio was worth much more to the Yankees than $17,500, and Ruppert knew it. Still, he declared DiMaggio's request to be "ill-advised" and added, somewhat disingenuously, "There isn't a man on the team who can't be replaced."[1]

But Ruppert had bigger worries that spring. Gehrig was holding out for $50,000, $19,000 more than Ruppert's offer, and Ruffing wanted $30,000. Because he couldn't afford to quibble with DiMaggio over a few thousand dollars, Ruppert agreed to pay DiMaggio $15,000, making Joe the highest paid second-year player in baseball. DiMaggio's holdout ended a week into spring training, but it had also set the stage for a far more acrimonious salary conflict the following year.

In the meantime, Joe set his sights on improving on his 1936 performance. To avoid another late-season slump, he switched to a lighter, 37-ounce bat. He also widened his stance at the plate, moving his front foot forward a few inches and pointing it a little bit more toward left field. With this modified, more open stance, Joe hoped to get a better look at the ball, and thus to become more selective at the plate. "[One] thing I must do is to lay off those bad balls I went after [last year]," DiMaggio said during spring training. "I was too anxious. Now I appreciate that the percentage is altogether with me."[2]

For the second consecutive year, an injury delayed DiMaggio's regular-season debut. This time, it was his throwing arm which started causing him trouble, following a strong toss made during an exhibition game on April 2. In a reflection of the era's crude understanding of the human body, doctors attempted to repair the damaged wing by removing his tonsils and extracting one of his teeth, hoping that the soreness was being caused by an irritated nerve. Not surprisingly, that didn't do the trick, and when DiMaggio did make his regular season debut on April 30, the arm still gave him trouble. To compensate for the injury, DiMaggio started throwing with a three-quarters delivery, rather than overhand, and as a result his throwing effectiveness, once considered the very best in baseball, gradually diminished. Over the next several seasons, his outfield assist totals slowly declined. The precise nature of the injury can only be guessed at, but one thing is clear: his ability to throw a baseball never returned to its pre-1937 level.

While his throwing ability declined, his batting reached new heights. In the month of June, with the Yankees already establishing a cushion in the American League standings, DiMaggio went on a home-run tear. After homering twice against the St. Louis Browns on June 11, DiMaggio connected for a career-high 3 home runs on June 13, giving him 14 for the season, 9 in as many games, and a 16-game hitting streak. The hitting streak ended the next day, but DiMaggio's home run barrage soon resumed. He connected for 15 home runs in the month of July, including a ninth-inning grand slam off 18-year-old Bob Feller in front of a reported 59,884 at Cleveland's Municipal Stadium on July 18. With the score tied 1–1, DiMaggio "crushed a high curve 350 feet into the left field stands," one account of the game noted. "Feller was undone. The crowd was stunned."[3] By August 18, he had pushed his season's total to 35, tops in the American League, and already 6 more than he had hit in his entire rookie season. He was still 25 round-trippers shy of the single-season mark established by Babe Ruth in 1927, but that didn't stop the New York media, already hyperventilating with DiMaggio–Ruth comparisons, from speculating if DiMaggio could make a run at the record.

He couldn't. Aside from the fact that DiMaggio simply wasn't as good a home-run hitter as Ruth, Joe also had to contend with the dimensions of Yankee Stadium. The same "Death Valley" in left center field that afforded him ample space to track down fly balls also deprived him of many home runs during his career. Like today, in 1937 Yankee Stadium was heaven for left-handed hitters, with its 295-foot porch giving way to a 407-foot right-center power alley. But it was a morgue for righties, who had to contend with a left-center-field alley that stretched some 460 feet from home plate. There is no doubt that DiMaggio's power numbers suffered as a result of this home-field disadvantage. Four times during his career he led the league in road home runs, and of his 361 lifetime roundtrippers, only 41 percent were hit at Yankee Stadium.

In assessing DiMaggio's place in history, some have used this handicap to exaggerate his true abilities. "In the years that he played, he must have hit three hundred balls out in that area [deep left-center field] that were caught as long flies," sportswriter Jack Lang told writer David Cataneo. "I realized what a home run total he would have had if he played in a ballpark with fairer fences. If DiMaggio had played in Fenway Park, he would have hit nine hundred home runs."[4] But even a cursory glance at DiMaggio's career totals reveals the absurdity of such speculation. Perhaps the best measurement of DiMaggio's "true" home run power is his performance on the road, where he was unencumbered by Yankee Stadium's cavernous dimensions. For his career, DiMaggio hit 213 home runs on the road. If that figure is doubled, DiMaggio still would still stand approximately 75 home runs shy of the 500 home-run club, light years away from Ruth's career total of 714. DiMaggio, with his level swing that tended to generate line drive bullets more often than soaring fly balls, simply was not that caliber of power hitter.

Though he hit only 11 home runs over the season's final seven weeks, DiMaggio finished the 1937 campaign with a league-leading 46 circuit clouts. His spring-training resolution to lay off bad pitches paid immediate dividends. Though his aggressive approach to hitting precluded him from ever having a high walk rate, his 64 bases on balls represented a significant improvement over the 24 free passes he collected in his rookie year. More importantly, as DiMaggio forced pitchers to throw him more strikes, his overall offensive performance improved dramatically. In addition to home runs, DiMaggio also led the league in slugging percentage (.673), total bases (418), and runs scored (151), while bettering his 1936 batting average by 23 points, and his on-base percentage by 60 points. His 167 RBIs represented a career-high, but alas, were not enough to lead the league, as Detroit's Hank Greenberg drove in 183 runs.

Defensively, DiMaggio also showed himself to be a superior center fielder. His league-leading 17 errors can be partially explained by his outstanding range: his 413 put-outs also led the league. Both on offense and defense, DiMaggio was fulfilling the extravagant fantasies of the sports writers who had hyped him before he ever played a major league game. Some in the press, particularly the *Washington Post*'s Shirley Povich, who bizarrely complained that DiMaggio wasn't drawing fans to the ballpark—an assertion drowned out by the noise of clicking turnstiles at Yankee Stadium—still groused that DiMaggio lacked the "color" necessary for true stardom. But such critics increasingly found themselves in the minority. "When it comes to that personal magnetism, you've either got it or you ain't," Jack Miley asserted in the *New York Daily News*. Like love, you can't buy it in a store. Roosevelt has it; Hoover hasn't . . . DiMaggio, like Ruth, has."[5]

The magnetism that Miley perceived was a product of DiMaggio's graceful play: that beautiful swing, his long-legged, loping gait as he ran the basepaths or waltzed after a fly ball. Amidst the bleakness of the Great Depression, the reticent DiMaggio embodied an aesthetic that New Yorkers could embrace. Like many of them, he came from an immigrant background, and yet his daily achievements, breathlessly chronicled by the city's numerous newspapers, suggested a transcendence of the dirt and squalor that was home for many New Yorkers. As future teammate Jerry Coleman later told David Cataneo, "His presence, his posture, his demeanor on the field was unlike any athlete I've ever seen. He had an imperial presence on the field that no athlete ever had."[6]

As his popularity swelled, that unique, indefinable "presence" translated into endorsement dollars. By the end of the decade, DiMaggio was already lending his name to Louisville Slugger, Wheaties cereal, and Chesterfield Cigarettes, billed as "The Baseball Man's Cigarette." In 1937, he also made his Hollywood debut with a cameo appearance in the film *Manhattan Merry-Go Round*. Gaining more confidence in himself off the field, DiMaggio began venturing out on the town without his usual chaperone, Lefty Gomez. According to biographer Richard Ben Cramer, DiMaggio even found his way to Polly Adler's notorious whorehouse on Manhattan's Upper West Side. Adler, a Russian immigrant whose brothel, with its decor of plush carpets and expensive furniture, bore more resemblance to an exclusive club than a typical house of ill-repute, kept a special set of plain cotton sheets on hold for DiMaggio, who complained that the expensive satin ones normally used caused his knees to slip.[7]

Adler's business was an open secret in New York in the 1930s, and she numbered among her clients some of New York's biggest names, many of the same high-society types that DiMaggio rubbed elbows with nightly at Toots Shor's restaurant. ("Going to Polly's?" became a popular catch-phrase in town.) Of course, none of this was reported by the New York media, who were already well-versed in the art of covering up the private foibles of the city's most glamorous stars. Just as Babe Ruth's bouts with syphilis might have been passed off as "stomach trouble" in the 1920s, so too could DiMaggio count upon the New York writers to look the other way when it came to his own sexual indiscretions.

At any rate, the sportswriters had more momentous things to cover in 1937, as the Yankees cruised to their second consecutive pennant. DiMaggio later described the 1937 Bombers as the best team he ever played for, and the available evidence certainly does nothing to contradict that claim. Finishing with a 102–52 record, thirteen games better than second-place Detroit, New York was once again powered by a magnificent offense, which led the league with 979 runs scored. Led by DiMaggio and Gehrig, who batted .351 and led the American League with a .473 OBP, the Yankee offense also got an exceptional performance from Bill Dickey, who enjoyed perhaps the finest year of his Hall of Fame career, posting a .332 batting average and collecting 133 RBIs. Once again the Yankees pitching staff led the league in fewest runs allowed, as Lefty Gomez rebounded from his subpar 1936 performance to win pitching's Triple Crown, leading the league in wins (21), earned run average (2.33), and strikeouts (194).

For the second consecutive year, the Yankees faced the New York Giants in the World Series, and for the second consecutive year, they easily dispatched their cross-town rivals, taking the Series in a tidy five games. DiMaggio batted .273 for the Series, blasting his first career World Series home run in the Yankees 4–2 championship-clinching victory in Game 5. He took home an additional $6,471 for his winner's share of the Series gate receipts, and once again made plans for another winter relaxing at home in San Francisco. The extra money would go towards the purchase of a new, larger house for the DiMaggio family, on San Francisco's Beach Street.

If DiMaggio experienced any disappointment in 1937, it came with the news that he had narrowly missed winning his first Most Valuable Player Award, finishing four points behind Detroit's Charlie Gehringer for that honor. In contrast to later seasons, when DiMaggio would beat out superior players for the MVP, Joe may actually have been more deserving of the 1937 trophy. Though

Gehringer won the batting crown and posted an on base percentage thirty-six points higher than DiMaggio, he trailed Joe in basically every other statistical category, scoring fewer runs, driving in 71 fewer runs, and posting a slugging percentage 153 points lower than DiMaggio's league-leading figure.

But if the writers couldn't agree that DiMaggio was the league's most valuable player, baseball fans expressed a decidedly different opinion. In a poll conducted by the American Institute of Public Opinion, DiMaggio easily outdistanced Gehrig, Giants pitcher Carl Hubbell, Cardinals outfielder Joe Medwick, Gomez, Gehringer, and Cubs catcher Gabby Hartnett as the fans' choice for MVP. In response to the poll, sportswriter Gordon Cobbledick, a Gehringer supporter, attributed DiMaggio's popularity to "ballyhoo," rather than his actual achievements. "If the power of ballyhoo can so exaggerate the worth of a DiMaggio," Cobbledick snorted, "is it any wonder that some of our public offices are filled by mountebanks, scoundrels, incompetents and plain fatheads?"[8]

Such criticisms aside, 1937 had been a good year for the DiMaggio clan. After toiling in the minor leagues for several seasons, Vince finally reached the major leagues, earning an every day spot in the Boston Braves line-up, and establishing himself as a center fielder arguably superior to his more-heralded younger brother. (Vince's hitting, on the other hand, was problematic, and would remain so for the rest of his ten-year big league career.) Meanwhile, Joe's younger brother Dominic, who at 5'9" and 168 pounds lacked his older brother's heft, made his debut with the Seals, playing the outfield and slapping his way to a .306 batting average. In a reflection of the growing marketability of the DiMaggio name, Joe opened a restaurant, DiMaggio's Place, on Fisherman's Wharf. In reality, Joe lent little to the operation other than his name. The restaurant, which specialized in seafood, was operated by his older brother Tom.

When Ruppert mailed DiMaggio his contract for the 1938 season, Joe once again returned it, unsigned. This time around, following his superlative performance in the 1937 season, and no doubt keeping in mind the nearly one million fans who had paid to watch him play that summer, Joe decided he was not going to settle for a few extra thousand dollars over his 1937 pay. No, this time he was going to go for the gold: $40,000, 267 percent more than his previous year's pay.

Ruppert was outraged, and the press was astonished, that a third-year player would ask for so much money, even more than Lou Gehrig's $36,000. (Left out of the discussion was the fact that Gehrig had asked for $50,000 in 1937, before being bargained down to the lower figure.) But if DiMaggio drew any lessons from Gehrig's failed holdout, it was only that Lou should have been more obstinate in insisting upon his asking price. Joe intended to engage Ruppert in a battle of wills, holding out until the stubborn owner acceded to his demands.

It was a battle that DiMaggio could not win. Too many forces were arrayed against him. In addition to the reserve clause, which precluded DiMaggio from soliciting other offers for his services, Joe also had to contend with a press that was sure to abandon him the instant he defied his owner, and a sporting public still smarting from the withering impact of the Great Depression. Though the nation's economy had begun its slow recovery, by 1938 the average American still earned just $901 annually, and thus could hardly identify with the gripes of a highly paid baseball player like DiMaggio. Finally there was Ruppert himself. Although hardly the most penurious of the game's owners, Ruppert, who fashioned himself a "Colonel" for his rank in the seventh regiment of the National Guard, could be counted on to protect his own purse. He countered DiMaggio's demands with a $25,000 offer.

When Joe rejected Ruppert's counter-offer, the Colonel slammed DiMaggio in the press. "DiMaggio is an ungrateful young man who is very unfair to his teammates to say the least," Ruppert said. "He wants $40,000 and I've offered him $25,000 and he won't get a button over that amount."[9] With that, both sides dug in their heels. The standoff lasted through spring training, drawing the ire of McCarthy and DiMaggio's teammates, one of whom groused that Joe seemed to have "get-rich-quick ideas." Even Babe Ruth, that grizzled veteran of salary disputes who had squared off against Ruppert on numerous occasions, declared that "Joe is pulling a boner."[10]

On April 6, with Opening Day less than two weeks away, a reporter knocked on DiMaggio's door to see if there was any progress toward a contract. "What time is it?" a groggy DiMaggio asked the reporter. "Ten thirty [in the morning]," came the answer. "Nuts, this is the middle of the night for me." There had been no progress.[11] The regular season opened on April 18, and still the two sides had not reached an agreement, though Ruppert had rejected a $150,000 offer from the St. Louis Browns for the rights to DiMaggio. More than anything else, that offer, and Ruppert's rejection of it, indicated DiMaggio's real value to the Yankees, but the reserve clause barred him from entertaining offers from other teams. Opening Day came and went, with still no indication of a settlement. Predictably, the New York press had backed Ruppert without exception, writing slanted articles designed to raise the ire of their readers, by depicting DiMaggio as lazy, ungrateful, and greedy. "This time the opinion is general that $25,000 is an adequate salary for any 23-year-old outfielder with only two years of major league play behind him, even if he does happen to be DiMaggio," sportswriter Frank Graham wrote, "and that Col. Jacob Ruppert would be unwise in tilting his offer by so much as a dollar."[12]

Reports that superficially offered both sides of the dispute clearly favored Ruppert's position. "Joe DiMaggio reluctantly left his feather bed yesterday in San

Francisco to yawn a bored denial of the story . . . that he planned to call up the Yankees office during the day and sign his contract," one story related. " 'I'm still holding out for $40,000,' said DiMaggio in a sleepy voice that betrayed recent communion with Morpheus." The article also contained a swipe by Ed Barrow against Joe's off-season conditioning program, such as it was. "He sleeps all day," Barrow said. "That's no way to get in condition—at least for playing the outfield."[13] For DiMaggio, however, the most disconcerting statement came as Opening Day approached, when McCarthy, the manager he had tried so hard to please since his arrival in 1936, told reporters that "The Yankees can get along without DiMaggio. And that $25,000 is final."[14]

DiMaggio knew when he was beaten. Two days into the regular season, he wired the Yankees, accepting their $25,000 offer. But Ruppert, angered by what he perceived as DiMaggio's importunate demands, refused to leave it at that. When DiMaggio reported to Yankee Stadium, Ruppert publicly embarrassed Joe by having him sign the contract in front of the press. According to one account of the conference, Ruppert treated DiMaggio brusquely, as if his best player was just a green farmhand. "Here's your contract, Joe DiMaggio," Ruppert said icily. "Now go ahead and sign it." When a reporter asked if DiMaggio was getting a bonus for signing, Ruppert turned to his young outfielder and barked, "Joe DiMaggio, are you getting any bonus for this?" "No bonus," came Joe's weak reply. "That's right," Ruppert lectured. "And furthermore Joe DiMaggio will not get a cent of pay until he starts to play ball."[15]

For DiMaggio, humiliation piled on top of humiliation. After the signing, McCarthy kept him out of the line-up for a week, contending that the center fielder's lax off-season conditioning program made him unfit for regular-season duty. As an additional slap in the face, the Yankees deducted $1,850 from his base salary, for the time he spent out of the line-up. When he did finally make his 1938 debut on April 30, he was involved in an outfield collision with second baseman Joe Gordon, which sent both players to the hospital. Fortunately, neither player was seriously injured, and DiMaggio was back in the starting line-up the next day. During his first two weeks back in the line-up, DiMaggio demonstrated his readiness, slamming 19 hits, 10 of them for extra bases, in his first 40 at-bats.

But his on-field successes came amidst a chorus of boos, both on the road and from the crowds at Yankee Stadium. DiMaggio, accustomed only to adulation from the fans, was mortified. "It got so I couldn't sleep at night," DiMaggio admitted to Joe Williams after the season ended. "I'd wake up with a start, with the boos dinning in my ears. I wouldn't be able to go back to sleep, so I'd get up, light a cigarette and walk the floor, sometimes til dawn. . . . You know there are times even now when I still hear those boos." To drown out the offensive noises, DiMaggio tried playing with cotton stuffed in his ears, "but that didn't do any good. Even if I couldn't hear the yells, I knew they were there all the same."[16] DiMaggio's confidence in himself and his abilities could help him look past his own failures, but not the hurled invectives of baseball's fickle fandom. Faced with similar circumstances, other stars might have lashed out in anger, adopting a more combative personality with fans and reporters, but DiMaggio simply determined never to get on the public's bad side again. "This was a season I wanted to forget but it was a season in which I learned something," he later wrote. "I knew that it wasn't doing me any good to draw the boos of the fans and I resolved that I would never again be their target."[17] More importantly, DiMaggio had learned that the surest way to satisfy the fans, aside from playing well, was to remain on good terms with the press. In a city where the news cycle was fed by several daily newspapers, the dozens of columnists and beat reporters who covered the Yankees could become a player's best friend, or his worst enemy. It was a lesson that would be learned by many a New York athlete in the twentieth century, but DiMaggio latched onto it early.

Despite the sleepless nights, DiMaggio put together another fine season in 1938, gradually winning back the admiration and support of Yankee fans. By the All-Star break, he was batting .324 with a .626 slugging percentage. With Gehrig mired in a perplexing slump at the plate, McCarthy quietly shifted around his batting order, moving Gehrig down to fifth and DiMaggio into the cleanup spot, where he would remain for the next twelve years. Picking up for Gehrig, whose combined on-base percentage and slugging percentage (OPS) fell by nearly 200 points, DiMaggio finished the year with 32 home runs, 129 runs scored, and 140 RBIs, while striking out just twenty-one times. With rookie second baseman Joe Gordon driving in 97 runs and smacking 25 home runs, the retooled Yankees cruised to their third consecutive American League pennant, finishing with a 99–53 record, 9½ games in front of the Boston Red Sox.

In that year's Fall Classic the Yankees attempted to become the first team in history to win three straight world championships. In what seemed a clear mismatch against the 89–63 Chicago Cubs, who were thirty years into their epic championship drought, the sporting press focused not on the overmatched Cubs, but on the Bombers run at history. "The chief question bandied about by the fans this week is not whether the Yankees can defeat the Cubs," *Sporting News* editor E. G. Brands noted, "but whether the Yankees can overcome the laws of chance and do what no other club in history has been able to accomplish."[18] McCarthy, who judged his 1938 squad to be the best he had ever managed, was supremely confident in his club. "I'm sorry my old friend [Cubs catcher and manager] Gabby Hartnett will have to take it, but we'll make it as short and snappy as we can."[19]

That they did. After taking the Series opener 3–1, the Yankees trailed the Cubs 3–2 heading into the eighth inning of Game 2. To that point, the powerful New York offense had been stymied by Dizzy Dean, the one-time Cardinals phenom who had been reduced to a soft-tossing junkballer by crippling arm injuries. "First it was astonishing, next incredible, then just plain annoying," wrote Joe Williams of the Yankee's clumsy efforts to hit Dean's assortment of "floaters," "half-speeders," "underhand drifters," and "sidearm twisters."[20] Finally with one man on in the eighth inning, Frank Crosetti caught hold of one of Dean's patented "slow balls" and sent it into the left-field bleachers for a two-run home run. In the ninth inning, DiMaggio followed up Crosetti by sending another Dean specialty into the stands for a second two-run home run, good enough to give the Yanks a 6–3 victory and two-games-to-none lead. After the game, astonished reporters witnessed the normally reserved, professional Yankees singing the Broadway hit, "East Side, West Side," in celebration of their come-from-behind victory. They went on to take the next two games easily, recording the first World Series sweep in six years.

After collecting his winner's share of the gate receipts, DiMaggio prepared for another relaxing off season, content that he had weathered the storm of what he later described as the toughest year of his career. The boos and catcalls of the spring and early summer had gradually given way to the cheers of October, and his Yankees were once again positioned at the summit of the baseball world. Putting aside any possibility of another contentious salary dispute, DiMaggio signed his 1939 contract, worth $26,500, and reported to spring training, pledging to put forth "my best season so far." Though he would make good on that promise, little did he know how much the Yankees universe was about to change.

NOTES

1. "Five Revolters Told to Get Into Line or Quit," *New York World-Telegram*, February 12, 1937.

2. Dan Daniel, "DiMaggio to Follow Advice of Cobb and Shift Scheme of 1937 Campaign," *New York World-Telegram*, March 20, 1937.

3. Dan Daniel, "Yankee Outfielder Routs Bob Feller Single-handed," DiMaggio Clippings File, National Baseball Hall of Fame Library.

4. Cataneo, *I Remember*, 82–83.

5. Cramer, *Joe DiMaggio*, 110.

6. Cataneo, *I Remember*, 5.

7. Cramer, *Joe DiMaggio*, 113.

8. Gordon Cobbledick, "Plain Dealing," *Cleveland Plain Dealer*, October 28, 1937.

9. Cramer, *Joe DiMaggio*, 116.

10. Dan Daniel, "Ruth Assails Joe DiMaggio," *New York World-Telegram*, April 15, 1938.

11. International News Service, "Sleepy-Eyed Joe," *New York Journal American*, April 6, 1938.

12. Frank Graham, "No Public Sympathy for DiMaggio," *New York Sun*, April 14, 1938.

13. "DiMaggio Denies Yielding on Terms," *New York Mirror*, April 19, 1938.

14. *New York Times*, April 15, 1938.

15. Dan Daniel, "Joe in Fold, But Not Forgiven," *New York World-Telegram*, April 28, 1938.

16. "DiMaggio Showed Grit in Winning Fans' Support," *New York World-Telegram*, November 8, 1938.

17. DiMaggio, *Lucky to Be a Yankee*, 93.

18. E. G. Brands, "Precedent Backs Cubs in Series with Yanks," *Sporting News*, October 6, 1938.

19. Robert Gregory, *Diz: Dizzy Dean and Baseball During the Great Depression* (New York: Viking, 1992), 353.

20. Ibid., 355.

THE BEST PLAYER IN BASEBALL

This DiMaggio lad is a changed ball player. Last year he affected a scowl. He was being razzed by the fans and appeared to nurse a grievance against the whole world. . . . But the jolter is a new man.

—Dan Daniel

The first bad news for the Yankees franchise came in January 1939, when Ruppert passed away from phlebitis at the age of 71. Though he had publicly embarrassed DiMaggio in the aftermath of the star's 1938 holdout, Ruppert had also overseen the buildup of the Yankees dynasty, from the acquisition of Babe Ruth and the construction of Yankee Stadium, through the franchise's rejuvenation under Joe McCarthy. In the wake of his passing, Ed Barrow, the man Ruppert had signed to serve as the team's general manager in 1920, took on the role of team president. Considering that Barrow had been Ruppert's right-hand man for the previous two decades, it was a remarkably smooth transition of power.

Lou Gehrig would not be so easily replaced. The team's captain, clubhouse leader and ambassador with the press following Ruth's departure, the 35-year-old Gehrig had also become the sport's most admired superstar by the end of the decade. Approaching the game with a methodical intensity that allowed him to perennially outrank the league's best sluggers, even as he amassed a string of consecutive games played that approached the limits of human endurance, Gehrig nonetheless carried himself with boundless humility and grace. If the

DiMaggio in the batter's box. *National Baseball Hall of Fame Library, Cooperstown, N.Y.*

New York press' endless hyping of DiMaggio as the "next Babe Ruth" offended Gehrig, he never betrayed his emotions to Joe, whose locker was situated next to his in the Yankee clubhouse. Though hardly the best of friends, the quiet first baseman and equally reserved outfielder had developed a mutual respect for one another, born out of their common talents and shared star status, and nurtured in the warm spotlight of three successive world championships.

DiMaggio, like the rest of his teammates, knew something was seriously wrong with Gehrig soon after the Yankees broke for spring training in early March. How could you miss it? The physical troubles of the "Iron Horse" were plainly visible every time he tried to swing a bat or field a ground ball. "Everybody knew something was wrong, although we tried not to let Lou know it," DiMaggio later remembered. "He didn't have a shred of his former power or his timing at the plate and [he] had slowed down amazingly in the field."[1]

After gathering just four singles in his first 28 regular season at-bats, Gehrig pulled himself from the line-up on May 2, ending his consecutive games streak at 2,130, and with it his career with the Yankees. In June the Mayo Clinic diagnosed Gehrig with amyotrophic lateral sclerosis (ALS), the fatal nervous system disorder that would one day bear his name, and the public mourned with Gehrig as he began his slow, crippling descent into the grave.

Gehrig would officially remain the team's captain up until his death in 1941, and in his honor that position would remain vacant for several decades. But with Gehrig's demise, DiMaggio became, in a very real sense, the living embodiment of the franchise, its most public symbol and spokesman. To be sure, it was a uniquely morbid way to assume the mantle of leadership, but the timing proved to be propitious for DiMaggio, who had just endured the harsh lessons of his protracted 1938 salary holdout and the nasty public fallout that ensued. In 1939, DiMaggio rededicated himself to his profession, playing with a new level of intensity that simultaneously elevated his hitting and fielding to new heights, while also landing him on the injured list for the third time in four seasons.

This time the injury came not in training camp, but nine days into the regular season. In an April 29 game against the Washington Senators at Yankee Stadium, DiMaggio badly injured his right ankle while chasing a long fly off the bat of Bobby Estalella. When he turned to make the catch, DiMaggio's spikes caught in the Yankee Stadium turf, causing his calf muscles to tear away from the tibia bone. DiMaggio had to leave the game, and two days later the newspapers reported that his leg had swollen up and he had "suffered intense pain throughout the morning" following the injury. On May 2, the same day Gehrig pulled himself from the line-up, DiMaggio was admitted to St. Elizabeth's Hospital for treatment.

Deprived of their two best hitters, the Yankees proceeded to do what absolutely no one expected of them: they won twenty-eight of their next thirty-five games. The Yankees run was partly fueled by sound pitching from Red Ruffing, Lefty Gomez, Monte Pearson, and Oral Hildebrand, but it was primarily due to an offense that continued to score runs at an astonishing rate. During the thirty-five games, the Yankee line-up scored 10 or more runs 10 times, including a 22–2 pasting of the Tigers, a 17–9 drubbing of the Red Sox, and a 17–5 shellacking of the Cleveland Indians. The offensive onslaught owed itself to some familiar names: Dickey, Gordon, and outfielder Tommy Henrich, and one unfamiliar one, rookie outfielder Charlie Keller, who would go on to bat .334 that season.

When DiMaggio finally returned to the line-up for good on June 7, the Yankees already enjoyed an 8½ game cushion in the American League standings, but the press treated him as if he was the savior come to rescue the club from a season-high two-game losing streak. Dan Daniel described the two-game skid as a "lamentable tailspin" that required "the magic influence and sovereign tonic" of DiMaggio's play to correct. Though undoubtedly some of this was intentional hyperbole, Daniel was already giving substance to one of the central myths regarding DiMaggio: namely, that the Yankees could not win without him. It was a view commonly shared throughout the American League. After DiMaggio's rookie season, Red Sox manager Joe Cronin had insisted that DiMaggio "upset the entire balance of the league. If we'd landed him, we'd have won. The Tigers would have [won] if they'd got him. The Indians would be champions if they had him."[2] But the Yankees consistent domination of the American League, season after season, refutes such easy formulations—and does an injustice to the rest of the Yankees team, which was formidable with or without DiMaggio. Charlie Keller probably came closest to the truth when he told Maury Allen, "You ask if the guys looked to DiMaggio to win a game. No. It wasn't that," Keller insisted. "It makes good reading how everybody depended on him, but that's not how it was. Everybody went out and did his own job and that's why we won. DiMaggio was the best player, but everybody had to contribute for us to win."[3]

By any measure, the 1939 Yankees were a remarkable team, breezing to the pennant despite replacing Lou Gehrig with the .235 hitting Babe Dahlgren and losing DiMaggio to an injury for thirty-five games. But when DiMaggio did finally return to the line-up, he unquestionably made them an even tougher team to beat. By the end of June, DiMaggio was batting .413 with a .697 slugging percentage. His hot hitting continued in the month of July, which began with his home run off Bill Lee in the American League's 3–1 All Star Game triumph at Yankee Stadium, and concluded with his batting average still holding steady at a league-leading .405.

Yet DiMaggio's excellent play was hardly limited to his performance in the batter's box. Both on the bases and in the field, DiMaggio was playing with a renewed energy and focus, as if he had something to prove. Though not a skilled base stealer, DiMaggio was coming to be regarded by many observers as the league's finest base runner, for his aggressive yet heady play on the base paths.

"He was the best base runner I ever saw," Joe McCarthy later asserted. "I've been in the game a long time. I never saw a man better on stretching a single into a double or going from first to third on a hit. If he went, you knew he would make it."[4] Despite the injuries he had sustained over the years to his knees and ankles, DiMaggio was an aggressive slider, hurtling himself feet-first into the bag on close plays, and undoubtedly doing extensive damage to his body in the process. "There were times when he went into me and I thought a truck ran over me," remembered Dario Lodigiani, a San Francisco native who played second and third base for the Philadelphia Athletics in 1939. "That's the way he played. Even if you were close friends, he was playing to win."[5]

But it was DiMaggio's improved fielding that elicited the most praise. Since his rookie season, DiMaggio had always been an above-average fielder, using his excellent foot speed to track down fly balls in the Stadium's deep alleyways. But his glovework had also been plagued by inconsistency, as he committed a league-leading 17 errors in 1937, and followed that up with 15 more miscues in 1938. In 1939, however, he committed only 5 errors, while collecting an impressive 2.80 putouts per game, more than he had recorded in any previous campaign, and the second-best total of his career.

What was responsible for his improved play in the field? Unlike hitting, which he always believed was primarily a God-given talent, DiMaggio held that a superlative outfielder could only get that way with intensive study and practice. From his constant study of the league's hitters and their tendencies he learned how to position himself appropriately on each pitch. He insisted that the team's infielders signal him the identity of the next offering (fast ball or breaking ball), so that he could get his feet moving in the right direction before the ball was even in the air. "Joe had this marvelous sense of anticipation," McCarthy later recalled. "That's because he studied the game."[6]

He also made an art form of footwork in the outfield, seemingly never making a wrong step or a wasted motion. Sam Suplizio, a long-time major league outfield instructor, recalled the lessons DiMaggio imparted to him as a Yankee prospect in 1956, five years after DiMaggio had retired from the game. "He could talk to you about outfield play like a professor," Suplizio said. "One of the finest things he taught me was, when you go back on a ball, to your left, right, or straight over your head, your feet should never sidestep. They should go like a track man, in the direction of the ball. Keep the ball off your shoulder, so you don't reach directly over your head for the ball."[7] Applying these principles, DiMaggio became a master at judging the trajectory of fly balls, and then using his superior foot speed to run to the spot where he was certain the ball was going to land. As DiMaggio later wrote in his instructional book, *Baseball for Everyone*, "Through experience and practice the outfielder acquires a working knowledge of the probable distance and speed of the hit from the first quick glance he gets at it as it begins its flight."[8] The same detailed study that Ted Williams applied to the art of hitting, DiMaggio applied to catching fly balls.

This fielding method, with its emphasis on anticipation, judgment, and footwork, soon gave rise to one of the most popular myths regarding DiMaggio, namely, that he never had to dive for a fly ball. As his own manager, Joe McCarthy, put it to Maury Allen, "He did everything so easily. . . . You never saw him fall down or go diving for a ball. He didn't have to. He just knew where the ball was hit and he went and got it. That's what you're supposed to do. The idea is to catch the ball. The idea isn't to make exciting catches."[9] While this myth undoubtedly highlights a real strength in DiMaggio's fielding—his extraordinary footwork and anticipation of the descending arc of a ball in flight—it also does great violence to the truth. The simple laws of physics, coupled with the limitations of the human body, sometimes demand that a fielder, no matter how gifted, dive for a fly ball. DiMaggio himself said so in *Baseball for Everyone*, noting that "there are times when [a dive] should be attempted," though he hastened to add that "unless the outfielder is really skillful at this type of catch, he should never gamble on making it unless the conditions are such that a base hit means the ball game to his club."[10] Presumably, DiMaggio thought himself a skillful enough outfielder to attempt a shoestring catch when the game situation warranted it.

As the 1939 season progressed, the extent to which DiMaggio's fielding had improved became more apparent. "The best defensive outfielder in baseball," was how sportswriter Edward T. Murphy characterized DiMaggio for his feature article on him in early September. Another report praised DiMaggio for his "exemplary" fielding, though it also noted that the outfielder's throwing "could be a lot better. He has been putting more on the ball these last few days, but still is far from the thrower he was in 1936."[11] Apparently, DiMaggio still had not recovered from the arm injury that sidelined him at the beginning of the 1937 season.

Despite all the praise, DiMaggio still had his skeptics. Tris Speaker, the Hall-of-Fame outfielder and consensus choice for the greatest-fielding center fielder of all time, chafed at those who tried to compare DiMaggio to him. "HIM?" Speaker disgustedly responded when questioned by a reporter about DiMaggio in July. "I could name fifteen better outfielders!"[12] DiMaggio's response to Speaker's challenge came on the field. On August 1, he recorded 10 put-outs in a game against the Detroit Tigers at Yankee Stadium, one shy of the major league record. Included among the ten catches he made that day was a "spectacular running catch" to rob Earl Averill of an extra base hit in the third inning, and a "shoestring catch of a low line drive" to deprive Pete Fox of a base hit in the fourth inning. But he saved his most sensational glove work for the following day, when he made arguably the most memorable catch of his career. With the Yankees trailing 7–2 in the top of the ninth inning, Detroit slugger Hank Greenberg came to the plate with a man on first and one out and blasted a pitch toward the 461-foot sign in deepest left center field. "Turning with the crack of the bat, DiMaggio raced to within two feet of the 461-foot mark on the wall and without looking backward, clutched the ball in his gloved hand just as it appeared about to hit the fence," the *New York Times* reported the next day, adding that the play was "probably the greatest catch ever made in the Stadium."

Apparently, DiMaggio himself was so stunned by the play that he forgot how many outs there were, and started trotting back toward the infield. His mental lapse allowed the Detroit runner, Earl Averill, enough time to scamper back to first. For Greenberg, DiMaggio's mental gaffe came as small consolation for a ball that he thought was going to go for a home run. "It was just about the only time I ever saw him make a mistake," Greenberg later told Maury Allen. "I was glad it happened. Just proved he was human."[13] DiMaggio's hard hitting had already gained him one nickname, "Joltin' Joe." His exemplary play in the outfield would earn him a second: "The Yankee Clipper," a reference to the speed and grace with which he tracked down fly balls in the expansive waters of the Yankee Stadium outfield.

Despite the Yankee's 7–2 loss on August 2, their record stood at an impressive 66–28, 7½ games in front of the second place Boston Red Sox. For the last two months of the season, that gap would only widen as the Yankees continued to bulldoze their way through the American League, while Boston faltered down the stretch. By the end of August, New York held an insurmountable twelve-game lead in the standings. With the pennant all but settled, attention shifted back to DiMaggio, who was putting together one of the finest offensive seasons of his career. He hammered 14 home runs in August, boosting his slugging percentage to .694. But by then the public was mostly interested in his batting average (.405 as August turned into September), and whether he could become the first hitter since Bill Terry in 1930 to bat better than .400. Winning his first batting crown had been DiMaggio's stated goal since spring training, but even he was surprised by his hot hitting. When Frank Graham asked him how it felt to be a .400 hitter, DiMaggio could only answer "Swell," before adding "I just hope I can bear up under [the strain.]"[14]

Once again injuries intervened and prevented DiMaggio from realizing his full potential. In early September, an infection in his left eye—his lead eye at the plate—left him with blurred vision. Then, on September 2, Joe slipped the cartilage in his knee, inviting the possibility that the leg would require surgical treatment. It didn't, but all the same DiMaggio's average plummeted twenty-four points in the season's final month. Though he still easily captured his first batting crown with a splendid .381 average, DiMaggio felt the injuries had cost him his chance at batting .400. Years later, when his rival Ted Williams received all the plaudits as baseball's last living .400 hitter, DiMaggio would grouse to acquaintances that McCarthy should have rested him in the season's final month. While Ted Williams was unwilling to preserve his .400 batting average by sitting on the bench in 1941, DiMaggio would have been more than happy to sit on the sidelines to protect his .400 mark in 1939. With the pennant already wrapped up, McCarthy had unnecessarily jeopardized his run at .400 by continually inserting his name into the line-up, Joe insisted. "It was a wonderful year, but hitting .400 would have been nice," a bitter DiMaggio complained, decades later. "I couldn't see, but McCarthy wanted to get the record for most victories in a season, so he kept me there, and my batting average dropped."[15]

It is hard to imagine that McCarthy believed the 1939 Yankees could have made a run at the record for most victories in a season. That mark was held by the 1906 Cubs, who had won an astounding 116 games. As of August 31, the Yankees stood at 87 wins. With only twenty-nine games left to play, the Yankees would have had to win every single game to tie the Cubs mark. As it worked out, the club won nineteen games in September, to finish the season with a record of 106–45, seventeen games better than second-place Boston, which had long since fallen off New York's blistering pace.

For the Yankees it was a record fourth consecutive American League pennant, and a fourth straight trip to the World Series against another overmatched opponent. This time, the Yankee's unfortunate victims were the Cincinnati Reds, winners of their first pennant in twenty years. For the second consecutive year, New York finished off their National League rivals with a four-game sweep, outscoring the Reds 20–8. For the Series, DiMaggio batted .313 with one home run and three runs batted in, but in keeping with his versatile play throughout the regular season, also shined in the field and on the base paths, particularly in the decisive fourth game. In the second inning, DiMaggio robbed Reds catcher Ernie Lombardi of an extra-base hit with a running grab up against the fence, then did the same to third baseman Billy Werber in the third. In the top of the ninth, with the Yankees trailing 4–2, DiMaggio singled to left, putting men on first and third with no outs. The next batter, Bill Dickey, hit a tailor-made double-play ball, but shortstop Billy Myers dropped the relay throw from second base when DiMaggio came barreling into him, and the Yankees cut the score to 4–3. After advancing to third on a deep fly out, DiMaggio scored the tying run on an infield grounder, sliding in ahead of the throw from Werber.

With that, the game headed into extra innings, and DiMaggio once again figured into the Yankees winning rally. With men on first and third and one out in the top of the tenth, DiMaggio singled to right field, scoring Crosetti from third base. On the play, Cincinnati right fielder Ival Goodman booted the ball, inducing Charlie Keller to also attempt to score. Keller and the ball arrived at home plate at the same time, and in the ensuing collision catcher Ernie Lombardi dropped the ball. As the dazed Lombardi struggled to retrieve his senses, DiMaggio, who had been running hard the entire time, rounded third and made a dash for the plate. Before Lombardi could regain his wits, DiMaggio slid across home plate with the third run of the inning, giving the Yankees a 7–4 cushion, and, after the Reds were retired in the bottom of the inning, their record fourth consecutive World Championship. After the Series, the press skewered Lombardi, labeling the tenth-inning fiasco "Lombardi's Swoon." But really it was DiMaggio's glove, bat, and legs, and not Lombardi's error, that were responsible for the Reds defeat.

After the Series' triumph, DiMaggio collected his winner's share ($5,542) of the gate receipts for the fourth consecutive year. He became the first (and, thus far, only) player in baseball history to win a World Series in each of his first four seasons in the major leagues. Yet, his contributions to the team's success aside, his 1939 campaign had also marked a personal triumph. Despite having missed a full month of the season because of injuries, DiMaggio easily won his first American League MVP, outdistancing Red Sox slugger Jimmie Foxx by more than 100 points on the baseball writers' ballots. Forgiven for his foolish 1938 holdout, the writers now ranked DiMaggio, still only 24 years old at the close of the season, among the game's all-time greats. "Every time you see Joe DiMaggio take that effortless swing of his or race back against the boards to rob some luckless batter of a triple," the Associated Press' Gayle Talbot gushed, "you can't help getting a sneaking feeling that here, perhaps, is the greatest all-around ball player there has been."[16]

DiMaggio's new status as a baseball immortal made his marriage that off-season to the actress Dorothy Arnold a big media event. DiMaggio had met Arnold in 1937 on the set of *Manhattan Merry Go-Round*, where the blonde starlet, lacking a speaking part in the film, had provided the picture with "atmosphere" (her term). She had never heard of DiMaggio, but Joe was instantly taken with her, and later declared that their meeting had been "a case of love at first sight."

She had been born Dorothy Arnoldine Olson, the second youngest of four girls, in Duluth, Minnesota. In her early years, she earned a reputation as a gifted entertainer, winning talent shows with her singing and dancing, and playing on the Minnesota vaudeville circuit. Spotted there by scouts for the producers of Chicago's *Bandbox Revue*, Dorothy joined the touring company when she was still just 16 years old, playing three shows a day, six nights a week. That gig earned her a screen test with Paramount in New York City, where the powers-that-be determined that her voice was too low for the movies. Undeterred, the ambitious Dorothy (who had now shortened her last name to the more marketable Arnold), modeled and did radio work for NBC, while occasionally landing bit parts in fluff pieces like *Manhattan Merry Go-Round.*

Encouraged to try her luck out West, in 1938 Dorothy moved to Hollywood, found an agent, and was signed by Universal Pictures. She appeared in three movies that year, *The Storm, Secrets of a Nurse,* and *Exposed,* and would appear in an additional six movies the following year. Her film credits, though numerous, included mostly minor roles (she was listed as the "debutante" in 1939's *You Can't Cheat an Honest Man*), and, like many another pretty face in Hollywood, true stardom eluded her. She would find it, but not in the way she expected.

DiMaggio began seriously courting her in 1938, making numerous trips out to Hollywood to spend time with her. They were engaged by the spring of 1939, and while Joe was having his big season, the 21-year-old Dorothy made several trips out to New York to watch him play, and also followed him between the Big Apple and Cincinnati during the World Series. DiMaggio enjoyed being seen with the beautiful actress, and Dorothy, in turn, relished the notoriety that came with being DiMaggio's girl. DiMaggio may have been hampered by a natural shyness, but the ebullient Arnold made it something of a personal project to turn this famous but uneasy athlete, this high school dropout, into a gentleman of society, someone who could carry a conversation about something other than baseball for longer than five seconds. She had her work cut out for her.

They were married November 19, at Sts. Peter and Paul Church, located in the heart of Joe's old San Francisco neighborhood. It was a madhouse scene at the traditional, twin-spired church, with two thousand people, including the mayor of San Francisco and Hollywood producer Darryl Zanuck, crammed into the narrow pews, and, according to one report of the nuptials, an additional 8,000 people milling around outside, anxious for a glimpse of the star-studded couple. At one point, the presiding priest, Father Francis J. Parolin, had to plead to the anxious crowd to remain calm. "I ask you in the name of the Lord, be quiet," he implored. "You are in the house of God."[17] Despite the theatrics, the wedding went off without a hitch, and the ensuing reception was marred only by the nervous Dorothy's attempt to cut the cake. Missing with the knife, she sliced her finger instead.

After the reception, the couple embarked for a honeymoon in Los Angeles, though Ciccio LaRocca, one of DiMaggio's groomsmen, later told Richard Ben

Cramer that the commotion at their wedding had upset Joe. "He didn't want to talk to her," Ciccio said. "I don't know why. But he was mad. They weren't talkin'."[18] After the honeymoon, Joe and Dorothy moved back to New York, into DiMaggio's Manhattan apartment. As far as Dorothy was concerned, her show business career was over. She told a reporter that she was abandoning her ambitions because she wanted "to be a real wife" and intended "to have children, because no marriage can be successful without them."[19] In time, however, Dorothy would discover that playing Mrs. DiMaggio wasn't as glamorous or rewarding a role as she first imagined.

As Dorothy went about setting up the DiMaggios new home in New York, Joe looked to improve upon his spectacular 1939 campaign. After a brief holdout, DiMaggio signed a $32,000 contract for the 1940 season, and reported to the Yankees spring training camp in St. Petersburg, Florida, determined to help McCarthy in his unprecedented drive for a fifth consecutive world championship. Both DiMaggio and his manager were confident that 1940 would witness another standout season for Joe and the Yankees. "Mechanically, physically, DiMaggio is perfection at the plate, and in the outfield," McCarthy told Dan Daniel. "This season he will begin to cash in seriously on his experience."[20]

It was an exciting spring for the entire DiMaggio clan. Vince was in the Cincinnati Reds spring training camp (he had been traded there from Boston in 1938), looking to come back from an injury-plagued 1939 season. Meanwhile, Joe's little brother Dominic had caught on with the Red Sox, and would join the team out of spring training, making the DiMaggio family only the second in baseball history to boast three simultaneous major leaguers. Prospects were particularly bright for Dominic, who had dispelled any notion that he was getting by on the family name. A center fielder like his older brothers, he was perhaps the best fielder of the three, and a good contact hitter with excellent speed who also drew a fair amount of walks—in other words, the ideal leadoff hitter. After watching Dom play in an exhibition game, National League umpire Babe Pinelli declared that the 23-year-old would "hit big league pitching and his fielding is already big league."

Unfortunately, Dominic was no more immune to injuries than his older brother, and before spring training was out, he found himself benched with a tendon injury that would limit him to 108 games his rookie season, though when he did play, he batted a solid .301. Worse for the Yankees, Joe once again failed to escape spring training without suffering an injury. This time, the mishap took place two days before Opening Day, when Joe tore some cartilage in his knee while sliding into second base. At first, the injury was judged to be very serious, with doctors at Johns Hopkins Hospital in Baltimore informing the club that DiMaggio would be out for "a long time." But when the Yankees got off to a slow start, winning only six of their first fifteen games (and making all the league's pitchers "look like Bobby Feller," according to one Dan Daniel quip), DiMaggio decided to risk further injury and return to the line-up on May 7.

Playing through the injury, DiMaggio carried a .300 batting average into the month of July, but it did little to reverse the team's fortunes. At the All-Star break, the Yankees found themselves in unfamiliar territory: fourth place, seven games back with a very pedestrian 37–34 record. The club's woes were primarily due to the sagging production of long-time regulars like catcher Bill Dickey, who batted just .247 with 9 home runs that year, and shortstop Frank Crosetti, who posted a horrible .194 batting average. On the pitching side of the ledger, Red Ruffing continued to admirably fill the role of staff workhorse, but Lefty Gomez, who had won 165 games for the Bombers in the 1930s, fell victim to injury and made only five starts.

Though DiMaggio was enjoying another standout season, he took the club's reversal in fortunes badly. In his first four years in the majors, he had become so accustomed to winning, and winning easily, that the sudden flood of losses nearly disrupted his worldview. Following a Yankees loss, DiMaggio became moody and uncommunicative. He would refuse to enter his usual hangout, Toots Shor's restaurant, and instead insist that Shor join him for long walks through the darkened city streets. No words were ever exchanged on these nighttime perambulations; the only communication DiMaggio was capable of following a loss was the surly dejection written all over his face. Even when he played well, both teammates and friends agreed, DiMaggio blamed himself for the Yankee's failures. "He always thought it was his fault," Shor remembered. "Keller could go oh-for-four or Henrich oh-for-four . . . it didn't matter. If the Yankees lost, Joe thought it was his fault."[21]

In the season's second half, the Yankees started winning again, helped in part by a DiMaggio hot streak. By August 31, DiMaggio had boosted his batting average to .344, and the Yankees moved up to third place, just five games behind the league-leading Cleveland Indians, and 2½ games behind the Detroit Tigers. For the month of September, DiMaggio batted a sizzling .381, lifting his average to a league-leading .352. He also finished the year with 31 home runs, 133 RBIs, and a very formidable .626 slugging percentage. But it wasn't enough. The Yankees finished the year at 88–66, two games behind the pennant winning Detroit Tigers, and one game behind second-place Cleveland. The three-way pennant race had come down to the season's final weekend, but a 6–0 loss at Philadelphia on Sept. 27 eliminated the Yanks, and denied them a shot at their fifth straight American League flag.

DiMaggio was not the league's MVP in 1940, not with Detroit's Hank Greenberg leading the league in slugging percentage, home runs, RBIs, and doubles, but he had enjoyed a fine season nonetheless. Considering that he had played much of the year with a bad knee, DiMaggio's constant production both at bat and in the field, as well as his inspired play down the stretch, had demonstrated beyond all doubt that his 1939 performance was no fluke. DiMaggio could now legitimately call himself one of the country's preeminent sports figures. But what did that really mean? With the nation's attention increasingly focused on the disturbing events in Europe and Asia, sports heroes seemed superfluous, their remarkable athletic deeds dimmed by the specter of a Nazi-occupied France and the raging Battle of Britain. How could a country so ill-at-ease, and standing on the precipice of another costly world war, find it within itself to root for an athlete, even one as gifted as DiMaggio? It would take the remarkable events of 1941 to reveal the answer. In the span of two giddy, inconceivable months, DiMaggio would find himself forever transformed in the eyes of the American public. No longer a mere "sports hero," he would become that rarest of cultural creations, a veritable national icon. After 1941, nothing would ever be the same again—not for America, and certainly not for Joe DiMaggio.

NOTES

1. DiMaggio, *Lucky to Be a Yankee*, 107.
2. Cataneo, *I Remember*, 59.
3. Allen, *Where Have You Gone,* 96.
4. Ibid., 41.
5. Cataneo, *I Remember*, 66.
6. Allen, *Where Have You Gone*, 42.
7. Cataneo, *I Remember,* 77–78.
8. Joe DiMaggio, *Baseball for Everyone: A Treasury of Baseball Lore and Instruction for Fans and Players* (New York: McGraw-Hill, 2002), 128–29.
9. Allen, *Where Have You Gone*, 40.
10. DiMaggio, *Baseball for Everyone*, 129.
11. Newspaper clipping reprinted in Wittingham, *The DiMaggio Albums*, 242.
12. Cramer, *Joe DiMaggio*, 137.
13. Allen, *Where Have You Gone*, 75.
14. Frank Graham, "Setting the Pace," *New York Journal-American*, August 31, 1939.
15. Engelberg and Schneider, *DiMaggio: Setting the Record Straight*, 33.
16. Cramer, *Joe DiMaggio*, 138.
17. Ibid., 145.

18. Ibid., 147.

19. "Meet the Missus," *Sporting News*, December 21, 1939.

20. Dan Daniel, ".400 mark seen for DiMag," *New York World-Telegram*, March 7, 1940.

21. Allen, *Where Have You Gone*, 62.

WE WANT HIM ON OUR SIDE

DiMaggio's streak is the most extraordinary thing that ever happened in American sports. He sits on the shoulders of two bearers—mythology and science. For Joe DiMaggio accomplished what no other ballplayer has done. He beat the hardest taskmaster of all, a woman who makes Nolan Ryan's fastball look like a cantaloupe in slow motion—Lady Luck.

—Stephen Jay Gould

Among all the major sports, baseball stands out for its cultivated quotidian aesthetic, the day-in, day-out repetitions of the game. Though this finely tuned and ritualized routine can reward the virtues of patience, restraint, and composure, it can also torment the player who is too easily unsettled by misfortune. Within the framework of a 154 (or 162) game schedule, each baseball player must stand always precariously balanced on the thin line that separates success from failure: a hitter who fails to reach base 60 percent of the time is flirting with greatness, while the batter who fails 70 percent of the time is in danger of losing his job. Because greatness and mediocrity are separated by the slimmest of fractions, the briefest of statistical burps can induce overconfidence or panic. Simply through random statistical fluctuation, a .250 hitter can suddenly find himself on a hot streak, with base hits dropping like acorns in autumn. Conversely, a .350 hitter, through no fault of his own, can find himself mired in an inexplicable, prolonged slump, as line drives consistently and infuriatingly seek out the gloves of the eight fielders arrayed against him. That these trends can

On July 1, 1941, DiMaggio matched Willie Keeler's all-time record by recording a base hit in his forty-fourth consecutive game. *National Baseball Hall of Fame Library, Cooperstown, N.Y.*

and often do reverse themselves at any moment—the next series, the next game, the next at-bat—constitutes what one noted baseball writer once called the "spooky music" underpinning the game. Its message is simple: never allow yourself to get too high or too low, because tomorrow's game just might humble today's hero, or glorify yesterday's goat.

All of which is to say, batting slumps and hitting streaks are as natural a part of the game as pine tar and rosin bags. Simply based on the laws of statistical probability and randomness, we can expect that each season will yield at least one or two lengthy hitting streaks of twenty games or more, and every few years, like the periodic passing of a comet, an even longer streak, of thirty or thirty-five games, will more than likely blaze its way across the sports headlines. But in 1941, Joe DiMaggio accomplished something that, statistically speaking, simply never should have happened. In his 1988 essay, "The Streak of Streaks," the noted evolutionary biologist and ardent baseball fan Stephen Jay Gould related the work of his colleague Ed Purcell, a Nobel Laureate in physics and fellow baseball afficianado, who calculated that all the streaks and slumps in baseball history could be explained statistically except for one. DiMaggio's fifty-six-game hitting streak, Purcell determined, should only have occurred in a universe that included either four lifetime .400 hitters (there are in fact none), or fifty-two lifetime .350 hitters (of which there are only three). At least thus far, Purcell's argument is amply supported by the evidence of history. In the sixty-five years of major league baseball prior to 1941, only four men assembled hitting streaks of forty games or more, and each of them (Ty Cobb's forty-game streak in 1911, George Sisler's forty-one-game streak in 1922, Bill Dahlen's forty-two-game streak in 1894, and Willie Keeler's forty-four-game streak in 1897) only barely crossed that threshold. In the more than sixty years that have passed since DiMaggio's record-shattering summer, only one batter has lurched past the forty-game threshold: Pete Rose, in 1978, with a forty-four-game streak.

With DiMaggio's closest historical rivals a distant twelve games, or more than 20 percent, removed from his record, it is no wonder that the fifty-six-game hitting streak stands, at least for a committed scientist like Gould, as a "legitimate legend," and a "central item of our cultural history." Gould's wonderment at DiMaggio's accomplishment, more than forty years after the fact, echoes the impressions the streak made on those who saw it unfold before their very eyes. In his remembrance of the 1941 season, author Robert Creamer recalls the friend who passed through a Montana coffee shop during the headiest days of the streak. "Almost every man who came into the café . . . would glance toward a newspaper lying on the counter and ask the proprietor, 'He get one yesterday?' He didn't have to explain who 'he' was, even though this was two thousand miles from New York. . . . Every day, all over the country, people asked 'Did he get one yesterday?' "[1]

To fully grasp the dimensions of DiMaggio's fifty-six-game hitting streak is to contemplate the event on multiple levels: as a baseball achievement that helped the Yankees recover from an early season swoon to win the 1941 American League pennant; as an extraordinary event that, through a combination of luck, talent and determination, held at bay, at least for a while, the exacting law of averages; as an impressive psychological achievement, in which DiMaggio continued to extend the streak despite the scrutiny and pressure that mounted with each passing game; and finally, perhaps most importantly, as a major cultural event that captivated an entire nation during one ominous summer. As Creamer notes, the streak not only transcended New York, "it transcended baseball." More than that, it transcended Joe DiMaggio himself. In the years that followed, the streak would become The Streak, carving its own niche in the American story, passing from history into mythology.

Not even the most fanciful of fiction writers could have envisioned such a tale on May 15, 1941, when DiMaggio collected an RBI single in the bottom of the first inning against Chicago White Sox left-hander Edgar Smith. It was DiMaggio's only hit in the game, and it scored the Yankee's only run, as Chicago bruised and battered New York pitching en route to a decisive 13–1 victory. The brutal loss marked a low point for the Yankees, who had dropped eight of their last ten and fallen 6½ games out of first place with a 14–15 record. The press, which had predicted a big season for the Yankees ever since DiMaggio joined the team in spring training after signing a $35,000 contract, now turned on the team with a fury. The Yankees were on a "non-stop flight toward the second division," groaned the *New York Herald-Tribune*. Going further, the *Daily News* described the Yanks as "ghastly"; their play a "shameless shambles."[2] Much of the blame fell squarely on DiMaggio's high-priced shoulders. Now the game's second-highest paid player (behind only Detroit's Hank Greenberg, who would find himself drafted into the Army and out of baseball that summer), DiMaggio had started out the season red-hot, collecting 19 hits in his first 36 at-bats. But from April 22 to May 14, he fell into one of the worst slumps of his career, gathering just 14 hits in 72 at-bats for a .194 batting average. As Dan Daniel succinctly put it, "Joe DiMaggio isn't hitting his weight," although in another column he added hopefully, "Slumps are overcome suddenly, and once the bellwether shows the way, a whole club very often will follow him. It is possible that when Joe DiMaggio begins to hit again he will pull the other Yankees with him."[3]

Though the streak began inauspiciously with that lone single off Edgar Smith on May 15, it wasn't long before DiMaggio was tearing into the ball again. Over the next twelve days he collected 18 hits in 45 at-bats, culminating in a 4-for-5 afternoon, including his seventh home run of the season, at Griffith Stadium in Washington. More importantly, the Yankees had started to turn their season around, winning eight of eleven games to inch back toward the top of the standings. On May 28, the streak received its first mention in the press, as Daniel noted in the *World-Telegram* that Crosetti was carrying a ten-game hitting streak, first baseman Johnny Sturm an eleven-game string, and DiMaggio had hit safely in thirteen consecutive games.

Most of the lucky breaks, which must accompany any sustained hitting streak, came DiMaggio's way early on, before the string had attracted much attention. In the fourteenth game, DiMaggio just beat out an infield single in the fourth inning of a 2–2 game at Griffith Stadium. One inning later, the skies opened up and the resulting downpour forced officials to declare the five-inning game a tie. In the sixteenth game, the second end of a double-header at Fenway Park, DiMaggio's only hit came on a wind-blown fly ball that Red Sox rightfielder Pete Fox misplayed into a single. The hit came in the midst of a horrendous afternoon for DiMaggio, who committed four errors, two on throws that clanged against the box seat railings. In a cartoon the next day, Gene Mack of the *Boston Globe* remarked, "Seldom on any field has anyone equaled his wild throwing." Concerning the Fox misplay, Mack added, "Not since Snodgrass in 1912 has a muff at Fenway caused such a furor as Fox's of Joe DiMag's." Mack was referring to Fred Snodgrass' infamous error that cost the New York Giants the 1912 World Series, but in this case, DiMaggio had been rewarded with a hit. And for a streak still in its nascent stage, that was all that mattered.

More lucky breaks would come DiMaggio's way in the ensuing days and weeks. On June 10, for instance, DiMaggio hit a bouncer to White Sox third baseman Lodigiani. When a tricky hop handcuffed the normally slick-fielding Lodigiani, DiMaggio beat it out for an infield single. On June 17, DiMaggio beat out a grounder to Chicago shortstop Luke Appling in the seventh inning for his only hit, and on June 21, a lone bloop single over the head of Detroit Tigers first baseman Rudy York extended the streak to thirty-four games. All told, in thirty-four of the streak's fifty-six games DiMaggio could muster only one hit to extend the string.

Nonetheless, DiMaggio's streak demanded much more than a healthy dose of good fortune, it also required sheer talent and determination. As the streak started to attract attention, DiMaggio began ripping into the ball with astounding regularity. Always a great contact hitter—DiMaggio never struck out more than thirty-nine times in a single season during his career—in 1941 he whiffed a career low thirteen times, and only five times during the streak. From June 2, 1941 (the day, coincidentally, that Lou Gehrig finally succumbed to

ALS), through June 20, DiMaggio collected 26 hits in 60 at-bats, including 7 home runs, 5 doubles, and a triple, good for a .900 slugging percentage during that span. During those three weeks, DiMaggio tagged some of the best pitchers in baseball, including Bob Feller (3 for 6 with two doubles) and 22-game-winner and 1941 ERA champion Thornton Lee (3 for 7 with a home run).

The streak became big news in Game 30, on June 17, when newspapers reported that DiMaggio had surpassed what was believed to be the Yankees franchise record of 29 games, set by Roger Peckinpaugh in 1919 and tied by Earle Combs in 1931. (In fact, the newspapers missed a longer streak, Hal Chase's thirty-three-game string in 1907.) But even then, news of DiMaggio's hitting streak rode piggy-back with that of another streak; the Yankees as a team had smashed a home run in each of their last thirteen games. The Bombers homer string would not run out for another twelve games, establishing a major league record of twenty-five consecutive games with a home run. But when that streak finally ground to a halt, DiMaggio's was still going, and by then it was the only streak that mattered.

As DiMaggio's streak climbed into the thirties, it crowded its way into a busy news cycle that featured daily dispatches from war-ravaged Europe. A few weeks earlier, President Franklin D. Roosevelt, in a speech heard by an estimated 85 million Americans, had declared a state of "unlimited national emergency." Though falling short of declaring war, Roosevelt bluntly stated that "We are placing our armed forces in strategic military positions. We will not hesitate to use our armed forces to repel attack." With Nazi U-boats harassing and sometimes sinking British and Allied supply ships on an almost daily basis, formal U.S. entry into the conflict increasingly seemed a matter of when, not if. On June 22, when Hitler's armies launched Operation Barbarossa, a sudden and massive invasion of the Soviet Union, Roosevelt signaled the new urgency by refusing to invoke the Neutrality Act, and instead extending to Joseph Stalin's besieged country the same Land-Lease agreement previously forged with Winston Churchill's Great Britain. On that same day, Joe DiMaggio smashed a 3–2 pitch from Detroit lefthander Hal Newhouser over the right-field fence at Yankee Stadium, extending his streak to thirty-five games and lifting the Yankees to a 5–4 victory. With their record now at 36–25, the Yankees stood just two games out of first place, and had just notched their first victory of what would become a blistering 30–3 stretch that settled the American League pennant before the end of July.

Undoubtedly, DiMaggio's hot hitting had been one of the main catalysts that turned the Yankee's season around, but he was not the only player in pinstripes who was aiding the cause. Outfielders Tommy Henrich and Charlie Keller, who had also been mired in inexplicable slumps through late April and into May, caught fire just as DiMaggio embarked on his streak. During the Yankee's twenty-five-game home run outburst, Keller and Henrich each blasted nine round-trippers, on their way to respective 30-home run seasons. At the top of the line-up, rookie shortstop Phil Rizzuto supplanted the aging Frank Crosetti and batted better than .300, while providing the best defense at the position in the history of the franchise. His double-play partner, Joe Gordon, had something of an off-year, leading the league in errors but still smacking 24 home runs and driving in 87 runs.

Meanwhile, Joe DiMaggio kept collecting his base hits, and all the other sub-plots—the Yankee's home run barrage, their sudden ascendancy in the standings—started to fade into obscurity. On June 25, DiMaggio extended the streak to thirty-seven games with a fourth-inning home run off St. Louis Browns right hander Denny Galehouse, leaving him just four games behind the American League record of 41, established by George Sisler in 1922. "Now the spotlight is trained on DiMaggio," Dan Daniel emphatically remarked in the *World-Telegram*. "[His] unbroken skein has intrigued fans more than they have been thrilled by any individual feat here since Babe Ruth bettered the home run record with 60 in 1927." The following day, the streak assumed national significance for the first time, as radio broadcasters throughout the country began interrupting their scheduled programming to deliver the latest bulletins from the Bronx. It was a breathless afternoon, tinged with tension and drama. With the streak standing at thirty-seven games, Browns right-hander Eldon Auker, who threw with a "submarine" style motion, nearly halted it. In his first three at bats, Joe flied out to left, reached on an error by shortstop Johnny Berardino (it was an obvious muff, but when the official scorer signaled "E," the Yankee dugout and much of the crowd erupted in indignation), and grounded out to third in the sixth inning, leaving open the possibility that he would not get another opportunity to extend the streak. In the bottom of the eighth inning, with the Yankees leading 3–1, a man on first and one out and DiMaggio standing in the on-deck circle, Henrich took the first move calculated solely to benefit the streak. Horrified at the prospect of grounding into an inning-ending double play, and thus depriving DiMaggio of one more chance at bat, Henrich conferred with Joe McCarthy and then laid down a sacrifice bunt. After that unorthodox bit of strategy, DiMaggio promptly lined the first pitch (at this point, he was swinging at anything near the strike zone, because a walk would also likely finish off the streak) past the third baseman for an RBI double. He was now just three games shy of Sisler's record.

That afternoon's high dramatics signaled the transformation of the streak from a big sports story into a veritable national obsession. As sellout crowds crammed their way into Yankee Stadium, and hordes of reporters descended on

DiMaggio from around the country, the normally unflappable star began to suffer from the pressure that mounted with each passing game. In fact, Daniel reported after the thirty-seventh game that "Joe McCarthy is of the opinion that DiMaggio's anxiety over his spree is not helping his general average."[4] In retrospect, this seems an unfair assertion, given DiMaggio's .384 batting average during the streak to that point. But nonetheless, it does highlight the strain DiMaggio shouldered in trying to meet the day-in, day-out expectations that maintaining the streak demanded. As Gould later observed, "Achievements of a full season . . . have a certain overall majesty, but they don't demand the unfailing consistency every single day; you can slump for a while, so long as your average holds. But a streak must be absolutely exceptionless; you are not allowed a single day of subpar play, or even bad luck. . . . You cannot make a single mistake."[5] For Joe DiMaggio, this improbable streak, born of a few lucky breaks scattered amidst a burst of exceptional hitting, became a daily burden that he alone had to bear. The struggle to defy the immutable law of averages took its own psychological toll. To most outsiders, DiMaggio remained imperturbable even in the eye of the storm. "He didn't show any pressure," Henrich remembered years later. "He never talked about it. From what I know of Joe, he wasn't built that way. He never let us in on his inner thoughts or anything. He never said anything."[6] Henrich's testimony, though authentic, is contradicted by Yankee clubhouse attendant Pete Sheehy, who recalled that "Before the games [during the streak], Joe was always gulping coffee. Maybe as much as ten cups. And he would smoke up a storm. A pack easy."[7] As for DiMaggio, he minimized his struggles. "There was pressure, but I could sleep—when I had the chance. The fans kept knocking on my door." For a born and bred ballplayer like Joe, the easiest moments came during the games: "Pressure on the field? On the ball field, I felt safest."[8]

If the results are any indication, DiMaggio was speaking the truth. After his narrow escape in game 38, DiMaggio made things considerably easier on himself in the ensuing days. He connected for a first inning single and a seventh inning home run the following day, and doubled off Philadelphia's Johnny Babich in the fourth inning the day after that, to move the streak to forty games. That hit was particularly sweet for DiMaggio, as Babich, a former rival from the Pacific Coast League, had promised to end the streak by walking DiMaggio, if necessary. After inducing him to pop out with two men on in the first, Babich ran the count to three-and-oh in the fourth and then threw what he thought was ball four outside. But DiMaggio reached out for it and hit it so hard that, though it rocketed within a few inches of the pitcher's crotch, it rolled far enough into the gap for DiMaggio to reach second base. Joe later gloated that Babich was "white as a sheet" as he stood triumphantly on second base, listening to the cheers from the appreciative Shibe Park crowd.[9]

The following afternoon the Yankees played a double-header in near 100-degree heat at Washington's Griffith Stadium, before an anxious, overflowing crowd. "When he stepped onto the field, they swarmed from the stands, pulling and tugging at him, pleading for autographs," one reporter observed. "All thru batting practice, kids and oldsters alike were hopping from their seats and flocking around the batting cage."[10] In his first at-bat against the Senators knuckleball pitcher, Dutch Leonard, DiMaggio uncharacteristically questioned umpire Johnny Quinn, when Quinn signaled a strike. "Sorry Joe," Quinn replied to DiMaggio's quizzical glance, "it was right over." After lining out to the center fielder and popping out to the shortstop, DiMaggio matched Sisler's modern record of forty-one games in the sixth inning when he ripped a line drive to left field on a one ball–one strike fastball over the outside part of the plate. The Yankees won the game, 9–4, but that hardly dampened the spirits of the crowd of 31,000, which suffered through the heat and humidity to see if DiMaggio could surpass Sisler in the second game.

By game time of the day's second contest, however, DiMaggio's bat—the same reliable Louisville Slugger model that had seen him through the streak's first forty-one games—was missing. It turned out to be stolen; an opportunistic fan who had driven down from Newark, New Jersey to watch the games had jumped into the dugout and snatched it while the players were cooling down in the clubhouse. A visibly upset DiMaggio was forced to borrow Tommy Henrich's bat to see him through the potential record-breaking forty-second game. Henrich's stick came through for Joe, but not before the Senators starting pitcher, Sid Hudson, held him hitless in his first three at-bats. The other Yankees tagged Hudson for several runs, however, so when DiMaggio came up for the fourth time, it was against right-handed relief pitcher Red Anderson. DiMaggio took the first pitch from Anderson high, then drilled the next one to left field for a clean single, extending the streak to forty-two games and establishing new modern and American League records. According to the *Washington Post*, the crowd responded to the hit with a "tremendous, rafter-shattering roar," while DiMaggio's teammates leapt from the dugout and commenced doing "their version of a jig."

After the game, a relieved but determined DiMaggio accepted the congratulations of teammates. "Here's where the big test comes," he noted. "It's going to be even tougher from now on, but I'd sure like to make it last a while."[11] His stolen bat would not be recovered for another week; a DiMaggio friend nabbed the thief after he had been overheard boasting of his prize in various

Newark watering holes. In the meantime, DiMaggio set his sights on Keeler's all-time record of forty-four games. After a day off, the Yankees met the Boston Red Sox for a double-header at Yankee Stadium. In the first game, DiMaggio received a gift single from the official scorer—who that day happened to be Dan Daniel—on a misplayed grounder to third in the fifth inning. That decision might still be debated to this day if DiMaggio had not come up again in the seventh frame and collected another hit, a clean, resounding single to left field. In the second game, DiMaggio wasted little time tying Keeler's mark, as he greeted Boston right-hander Jack Wilson with another line-drive single in his first at-bat. The following day, July 2, 1941, he surpassed Keeler and established a new all-time record with a line-drive home run over the left-field fence off Boston's 31-year-old rookie right-hander Dick Newsome. This time, even the writers in the press box joined the assembled throng of 52,000 in a standing ovation. As DiMaggio later recalled, "I played the rest of the game in a trance. Somebody said they saw a grin on my face, and for just a little while at least I was no longer 'Dead-Pan' Joe."[12]

He would never be that, again. In the eyes of the American public, who had been eagerly following his progress for the last week or more, through radio, newspapers, magazines, and dinner conversations, DiMaggio had become something more than a baseball star; he was now a nationally recognized hero. Besides the Cincinnati history class that voted him "The Greatest American of All Time" (ahead of George Washington and Abraham Lincoln), there was also the song "Joltin' Joe DiMaggio" by Alan Courtney and Ben Homer, that became the number one hit in the land that summer, its schmaltzy lyrics and silly tune echoing in the heads of millions of Americans.

There was a certain comfort to be found in his accomplishment. To be immersed in the streak was to forget, at least for a little while, that Hitler's armies were routing the Soviets near Smolensk, that the Brits had abandoned the island of Crete to Nazi occupation, or that one-time American hero Charles Lindbergh was now traveling the country, telling anyone who would listen that he preferred Hitler to Stalin, and that, like Hitler, he believed that there were superior and inferior races in the world. DiMaggio was a hero happily unassociated with the unpleasant question of bigotry in American society, someone who was free from the stench of politics, and unencumbered by the grim realities of foreign policy. No one knew Joe's opinion, if indeed he had one, about the ongoing catastrophe in Europe or the frightening militarism in Japan, and no one wanted to know. To a country shadowed by bloodshed, tears, and turmoil, DiMaggio represented an oasis of simplicity, grace and beauty, where weary minds could come to rest.

In surpassing Keeler, DiMaggio had already secured his legendary status, but his extension of the streak over the coming weeks would propel his achievement from the improbable to the seemingly impossible. "Joe is liable to extend the streak indefinitely," Joe McCarthy had boasted after DiMaggio broke Sisler's record, and for two weeks Joe seemed to prove his manager right. When would it ever end? After homering in the forty-sixth game, he went 6 for 9 in a July 6 double-header against the Athletics at Yankee Stadium, before a crowd of 60,948 fans who had come not only to see DiMaggio, but also for the unveiling of the center field monument to Lou Gehrig. That pushed the streak to forty-eight games, where it stayed for the next four days, as baseball took a breather for the All Star Game. Though it didn't count for the streak, Joe got a hit in that game as well, and was on base when Ted Williams hit a three-run home run off Cubs pitcher Claude Passeau in the bottom of the ninth inning to win the game for the American League.

Despite the layover, DiMaggio picked up where he left off, in a game at Sportsman's Park against the St. Louis Browns on July 10. The Yankees had arrived in town to find much of the city plastered with handbills trumpeting DiMaggio's arrival, and Joe didn't disappoint the crowd of 12,642 on hand for the game, as he beat out an infield grounder to short in his first at-bat, pushing the streak to forty-nine games. The following day, before a crowd of just 1,625 (as it turned out, the doormat Browns needed those handbills to get anyone to notice their games) he broke out with 4 hits in 5 at-bats, including his twentieth home run of the season, a ninth-inning blast off Browns relief pitcher Jack Kramer. After going 2 for 5 in the streak's fifty-first game, the Yankees traveled to Chicago's Comiskey Park, where DiMaggio went 3 for 4 with 2 runs scored in the first game, then collected a lone, sixth-inning single off Thornton Lee in the second contest, a tightly-played 1–0 Yankees victory before 50,387 fans. In the streak's fifty-fourth game, on July 14, DiMaggio beat out a slow grounder to third base, his only hit in three at-bats. The next day, however, he went 2 for 4 with a double, pushing the string to fifty-five games, and the day after that, at Cleveland's Municipal Stadium, he went 3 for 4, again with a double.

The streak now stood at fifty-six games, and showed no signs of stopping. Since surpassing Keeler, DiMaggio had actually started hitting even more, collecting 24 hits in 44 at-bats, for a .545 batting average and .818 slugging percentage. What kept him going? For one, DiMaggio still had his eye on surpassing the 61-game streak he had assembled with the Seals in 1933. After that, there was Joe Wilhoit's all-time professional record of 69 games, set in 1919. There were also financial considerations. While endorsement offers were flying at Joe left and right, the H. J. Heinz Company, maker of Heinz 57 ketchup, had promised him an extra $10,000 if his streak reached fifty-seven games. With each passing game, more opportunities figured to come Joe's way.

But it all came to an end for DiMaggio in the fifty-seventh game, on the night of July 17, before an announced crowd of 67,468 at Cleveland's Municipal Stadium. For a streak that had so often survived through white knuckle last at-bats, slow grounders beaten out for base hits, and lucky bloop singles just over the heads of infielders, the dramatic events of the fifty-seventh game provided a fitting, if somewhat ironic, conclusion. In this game, the streak would be stopped not by poor hitting, or exceptional pitching, but by the great fielding of Cleveland's star third baseman, Ken Keltner. Still only 24 years old on that night, the six-foot, 190-pound Wisconsin native had already earned a reputation as the American League's best fielding third baseman. In 1939, just his second full season in the majors, Keltner had led all third sackers in putouts, double plays and fielding percentage, and in 1941 he would lead the league in assists, double plays and fielding percentage. Aside from his brilliant fielding and adeptness at diving for ground balls hit to his right side, Keltner was most known for his attempt in 1939 to collect $15 a week in unemployment benefits during the off-season, while pulling down a $7,500 salary during the regular season. (When an indignant press demanded an explanation for his unusual request, Keltner replied, "It was all a joke," to which an outraged *Sporting News* responded, "It certainly wasn't a joke to persons actually in want.") Earlier in the streak, DiMaggio had gathered one of his base hits by blasting a ground ball past Keltner, who had been playing DiMaggio at medium depth. In the future, Keltner resolved to play deeper when DiMaggio was at the plate.

In his first at-bat against Cleveland lefthander Al Smith, DiMaggio pulled a low and inside curve hard down the third-base line. Keltner, playing so deep that DiMaggio would later exclaim, "Deep? My God he was standing in left field!", collared the ball, and then, with his momentum carrying him into foul ground, threw to first, the ball just beating DiMaggio to the bag. It had rained the previous day, and the still dampened turf slowed DiMaggio. "I couldn't get out of the box quickly because of the rains the day before," DiMaggio later recalled, "and Ken's throw just nipped me."[13] After drawing a walk in his next at-bat, DiMaggio faced Smith for a third time, in the seventh inning. Again DiMaggio hit a hard ground ball down the third base line, which Keltner deftly played on a short hop, before turning and firing to first, beating Joe by a step. Keltner's glovework had robbed him of two hits, but DiMaggio was given one more chance, in the eighth inning. With one out, the bases loaded, and the Yankees already ahead 4–1, DiMaggio hit a two ball–one strike fastball from relief pitcher Jim Bagby Jr. to shortstop Lou Boudreau. It was a hard-hit groundball, but right at the sure-handed Boudreau, who handled the chance cleanly, tossing the ball to second baseman Ray Mack, who then pivoted and threw to first baseman Oscar Grimes for the double play. DiMaggio almost got another chance to bat in extra innings, when Cleveland pulled to within 4–3 in the bottom of the ninth and placed the tying run on third with no one out. But three Indian batters in a row failed to bring that runner in, and with that, both the game and the streak were over.

"Well, that's over," DiMaggio announced to his teammates in the clubhouse following the game. Though the Yankees had won, the locker room had been like a morgue, with his teammates waiting for DiMaggio to say something. He expressed relief that the burden of carrying the streak had finally come to an end, but he wasn't happy. "I can't say I'm glad it's over. Of course, I wanted it to go on as long as it could."[14] After accepting the congratulations of his teammates, DiMaggio left the clubhouse with the rookie Rizzuto. As the two ballplayers started walking back to the Cleveland Hotel, DiMaggio suddenly stopped, and reached into his back pocket. "Son of a bitch,' he exclaimed. "I forgot my wallet. Phil, how much money you got?" Rizzuto had eighteen dollars. "Let me have it," DiMaggio said. Rizzuto complied, and then DiMaggio started to head toward a bar. When Rizzuto started to follow him, DiMaggio turned and said, "No, you go on back to the hotel. I want to relax a bit." DiMaggio wanted to mourn the passing of his streak alone, or at least, only among the company of strangers.[15]

As for Keltner, he exited Municipal Stadium that night surrounded by a police escort. When he emerged from the clubhouse, a crowd of fans, who had been waiting for DiMaggio to appear, began to boo him. "You know, Joe had lots of Italian friends in Cleveland," Keltner later explained.[16] Enlarged photographs of the two pitchers who had stopped the streak, Smith and Bagby, were prominently displayed in the next day's newspapers, as if, one sportswriter remarked, "they had just assassinated a king."

Heading into May 15, the date the streak began, the Yankees were in fourth place with a 14–14 record, 5½ games behind the front-running Indians. Following the streak's demise on July 17, the Yankees were in first place, with a 56–27 record, seven games in front of the fast-fading Indians. New York's remarkable insurgence owed much to DiMaggio's performance during the streak's fifty-six games. From May 15 to July 16, DiMaggio posted a .408 batting average, .463 on-base percentage, and a .717 slugging percentage. He had connected for 16 doubles, 4 triples, and 15 home runs, while driving in 55 runs and scoring 56. More than any other player, DiMaggio had turned the Yankees season from a struggle to stay above .500 into another rout of their American League rivals. But it was not the streak itself that accomplished this. That DiMaggio happened to gather at least one hit in fifty-six straight games is not what propelled the Yankees; rather it was the sheer force of his offensive production. If he had been deprived of a hit in one of the games in which he only went 1 for 4 in a Yankee loss—such as occurred in the streak's thirty-fourth game, when DiMaggio managed only a lone single in a 7–2 loss to Detroit—the failure would have ended the streak, but it would not have significantly lessened Joe's value, either as an individual or to the team. It has been suggested that DiMaggio's streak is the most extraordinary batting accomplishment in baseball history. On the psychological and phenomenological levels, this may well be true. But in terms of baseball value, it is demonstrably false. Players such as Babe Ruth, Ted Williams, and Barry Bonds have hit better over an entire season than DiMaggio did during his fifty-six games. Indeed, during that two-month time span, DiMaggio might not have even been the best hitter in his own league. From May 15 to July 16, Boston's Ted Williams actually out-hit DiMaggio, posting a .412 batting average and higher on-base percentage.

Yet much of DiMaggio's lasting fame owes itself to this streak because his accomplishment resonated not only in the alignment of baseball statistics, of numbers on a page, but also in the hearts and minds of a captivated public. His continued success, against all odds, flowed effortlessly into the deepest waters of the American imagination. "DiMaggio's hitting streak is the finest of legitimate legends because it embodies the essence of the battle that truly defines our lives," Gould wrote. "DiMaggio activated the greatest and most unattainable dream of all humanity, the hope and chimera of sages and shamans: He cheated death, at least for a while."[17] For that, DiMaggio entered the gallery of untouchable cultural artifacts, where he would reside for the rest of his life, and beyond.

After the streak ended, the Yankees coasted to the pennant, winning 101 games, and DiMaggio continued to lead them. On July 18, he began another hitting streak of seventeen consecutive games, and though an ankle injury sidelined him for seventeen games in late August and early September, he still finished the season with a .357 batting average, 30 home runs, and a league-leading 125 RBIs. It was arguably the finest year yet in his six-year major league career, but he was no slam-dunk choice for the AL MVP honors. Over the season's final months, the baseball world turned its attention from DiMaggio to Ted Williams, who was threatening to become the first player in a decade to bat over .400. Williams' chase extended into the season's final day, when he clinched the .400 mark with a 6-for-8 performance in a double-header at Philadelphia's Shibe Park. For the season, Williams batted .406, becoming the last man of the twentieth century to clear the .400 barrier, while also leading the league in home runs (37), runs scored (135), walks (145), and slugging percentage (.735), and setting a new all-time record with an on-base percentage of .551, a record that would stand for sixty-one years, until Barry Bonds broke it in 2002.

The comparisons between DiMaggio and Williams presented a tough choice for the sportswriters who cast their ballots for league MVP, but the results would not be announced until the end of the World Series. In the meantime, DiMaggio and the Yankees had business to attend to. Facing them in the Fall Classic were the surprising Brooklyn Dodgers, who had emerged from the dusty catacombs of the National League's second division to overtake the St. Louis Cardinals and win their first pennant in twenty-one years. Despite a record of 100–54, the Dodgers were the prohibitive underdogs against the 101–53 Yankees.

The Yankees did take the Series in a brief five games, but the result could have been very different if not for the unusual chain of events that took place in the top of the ninth inning of Game 4. Down two-games-to-one in the Series and holding a 4–3 lead in the game, the Dodgers seemed poised to tie up the Series with two outs, no men on base, and Tommy Henrich at the plate. Henrich swung at strike three from Brooklyn pitcher Hugh Casey, but the ball glanced off the glove of catcher Mickey Owen, and rolled all the way to the backstop, allowing Henrich to reach base. After Owen's passed ball gave the Yankees new life, DiMaggio singled, then Charlie Keller launched a double off the right field wall to score both runners and give the Yankees a 5–4 lead. The Yankees tacked on two more runs in the inning, and eventually won the game 7-4. They took the following afternoon's contest as well, defeating the demoralized Dodgers 3–1, and thus claiming their fifth World Series crown in six years. For the Series, DiMaggio batted .263 without an extra-base hit in 19 at-bats.

After collecting his $5,943 winner's share for the World Series, DiMaggio had renewed cause for celebration three weeks later, when Dorothy gave birth to the couple's first and only child, a son, Joseph DiMaggio Jr. On the day Joe Jr. was born, October 23, 1941, DiMaggio burst into Toots Shor's restaurant, handing out free cigars and accepting the well-wishes of friends and strangers alike. "Joe was a little excited when he announced it," the *Journal-American* reported the following day, "far more excited, in fact, than he was this year when he broke the consecutive hitting records of all time." In the ensuing days, Joe DiMaggio Jr. would become, in the estimation of San Francisco sportswriter Abe Kemp, "the most photographed child in the United States," with each picture featuring not only the little slugger, but also his happy, beaming parents.

Yet beneath the surface, all was not well in the DiMaggio household. Three years later, Dorothy would say that she had hoped Joe Jr.'s arrival would make DiMaggio "realize his responsibilities as a married man."[18] During their first two years of married life, DiMaggio had not been living up to Dorothy's expectations. He rarely took her out, preferring instead to hang out with his buddies at Shor's place, or to engage in casual dalliances with the beautiful women who threw themselves at his feet; when he did show her off in public, he would often criticize her for talking to the wrong people or saying the wrong things. As far as Joe was concerned, Dorothy was *his*. Coming from a Sicilian heritage that regarded the husband as the unquestioned ruler of his wife and household, DiMaggio could not reconcile his expectations with Dorothy's ambitious and independent nature. Though she had forsaken a promising film career for their marriage, she still sometimes talked with her agent about possible movie roles. If Dorothy hoped that Joe Jr.'s arrival would force him to realize his responsibilities, Joe hoped the baby would tie her down, domesticate her in a way that their marriage never had.

Three weeks after Joe Jr.'s birth, DiMaggio learned that the writers had selected him over Ted Williams as the American League MVP, by a vote of 291–254. The outcome was greeted with approval by sportswriter Joe Williams, who noted that "the plain truth is Williams isn't the ballplayer DiMaggio is. A better hitter, yes, but not too much of a better hitter . . . and from what we hear he isn't the team player the 'Frisco kid is, either."[19] Sportswriter Dave Egan disagreed, and gave his support to Williams. "Certainly DiMaggio sparked the Yankees to the pennant," he wrote, "but he was sparking a smart and nimble and intelligent and ambitious team. . . . On the other hand, Master Williams was carrying, on his slim, young shoulders, a lot of tired veterans and pleasant yes-men and family retainers. The Red Sox are not a baseball team; they are a country club."[20]

More than sixty years later, DiMaggio's MVP selection remains among the most controversial in the history of the award. Was he the right choice? Even the most sophisticated of modern statistical formulas, Bill James' Win Shares, has a difficult time providing us with a clear answer. By James' extraordinarily complex and complicated formula, which takes into account both offense and defense, Williams earned 42 Win Shares for the Red Sox in 1941, while DiMaggio earned 41 for the Yankees. As a hitter, Williams was significantly better than DiMaggio: his batting average was 49 points better, his on base percentage a staggering 111 points better, and his slugging percentage 92 points superior. But where DiMaggio was one of the game's best center fielders, ranking among the league leaders in putouts, Williams was a below-average left fielder. Far from studying the league's hitters to get the best jump on fly balls, as DiMaggio did, Williams could often be seen working on his swing in between pitches in the field.

They were very different players, and very different people. Especially following his disastrous 1938 holdout, DiMaggio had his superstar-role down pat, always giving the sportswriters what they wanted, never causing any trouble, while Williams could sometimes wear his emotions on his sleeve, reacting to misfortune or criticism with crude gestures and epithets. Yet, despite their differences, the two legends would be forever linked in history for their simultaneous exploits in the 1941 season. The Japanese bombing of Pearl Harbor on December 7, 1941, and America's subsequent entry into the world conflict, made their deeds seem even more heroic. Like a photographic process enveloping the past, the war served to color the pair's achievements in sepia tones, casting a glaze of bittersweet nostalgia over the entire summer of 1941, and all its improbable events. With all that followed the bombing of Pearl Harbor in American history, from the sacrifices and bloodshed of 1942 to 1945, through the cataclysmic social upheavals of the ensuing decades, the summer of 1941 would stand, for many Americans, as a simpler time, a time of lost innocence when heroes were good and villains were bad and it was easy to distinguish between the two. It was a cliché, of course, but for the rest of his life, Joe DiMaggio would be expected to live it.

The bombing of Pearl Harbor not only impacted DiMaggio's life in the long-term, it also had serious short-term ramifications as well. While many of his fellow players enlisted, DiMaggio's draft classification was 3-A, meaning that he wouldn't be called until all healthy single men had already gone before the draft board. Some of his fellow baseball stars, such as Cleveland's Bob Feller, opted to volunteer for active duty, but DiMaggio declined that option. As he explained, "Well, there's a little matter of the salary difference between what the army pays a private and what the Yankees pay me."[21] Following his stellar 1941 campaign, DiMaggio expected to be paid a lot. A holdout for the first week of spring training, DiMaggio reported to camp after receiving a raise of $7,000 from his previous year's pay, giving him a 1942 salary of $42,000.

The 1942 season would be the only one in DiMaggio's career in which he remained healthy all season, as he played in all 154 games for the Yankees. Yet it would also be one of his more disappointing years, as he failed to lead the league in a single offensive category, posting a .305 batting average with 21 home runs and 114 RBIs. Those numbers would constitute a career year for many other players, and even though the Yankees once again breezed to the pennant with a 103–51 record, DiMaggio started to hear the same boo birds from the crowd that had bedeviled him after his 1938 holdout. "Efforts to trace the strange conduct of so many of the customers toward DiMaggio have not led to rational sources," Dan Daniel reported in May. "Last season when he was setting that amazing record by hitting safely in 56 consecutive games he was the hero of the Stadium and the darling of the fans. Now his every appearance at the plate is accompanied by hoots. . . ." DiMaggio remained philosophical about the jeering. "Maybe some of the fans don't like my batting average," Joe surmised. "Well, neither do I, so in that respect the hooters and DiMaggio have the same feelings."[22]

But this was about more than batting averages. With a war going on, there were now new heroes, real heroes who were sacrificing their lives for their country while DiMaggio was getting paid $42,000 to hit a baseball, and even that he wasn't doing as well as he used to. Dorothy told him that he should enlist, contribute to the cause of the nation in some way. After that year's World Series, which the Yankees lost to the St. Louis Cardinals in five games, DiMaggio decided to listen to his wife. He would not step on a major league diamond again for more than three years.

NOTES

1. Robert Creamer, *Baseball in '41: A Celebration of the Best Baseball Season Ever—In the Year America Went to War* (New York: Viking, 1991), 6.

2. Michael Seidel, *Streak: Joe DiMaggio and the Summer of '41* (New York: Penguin, 1989), 37.

3. *New York World-Telegram*, May 15, 1941.

4. Dan Daniel, "Joe's Homer in 4th Keeps 3 Bomber Streaks Intact," *New York World-Telegram*, June 26, 1941.

5. Stephen Jay Gould, "The Streak of Streaks," in *Bully for Brontosaurus: Reflections In Natural History* (New York: W. W. Norton and Company, 1991), 464–465.

6. Cataneo, *I Remember*, 43.

7. Kahn, *Joe and Marilyn*, 221.

8. Cataneo, *I Remember*, 163.

9. Cramer, *Joe DiMaggio*, 171.

10. "Fans Come From Miles Around to See DiMaggio Make History," DiMaggio Clippings File, National Baseball Hall of Fame Library.

11. "DiMaggio Aims to Set Record That'll Stand," *New York World-Telegram*, June 30, 1941.

12. Joe DiMaggio (As told to Leslie Lieber), "The Big Streak," DiMaggio Clippings File, National Baseball Hall of Fame Library.

13. Seidel, *Streak*, 202.

14. Allen, *Where Have You Gone*, 105.

15. Cramer, *Joe DiMaggio*, 186.

16. Charles Alexander, *Breaking the Slump: Baseball In the Depression Era* (New York: Columbia University Press, 2002), 271.

17. Gould, "The Streak of Streaks," 472.

18. Associated Press, "Joe DiMaggio Divorced by Wife," *New York Sun*, May 1, 1944.

19. "Yankee Party Put Seal on DiMaggio Value," *New York World-Telegram*, November 12, 1941.

20. Ed Linn, *Hitter: The Life and Turmoils of Ted Williams* (New York: Harcourt Brace and Co., 1993), 169.

21. Kahn, *Joe and Marilyn*, 190.

22. Dan Daniel, "Yanks Expect to Get In Full Stride on Road," *New York World-Telegram*, May 9, 1942.

In his Army Air Force uniform, DiMaggio shakes hands with marine Corporal Andy Steinbach following a June 1944 game. *National Baseball Hall of Fame Library, Cooperstown, N.Y.*

OUT AT HOME

As to the players themselves, I know you agree with me that individual players who are of active military or naval age should go, without question, into the services.
—President Franklin D. Roosevelt, in his famous "green light" let-
ter to the Commissioner of Baseball Kenesaw Mountain Landis,
January 1942, urging baseball to continue during the war

Throughout the summer of 1942, Joe DiMaggio heard the boos. And though he wanted to pass them off as mere gripes over his high salary and sunken batting average, as the summer progressed the feeling gnawed up inside of him that something else was to blame. "There were times when it was plain hell. I'd read in the papers the next day that the cheers offset the boos, but you could never prove it by me. All I ever heard were the boos," he later said. "At first I thought it would wear off, but it didn't . . . and it didn't seem to make any difference whether I had a bad day or a good day. Pretty soon I got the idea that the only reason people came to the game at all was to give DiMaggio the works."[1]

That year Dorothy kept telling him that the only way to make it stop was to enlist. In actuality, though, this was more than a suggestion—it was an ultimatum. Toward the end of that year, Dorothy separated from Joe, moving into an apartment in Reno, Nevada, where divorces were easier to come by, and retaining the services of a prominent divorce attorney. As far as she was concerned, that year, 1942, proved to her that DiMaggio would never make the grade as a husband. Of course, he would pose for the cameras with the baby, and reporters would talk about how he doted over young Joe and wasn't afraid to change dirty diapers. But as soon as the cameras turned away, DiMaggio left Dorothy to deal with little Joe whenever he cried or fussed. As far as he was concerned, the baby was her problem, and if the noise got too bad, Joe would leave, complaining that he couldn't concentrate.

Dorothy's move to Reno was a wakeup call for DiMaggio, who flew out to Nevada and pleaded for a reconciliation. The newspapers got wind of the feud, and by the time the press showed up, Dorothy was singing a different tune, at least in public. "We're very happy about it all," she beamed to reporters as she announced their reconciliation in early January 1943. They even kissed for the cameras. But DiMaggio had only been able to secure a reprieve from a divorce by promising Dorothy he would enlist in the armed forces. Joe had resisted. He didn't want to fight in the Army; he was happy in New York playing for the Yankees. But Dorothy had insisted. If he didn't enlist now, he would look like a coward. After all, even the noted peace activist and folk singer Pete Seeger was now singing the patriotic tune with such songs as "So Mr. President," in which the singer asked for a gun "so we can hurry up and get the job done!"

It was not a good time for a professional athlete to hide behind his 3-A draft status, and Dorothy, who still had ideas of rejuvenating her moribund film career, wasn't about to see her hopes dashed because she was married to the nation's number-one coward. According to Richard Ben Cramer, DiMaggio began to weep when he realized he had no other alternative.[2] In his newspaper column, Dan Daniel agreed that DiMaggio had made the best—really the only—choice. "It is our notion DiMaggio will be happier in the Army than if he had come back for another season of baseball," Daniel wrote. "There was grave danger he would have been made a target. It would have been grossly unfair, but this is a world that knows more than its share of mental cruelty."[3]

He formally enlisted in the Army at the San Francisco Armed Services induction center on February 17, 1943, and one week later reported for duty at the Santa Ana Air Base, which served as headquarters for the Army Air Force's West Coast training center. "He is built for the soldier," Daniel noted of DiMaggio after his enlistment. "He has the temperament of the soldier. He has gone into the Army looking for no favors, searching for no job as coach. He wants to fight, and when he gets his chance, he will prove a credit to himself and the game and the Yanks and his family."[4] A less prescient statement could hardly be found. Soldierly temperament DiMaggio certainly had, but not necessarily the desire to fight, and he clearly wasn't going to turn down any favors. DiMaggio would one day earn the Presidential Medal of Freedom for his service in the Armed Forces during the war, but unlike fellow major leaguers Bob Feller, Cecil

Travis, Warren Spahn, and others, he never ventured anywhere near the battle-field. In fact, he spent his time in the Army doing the exact same thing he did before the war, and the same thing he would do after it—playing baseball. Only instead of earning $42,000 for his work, he now pulled in just $50 per month.

In the summer of 1943, DiMaggio played baseball for the Santa Ana Air Base team, the Seventh Army Air Force (AAF) Fliers, which boasted perhaps one of the most incongruous line-ups of all time, with major leaguers Joe DiMaggio, Red Ruffing, Dario Lodigiani, and Mike McCormick playing alongside AA minor leaguers and young kids, some of whom had never even sniffed professional baseball, much less the major leagues. In his first game with Santa Ana, DiMaggio went hitless against the Fullerton Junior College baseball team. He recovered the next week to make three hits in an exhibition game against the Pacific Coast League's Hollywood Stars, but the quality of play still unsettled him. "Our pitching was so bad I once had to spend forty-five minutes chasing base hits around the outfield," he later said.[5]

Yankee Stadium this was not, but nonetheless DiMaggio's initial experiences in the Army were positive, better than he anticipated. He took instruction well, and quickly became a favorite of his superior officers, who often invited him over for dinner and gave him frequent weekend passes. Those he often used to visit Dorothy. She was now living in Los Angeles with Joe Jr., trying to break back into the movie business and still contemplating a divorce. DiMaggio tried to convince her that he would change, that after the war he would work hard to be a better husband and more attentive father, but she remained skeptical. By then, Dorothy's Hollywood ambitions had been rekindled. The decision she made in 1939, when she was just 21 years old, to forego her movie career in favor of married life now looked like a bad one to her. Just as Joe wanted to have it both ways—a beautiful actress who could also be a doting, devoted housewife—so too did Dorothy fail to reconcile her professional ambitions with her personal commitments. As she maneuvered her way into a divorce, Dorothy simultaneously sought out acting work, auditioning for several roles. Success eluded her, but she kept trying.

In 1943, even with most of the game's top stars off serving in the armed forces, the Yankees continued to dominate the American League, winning another pennant and avenging their 1942 World Series defeat with a five-game victory over the Cardinals in the 1943 Fall Classic. With Spud Chandler winning the American League MVP, and Yankee Stadium's center field now being patrolled by former pitcher Johnny Lindell, DiMaggio was back page news. On September 30, five days after the Yankees clinched the American League pennant, the Associated Press carried a brief notice that DiMaggio had successfully recovered a penny from a San Francisco trolley car coin box while on leave from the Army. In an article headlined, "DiMaggio Recovers Penny," the AP reported that DiMaggio had accidentally placed a 1905 Indian head penny into the locked coin box. After Joe demanded his lucky "home run" penny back, Municipal Railway Officials successfully excavated the coin from the box three days later. A further indignity came in November, when DiMaggio was accidentally left off the Army's list of All Star baseball players, because somebody had neglected to submit his name.

But by then, DiMaggio was suffering deeper embarrassments. Despite his pleas and promises, Dorothy formally filed for divorce in a Los Angeles court on October 11, charging Joe with "mental cruelty" and demanding custody of Joe Jr. When the case was heard before a judge the following May, DiMaggio declined to appear in court and face Dorothy, the judge, or the press that eagerly covered the event. This was an era when divorce was still a relatively rare event, especially for a nominal Catholic like DiMaggio. Far from the routine procedure it is today, divorce in 1940s America entailed a good deal of embarrassment, especially for a public figure of Joe's stature. On May 12, a weeping Dorothy explained in open court that DiMaggio had wrecked their marriage through "cruel indifference." "Joe never acted like a married man," she explained. "He would stay out until the early morning hours with his men friends, leaving me at home alone. He rarely took me out evenings and when he did, he would embarrass me by criticizing everything I did." She added that she had hoped that Joe Jr.'s arrival would lead DiMaggio to change his ways. "But even the baby's arrival didn't change him," she testified. "He became ill-tempered, refused to talk to me for days at a time and several times asked me to get out of the house."[6]

In his ruling, Superior court Judge Stanley Mosk granted Dorothy a divorce, adding that "As a rabid baseball fan it is difficult for me . . . but the evidence is so overwhelming it must be done."[7] Mosk granted Dorothy custody of Joe Jr., ordered DiMaggio to pay $150 a month in child support, and approved a property settlement that granted Dorothy a lump sum payment of $14,400. Technically, the ruling was an "interlocutory decree" which meant the divorce would not be finalized for another year. DiMaggio saw this as another reprieve, an extra year that he could use to try to convince Dorothy to call the whole thing off. But she would remain unswayed. Even when DiMaggio was seen escorting her in public in early September of that year, she made sure to tell reporters that the "status quo" still was in effect. "Any announcement of our reconciliation is premature," she said. The following spring, the divorce was finalized.

The Hollywood success Dorothy Arnold hoped for would elude her for the rest of her life. After the divorce, her film credits list only one picture, 1957's *Lizzie*, a poorly received Hugo Haas film about a woman with a split personality. Thirty-nine years old by then, much of the bloom had fallen off her rose. Six years earlier, she had even dropped a hint to a gossip columnist that she would like to get back together with DiMaggio, but by then Joe had moved on. Married twice more, Dorothy ran a successful supper club in Palm Springs, Florida, called Charcoal Charlie's, where she continued to sing show tunes and dance for the crowds, until she contracted pancreatic cancer. After seeking non-traditional treatment for the disease in Mexico, Dorothy Arnold died in 1984, at the age of 66. By then, she had become a mere footnote to a larger story, the DiMaggio story, and she was also no longer the blonde actress the public most associated with the DiMaggio mystique.

With the divorce proceedings still weighing heavily on him, DiMaggio continued to play baseball for the Army in the spring and summer of 1944, but not at the same Santa Ana base where he had lived and worked the previous year. That spring the Army decided to move the Seventh AAF baseball team, which now also included DiMaggio's old teammate Joe Gordon, to Hawaii, where the ballplayers would tour the islands playing for troops soon to be headed for combat in the waters of the South Pacific. Now promoted to the rank of Sergeant, DiMaggio played well, batting .441 in his first 34 times at bat. But stomach troubles soon forced him to the sidelines. In an unmistakeable sign of the stress DiMaggio had endured in his on-again, off-again relationship with Dorothy—not to mention the strain that accompanied maintaining his composure during the 1941 batting streak, when he guzzled coffee and puffed on cigarettes like both were going out of style—he had developed ulcers. By August 17, DiMaggio found himself hospitalized in Honolulu. He stayed there for six weeks, living next to wounded GIs, some of whom would wake up screaming in the middle of the night, thinking they were still under attack. DiMaggio later described this as the worst part of the war for him. Sequestered in his hospital bed, thinking constantly about Dorothy and his infant son thousands of miles away, the war "never seemed to move at all."[8]

Finally DiMaggio convinced his superior officers to transfer him to another hospital, on the West Coast, where he stayed for an additional three weeks' treatment. After that, he convinced the Army to transfer him again, to the Special Services AAF Redistribution Station, in Atlantic City, New Jersey. While he spent the rest of the war as a "physical training instructor" in Atlantic City, his old unit, the Seventh AAF, moved closer to battle, eventually serving the important role of fueling the bombers that methodically blasted the Japanese in the Pacific Theater during the closing days of the conflict. In all, DiMaggio played only about 100 games for the Army during the war.

When the star sat down with Dan Daniel in November 1944, the reporter thought DiMaggio looked "thin, even peaked." Joe had weighed 210 pounds when he joined the Army; now Daniel doubted "he could have tipped the beams at 180." When asked if his relocation to New Jersey signaled a return to the Yankees in 1945, DiMaggio dismissed the possibility, "scoffing at it," according to Daniel. He had only one question for the reporter: "How did the Yanks lose four straight to the Browns in that final series?"[9] It was a good question. The 1944 Yankees had finished in third place, six games out, and handed the St. Louis Browns their first ever pennant by getting swept in the season's final series.

Clearly, the 1945 Yankees could have used DiMaggio's services, but they needed the 1942 DiMaggio, strong and healthy, and not the sickly 1945 version. After a few months at his new position in Atlantic City, ulcers again landed Joe in the hospital. This time Joe was moved to a clinic in Sarasota, Florida, just a few miles from the Yankee's spring training facilities. Joe arrived in Florida a few days after the bombs fell on Hiroshima and Nagasaki, signaling the end of the bloody, protracted conflict. With peace at hand, baseball writers could afford to start thinking about the game's great stars playing in the big leagues again. At the end of August, the Yankees found themselves in fourth place, but only four games out, leading Daniel to speculate that a well-timed return of the recuperating DiMaggio and Charlie Keller, who had spent the war with the Merchant Marines, could lift the Yankees to another pennant.

If the Yankees did not go to the same lengths to fill their wartime labor shortages as the Cincinnati Reds, who experimented with 15-year-old pitcher Joe Nuxhall, or the St. Louis Browns, who employed the one-armed outfielder Pete Gray, they still struggled to field a respectable team. Prior to the war, their outfield of Henrich, Keller, and DiMaggio had been the best in baseball. By 1945, the green pastures of Yankee Stadium were being patrolled by the utterly pedestrian trio of Bud Metheny, Hersh Martin, and Tuck Stainback, while the catcher's position, once the proud domain of Hall-of-Famer Bill Dickey, was now being manned by the .216-hitting Mike Garbark. The one gem the Yankees had uncovered was their replacement for Joe Gordon at second base, George Henry "Snuffy" Stirnweiss, who won the 1945 batting title with a .309 average.

Nonetheless, the Yankees stood poised to take the pennant if they could get Keller and DiMaggio back for the season's final month. Keller did return, but DiMaggio did not. Initially, Joe was supposed to have been discharged from the Army on August 21, but that date got moved to August 27, at which point the Army lost his discharge papers. Another three weeks passed before the matter was sorted out, and Joe DiMaggio was finally discharged from the Army on September 14. By that time, the Yankees had fallen out of contention, and though DiMaggio offered to come back and play for the season's final two weeks, the organization told him to rest and regain his strength. In the end, the 1945 American League pennant race was decided by a different returning star, Detroit's Hank Greenberg, who reemerged from a four-year hiatus from the game to belt a crucial game-winning home run in the season's final weekend to secure the Tigers their first pennant in five years.

DiMaggio spent the 1945 off-season checking up on his San Francisco restaurant, (which was still being run by his older brother Tom), coaching for Bob Feller's free baseball school in Tampa, Florida, and haggling over his contract for the 1946 season. As Dario Lodigiani recalled for Richard Ben Cramer, during the war a disillusioned DiMaggio nursed visions of a sizeable pay increase when he returned to the Yankees. "One night, we're lyin' around on the cots," Lodigiani recalled, "and DiMaggio says, 'Somebody's gonna pay me for all this time I lost.'

"I said, 'Well Joe, the GI Bill of Rights says you get your job back, same pay and everything.'

" 'The hell with the same,' he says. 'They're gonna pay me. I'm gonna get a twenty-five-thousand-dollar raise.'

"I said, 'Good night! Twenty-five thousand, that's a lot of money, Joe.'

" 'Cost me three years. They're gonna pay for it.' "[10]

Though he never came within a thousand miles of actual combat, DiMaggio resented the war with an intensity equal to the most battle-scarred private. It had robbed him of the best years of his career. When he went into the Army, DiMaggio had been a 28-year-old superstar, still at the height of his athletic powers. By the time he was discharged from the service, he was nearly 31, divorced, underweight, malnourished, and bitter. Those three years, 1943 to 1945, would carve a gaping hole in DiMaggio's career totals, creating an absence that would be felt like a missing limb.

As a player, one of DiMaggio's greatest attributes was the calm, composed, and confident way he went about his business on the baseball diamond. But off the field, those same qualities, augmented by his status as a privileged celebrity and American icon, could become mere self-absorption. While he was getting paid $50 a month to play baseball, millions of Americans were putting their lives at risk combating tyranny both in Europe and the seas of the Pacific. During the war, an estimated 1,078,000 Americans had either been killed or wounded. Balanced against such an unthinkable loss of human life, DiMaggio's gripes over low pay and lost years sound selfish and utterly disconnected to the epochal, world-shattering events that had taken place while he was playing baseball or laying prostrate in a hospital bed.

By November 1945, DiMaggio had agreed to return to play the 1946 season for $42,500, the same pay he received in 1942. Though he didn't get the extra money he hoped for, his salary still carried considerable risk for the Yankees. Away from the game for three years, no one could be sure how he or other returning stars would bounce back from their prolonged absence from the game. "Bob Feller's right arm, the impetus for baseball's fastest pitch, and Joe DiMaggio's powerful wrists, the source of the Yankee Clipper's batting fame, have performed unfamiliar tasks in answering the country's needs," wrote one reporter, apparently unfamiliar with DiMaggio's war-time activities, late in 1945. "What war chores have done to such ball players is a constant question."[11]

Weighty questions hung over the entire sport that off-season. In late October, Branch Rickey, president of the Brooklyn Dodgers, signed one of the Negro Leagues' star players, Kansas City Monarchs infielder Jackie Robinson, to a deal that would send Robinson to the minor league Montreal Royals in 1946, and the big league Dodgers in 1947. The stunning move shattered Organized Baseball's decades old "gentleman's agreement" that excluded African Americans from the major leagues, casting a shadow over the achievements of all the white players who came before Robinson that historians have been struggling to resolve ever since. During his first seven years in the big leagues, DiMaggio had never had to face the best pitchers in baseball, only the best *white* pitchers. Instead of competing against great black hurlers such as Satchel Paige, Leon Day, Raymond Brown, Hilton Smith, Bill Byrd and others, DiMaggio, like all his fellow hitters in the American and National League, had feasted on many mediocre white pitchers who otherwise would have been in the minor leagues.

Despite Robinson's emergence in 1947, the status quo would pretty much hold for the remainder of DiMaggio's career, as few American League teams initially followed the Dodgers lead in signing black players. Indeed, DiMaggio would be long-retired before the Yankees finally played their first African American, catcher Elston Howard, in 1955. Nonetheless, other momentous changes were in store for him and the Yankees when DiMaggio reported for spring training in 1946.

NOTES

1. Cataneo, *I Remember*, 167.
2. Cramer, *Joe DiMaggio*, 208.
3. DiMaggio Clippings File, National Baseball Hall of Fame Library.
4. Ibid.
5. Kahn, *Joe and Marilyn*, 232.
6. Associated Press, "DiMaggio is Divorced; Indifferent, Wife Says," *New York World-Telegram*, May 12, 1944.

7. Cramer, *Joe DiMaggio*, 210.

8. Ibid., 213.

9. Dan Daniel, "DiMag Back in New York as GI Joe," *Sporting News*, November 30, 1944.

10. Cramer, *Joe DiMaggio*, 213.

11. Newspaper clipping reprinted in Wittingham, *The DiMaggio Albums*, 468.

Back from the war: DiMaggio and teammate Charlie Keller take a break in the shade during the Yankees 1946 spring training. *National Baseball Hall of Fame Library, Cooperstown, N.Y.*

COMING BACK

Joe was the team leader but he never said much. Players just watched what he did and they tried to imitate him. If he took a bunt and five swings [during batting practice], they took a bunt and five swings.

—Phil Rizzuto

From the moment Joe DiMaggio reported to the Yankees for spring training in 1946, he could sense the changes that had transformed the organization during his absence, carrying with them new and unfamiliar tensions. Instead of limbering up in Florida as they had in years past, the Yankees flew to Panama in late February, where they prepared for the coming season by playing in tropical heat against baseball teams from the U.S. services. The move was not a popular one with most of the Yankees, who preferred the comfortable familiarity of Florida to the oppressive heat they found in the Central American country. The Panama exhibition had been the brainchild of the Yankee's new president, Larry MacPhail, who had replaced Ed Barrow after the estate of Jacob Ruppert sold the club to Del Webb and Dan Topping following the 1944 season.

Joe McCarthy, still the Yankee's skipper after suffering through three long years of brutal wartime baseball, detested MacPhail and the new owners who hired him. Throughout "Marse Joe's" long and successful tenure with the club, the Yankees had become synonymous with a certain brand of quiet professionalism and staid conservatism. Soon after assuming control of the club's operations, however, MacPhail stood all that on its head. Loud, arrogant, and a born risk-taker (during World War I, MacPhail had led an unsuccessful plot to kidnap Germany's Kaiser Wilhelm), MacPhail had already profoundly impacted the sport during his previous stints with the Cincinnati Reds and Brooklyn Dodgers, by introducing night baseball and broadcasting regular-season games live on the radio, thus revolutionizing the way the game would be marketed to a whole generation of fans. Though he also helped turn both the Reds and Dodgers into pennant winners, the hot-headed MacPhail rarely lasted long in any one job. Fired by the Reds in 1936 after punching a police sergeant in a hotel elevator, he abandoned his post with the Dodgers to join the Army after 1942, where he served as a special assistant to the secretary of war. As Leo Durocher, Dodgers manager under MacPhail, succinctly put it, "MacPhail was a wild man . . . a man of physical action."[1]

He was not Joe McCarthy's type of man. After Webb and Topping hired MacPhail, McCarthy threatened to resign, but was convinced to stay on. Prior to the 1946 season, MacPhail started to work his magic. First, he boosted Yankee Stadium's seating capacity to 80,000, by installing 10,000 new box seats and adding a second deck to the outfield bleachers. Then, just as he had done with Cincinnati and Brooklyn, he brought in the lights. After introducing night baseball to the Bronx, MacPhail also held special promotional days, including a "Ladies Day," in which the club gave away 500 free pairs of nylons and held a pre-game fashion show, complete with models parading around the infield in Jeeps. Not stopping there, MacPhail also began chartering flights for road trips; at least one player, Frank Crosetti, refused to fly and insisted on taking a train instead.

When the club got off to a slow start in April, the increasingly nervous and irate McCarthy started drinking heavily, often flying into violent drunken rages on airplanes and in hotel lobbies, loudly cursing "that son of a bitch MacPhail" to anyone who would listen. On one particularly painful road trip in May, McCarthy actually failed to show up for a few games, then embarked on a three-day bender, at the end of which he telegrammed his resignation to the Yankees front office. Bill Dickey was named his replacement on an interim basis.

Amidst the chaos, DiMaggio emerged as the undisputed leader of the clubhouse, the calming influence on a roster in flux. Ten years after his major league debut, DiMaggio remained the only regular from the 1936 team. His old roommate, Lefty Gomez, had retired as an active player after the 1943 season, and the aging Dickey and Crosetti were now relegated to the bench. With Gomez managing the Binghamton Triplets of the Eastern League, DiMaggio now roomed with the hard-throwing relief pitcher Joe Page, who made no effort to hide his great admiration for his roommate. As Maury Allen noted, Page "would dress like Joe, imitate him, and do his bidding under the guise of friendship. Teammates started referring to Page as 'DiMaggio's Porter,' but the pitcher didn't seem to mind."[2]

There was little reason for Page to feel ashamed. Up and down the Yankee roster, old veterans and younger players alike looked to DiMaggio for leadership. Although reticent and soft-spoken as always, DiMaggio managed to lead by example, as his knowledge of the game and consummate, unflappable professionalism on the field commanded the respect of his fellow teammates. To them, DiMaggio was not DiMaggio but "The Big Dago," or sometimes just "Daig," an ethnic slur that in this instance connoted respect and awe rather than bigotry. "All you had to do was follow what he did," Tommy Henrich later remembered. "He never preached, 'Hey you didn't run that out.' I never heard him say anything like that. But I'll tell you, one look from him, and if you were a rookie and you were guilty of not hustling, a look from him was enough."[3]

DiMaggio also developed a reputation for protecting his teammates. As a rookie in 1941, Phil Rizzuto became a target for some of the team's veterans, who tried to prevent the diminutive shortstop from getting his regular turn in batting practice during spring training. Finally, DiMaggio walked over to Rizzuto and said "Get in there and hit, kid," and with that, the attempted shutout of Rizzuto came to an end. Infielder Jerry Coleman, who joined the Yankees in 1949, remembered DiMaggio as the player who could be counted on to deliver retribution when necessary. "Against the Red Sox, Johnny Pesky took out Rizzuto. It was a tough slide. Just barreled him. I don't know if it was on purpose or whatever," Coleman related to David Cataneo. "So the next inning, DiMaggio came up and hit a single to left field. He never stopped. He went into second and took Doerr into left field. And that kind of thing, when you're a young player, you think, 'Oooooh. Wow. That's our guy.' "[4]

Amidst all the turmoil engendered by the McCarthy-MacPhail feud and the manager's subsequent resignation, DiMaggio remained seemingly imperturbable, a rock of stability in an ocean of chaos. From the beginning of the 1946 season, the writers covering the Yankees detected a new sense of awareness and calm emanating from the Yankee Clipper. Undoubtedly relieved to be out of the Army and back with the Yankees again, he enjoyed a spectacular spring training at the plate. To the writers, he gave every indication that 1946 would mark his triumphant return to baseball. "There is a polish and savoir faire to Joe now that one cannot help but notice," sportswriter Abe Kemp wrote. "He is an agreeable host, certain of himself and free in his conversation."[5] Ten years into his major league career, DiMaggio had indeed come a long way.

Unfortunately for DiMaggio and the Yankees, "polish" and "savoir faire" did not translate into victories. While the Yankees got off to a sluggish start, falling 6½ games behind the frontrunning Boston Red Sox by the last week of May,

DiMaggio struggled with them. As of May 28, his batting average stood at just .261, with only 14 extra-base hits in his first 153 at-bats. Though probably rusty from his extended three-year sabbatical in the Army, DiMaggio also had new physical ailments hampering his performance. In May, DiMaggio experienced a new and perplexing injury that would plague him for the rest of his career: bone spurs in his heel. He first noticed it while trying to round second base, a throbbing pain in his left heel caused by calcium deposits that were digging into his flesh. Though he played through the pain, by the All-Star break DiMaggio's batting average was still stuck in second gear, at .271. Though he was voted onto the All-Star squad that year anyway, largely on the basis of his past exploits, DiMaggio was prevented from playing in the game by another injury. This one occurred in the first game of a double-header against the Athletics on July 7, when DiMaggio sprained his ankle and tore some cartilage in his knee while sliding into second base on what was just his sixth double of the year. Adding a touch of insult to injury, DiMaggio's place in the American League starting lineup was taken by his younger brother Dom, who was enjoying a better season anyway, as he was in the process of setting career highs in batting average and on base percentage for the first place Red Sox.

The rivalry between the DiMaggio brothers had always been something less than friendly. Though Joe himself acknowledged that Dominic was a better fielder, he still chafed whenever his younger brother got the best of him. As Toots Shor later recalled for Maury Allen, "One time Boston was in town for a series with the Yankees, and Joe and I had made a date with his brother Dominic to have dinner at my joint and then go out to a few places around the town. It was a big deal for Dom. He was a kid then," Shor remembered. "That was the day Dom robbed him of two triples with two terrific catches way back in center field in Yankee Stadium. I knew what to expect. All of a sudden here comes a phone call from Joe. 'I'm not going out tonight.' I tried to talk him out of it. Joe was stubborn that way. That was it."[6]

Following the All Star Game, DiMaggio remained on the injured list into the first week of August. By the time he returned to the lineup on August 2, the Yankees found themselves a distant 11½ games behind the seemingly unstoppable Boston juggernaut. Though he would play much better in the season's final two months, as he boosted his batting average to .290 and finished the year with a respectable 25 home runs and 95 RBIs, there was nothing he could do to lift the Yankees back into the pennant race. In addition to the injuries and rustiness that plagued DiMaggio that summer, teammate Tommy Henrich later contended that Joe's performance also suffered from a failure to adapt his hitting style to the slider, the new pitch now being sported by many of the league's top hurlers. First employed by St. Louis Browns right-hander George Blaeholder in the late '20s and early '30s, the slider did not become a popular pitch until top hurlers such as Bob Feller began using it after the war. Thrown with the same grip as a curveball but with a stiff wrist, the slider looked like a fastball until it neared the plate, when it suddenly broke down and away from a right-handed batter (if he was facing a right-handed pitcher). In the endless cat-and-mouse game between batters and pitchers, the slider was a devastating new weapon for the hurler who could effectively control the pitch. In response, a whole new generation of hitters would have to adjust their swings to hit the slider, but, at least according to Tommy Henrich, Joe DiMaggio never modified his approach at the plate. Perhaps because he believed that a hitter needed only a "good eye" and a "level swing," DiMaggio never bothered with the practice and training necessary to combat the new pitch. "Joe D. never changed anything in his swing, and he never hit the slider well," Henrich later claimed.[7] For the rest of his career, the scouting reports on DiMaggio would testify that he could be beaten with the low-and-away slider.

Sinking into third place and finishing with a disappointing 87–67 record, the season ended badly for the Yankees. With two weeks left to play, Dickey resigned his post as manager, and was replaced on an interim basis by Johnny Neun. Dickey's resignation marked both the end of his spectacular playing career and also the end of his abbreviated and unsuccessful foray into managing. To replace him at the catcher's position, the club started playing a 26-year-old Alabaman named Gus Niarhos. When he proved inept, they turned to a pudgy, funny-looking 21-year-old kid from St. Louis named Lawrence Peter "Yogi" Berra. Already, the Yankees were assembling the pieces that would form their next great dynasty.

Larry MacPhail was rapidly making his fair share of enemies within the organization through his abrasive style, but in the winter following the 1946 season he busied himself making moves that would dramatically improve the Yankees by Opening Day 1947, and also in the years to come. Shortly after the Cardinals beat the Red Sox in the 1946 World Series, MacPhail traded second baseman Joe Gordon to the Cleveland Indians for pitcher Allie Reynolds. Reynolds would join a reworked Yankees rotation that also included Spec Shea, Bill Bevens, Spud Chandler, and Vic Raschi. That same winter, MacPhail signed an amateur free agent left-handed pitcher named Edward Charles "Whitey" Ford, who would later anchor the Yankee's pitching staff for more than a decade. Finally, he hired Bucky Harris as his new manager. Once considered baseball's "Boy Wonder" for managing the Washington Senators to their first and only World Championship in 1924 at the age of 27, by 1947 Harris was one of baseball's most experienced and respected managers, having served as skipper for four different teams over a span of twenty seasons.

Amid this flurry of activity, MacPhail nearly made another deal that would have shocked the baseball world, and likely rewritten much of baseball history, if it had come to pass. In the spring of 1947, MacPhail met with Boston Red Sox owner Tom Yawkey to discuss the possibility of trading DiMaggio to the Red Sox for Ted Williams. With Williams coming off an MVP season, and DiMaggio hampered by numerous injuries, the Yankees were anxious to make the trade, but Yawkey backed off at the last minute. "Well, I want to make it, but I just can't make it even up," Yawkey explained to Yankees co-owner Dan Topping. "The people in Boston think Williams is better." Yawkey then offered to make the deal if the Yankees threw in another player, but the Yankees balked: they could justify trading their most marketable star for Williams even-up, but not if they had to include another player in the deal. With that, the proposed trade was abandoned.[8]

In the ensuing years, the aborted Williams-for-DiMaggio deal has become a favorite topic for fans and historians. What would have happened if the trade had gone through? Some historians have suggested that the deal would have benefited both players. Williams, a left-handed hitter, would have had the luxury of taking aim at Yankee Stadium's short right field porch for the rest of his career, while DiMaggio would have escaped the Stadium's Death Valley in left center, for Fenway Park's much more inviting Green Monster. The 37-foot high wall stood just 315 feet from home plate down the foul line, before jutting out to a mere 379 feet in left center. In many respects, this analysis is sound. Williams likely would have seen his home run totals boosted at the Stadium, and DiMaggio's batting average certainly would have benefited from Fenway Park's cozier dimensions. But his power numbers probably would not have improved, and might even have decreased, had the trade been consummated. As we have seen, DiMaggio's approach to hitting, which he never significantly altered during the course of his career, produced line drives more often than fly balls, and it is doubtful that many of DiMaggio's hits could have cleared the fence. Instead, many of the line drive home runs and extra-base hits he collected at the Stadium would have become merely hard hit singles at Fenway. Indeed, DiMaggio himself agreed with this assessment. "I was a line-drive hitter," he noted. "I didn't get the ball high. My line drives rose, but the high fence at Fenway would have kept them from going over."[9]

In January 1947, on the advice of MacPhail, DiMaggio underwent surgery to have the calcium deposits in his aching left heel removed. By all accounts, the surgery was a disaster. When DiMaggio arrived for spring training in late February 1947 (this time in San Juan, Puerto Rico), he was still limping. Mal Stevens, the club's physician, examined the heel, and to his dismay discovered the surgeon's incision had left an open and granulating wound, which was now badly infected. "His heel was grotesque," Yankees traveling secretary Frank Scott later remembered. "It was stitched up like a bad shoemaker had fixed it."[10]

Stevens sent DiMaggio back to the United States, where his heel underwent a second, more successful operation on March 17, at Baltimore's Johns Hopkins Hospital. This time, doctors took a piece of skin from the back of Joe's right thigh and grafted it over the infected wound on his heel. Initially, doctors hoped DiMaggio would be ready to play once the regular season began, but Joe, sporting a cane to help him move around, told Dan Daniel that he felt "a little discouraged, and, quite bewildered" by the setback. "There is still some seepage through a small hole in the new skin," DiMaggio explained. "In a few days that should heal, and the crust should harden. Meanwhile I dare not step down on my heel, and I need this cane to navigate."[11] By early April, DiMaggio was able to take batting practice, but he still couldn't put a baseball shoe on his wounded foot, nor perform any running.

The Yankees were clearly worried about DiMaggio's future. Though still only 32 years old, DiMaggio had suffered through numerous injuries in his professional career; by all accounts, he had torn the cartilage in his knee at least three times, injured his ankles at least twice, been hospitalized on more than one occasion for ulcers, suffered an eye infection, and hurt both his right shoulder and right elbow. There was scarcely a part of his body that had not experienced some injury, ailment, or mishap, making pain—and playing through it—a constant theme of DiMaggio's career. "Joe played hurt almost all the time," one team physician, Dr. Sidney Gaynor, later testified. "He had a high tolerance for pain and could play when other people wouldn't. That's just something built into the man."[12]

Though he was forced to favor his right leg while the injured left heel continued to mend, DiMaggio missed only four games at the start of the 1947 season before returning to the line-up. At first, he struggled. On May 15, his batting average stood at just .259, and he had connected for only 2 home runs. But as the weather warmed, DiMaggio's play improved dramatically. By the end of June, his batting average stood at a resounding .324, while a barrage of 18 doubles and 9 home runs boosted his slugging percentage to .527.

Under Bucky Harris' laid-back managerial style, the resurgent Yankees reclaimed their perch atop the American League standings. By the All Star break, New York was in the midst of a franchise-record nineteen-game winning streak, also tying an American League record that would not be broken until the Oakland Athletics won twenty straight in 2002. At the end of their mid-summer surge, the Yankee's record stood at 58–26, a commanding 11½ games ahead of the second place Detroit Tigers. From there, the Bombers coasted to their first pennant in four years, finishing the season with a 97–57 record, twelve games ahead of the Tigers. During the pennant-deciding win streak, DiMaggio had aided the cause by posting a .382 batting average with 4 home runs and 17 RBIs.

As with years past, the Yankees dominated the league with a balanced attack. Though their rotation did not boast a single 20-game winner (off-season acquisition Allie Reynolds led the club with 19 wins), New York received superlative performances from Spec Shea (14–5, 3.07 ERA), Spud Chandler (9–5, 2.46 ERA), midseason acquisition Bobo Newsom (7–5, 2.80 ERA), and closer Joe Page, who led the league with 17 saves while notching 14 wins and registering a 2.48 ERA over 141⅓ innings of work.

On offense, DiMaggio led the way with a .315 batting average, 20 home runs and 97 RBIs. His chief support came from long-time teammate Henrich, who batted .287 with 16 home runs and 98 RBIs, first baseman George McQuinn, who posted a team-high .395 on-base percentage, and third baseman Billy Johnson, a holdover from the war years, who batted .285 with 10 home runs and 95 RBIs. After giving Yogi Berra a brief look in the outfield, the Yankees pushed him into the backup catcher role, where he excelled offensively, batting .280 with 11 home runs in 83 games.

Henrich later insisted that the aspect of DiMaggio's play that impressed him the most that year was his defense. For the year, DiMaggio committed only one error, leading the league with a .997 fielding percentage, but this was more an indication of his reduced range in the outfield than anything else. Slowed by his sore left heel, DiMaggio posted just 2.3 putouts per game, the lowest total of his entire career. Even more troubling, his outfield assists total dipped to a career low of two. Some argued that the decline was caused by opposing runners' trepidation over challenging DiMaggio, but it wasn't that. While the heel injury prevented DiMaggio from firmly planting his left foot on his throws from the outfield, he also suffered other injuries that hampered his throwing ability. In early August, he strained a muscle in his neck, sidelining him for several games. Additionally, after the World Series DiMaggio admitted to a reporter that he had been bothered by a sore arm for the last several weeks of the season.

The 1947 World Series proved to be a classic, pitting the Yankees against their crosstown rivals from 1941, the Brooklyn Dodgers. That '41 Dodgers team bore the imprint of then-president MacPhail, who had assembled the pennant-winning roster around hitting stars such as Dolph Camilli, Pete Reiser, and Joe Medwick. By 1947, the club bore the distinct imprint of the new head of baseball operations, Branch Rickey, who had promoted Jackie Robinson to the parent club that spring. "The Rickey experiment," had proved a resounding success, as the first baseman collected the inaugural Rookie of the Year award, finishing the season with a .297 batting average, .383 on-base percentage, and a league-leading 29 stolen bases.

Though they were each their team's biggest stars, neither Robinson nor DiMaggio played particularly well in the seven-game Classic. Jackie, who once said that DiMaggio was the player he most admired in the major leagues, batted .259 with three runs scored, while Joe batted just .231, albeit with two home runs. Instead, the Series turned on the play of each club's supporting cast. With the Yankees holding a two-games-to-one advantage in the Series, the unheralded Bill Bevens took the mound for New York in Game 4. Bevens had pitched poorly out of the rotation in 1947, posting a 7–13 record with a 3.82 ERA, and his start at Brooklyn's Ebbets Field would prove to be the last of his major league career. He made it a memorable one. Though he walked 10 batters in the game, Bevens held the Dodgers hitless for 8⅔ innings. He needed just one more out to secure the first no-hitter in World Series history, but with runners on first and second and the Yankees clinging to a 2–1 lead, he surrendered a double to pinch-hitter Cookie Lavagetto, scoring the tying and winning runs for Brooklyn. One out away from immortality, Bevens instead ended up with the loss.

With the Series tied at two games apiece, Spec Shea took the mound for the Yankees in Game 5, and delivered a masterful four-hitter for a 2–1 victory, with one of the runs coming on a DiMaggio home run. The Series returned to Yankee Stadium the next day for Game 6. The Dodgers took an 8–5 lead heading into the bottom of the sixth inning, when the Yankees put two runners on base with two men out, and DiMaggio at the plate. What followed has long since entered baseball lore as one of the greatest plays in World Series history. Facing the Dodgers fireballing left-hander Joe Hatten, DiMaggio smashed a line drive into deep left field, toward the 415-foot sign and low chain-link fence separating the field from the Brooklyn bullpen. It looked sure to go for extra bases, but Al Gionfriddo, a seldom-used outfielder who had just been inserted into the game as a defensive replacement for Eddie Miksis, raced under the ball, stuck out his glove, and caught it within a few feet of the fence. The Yankee's rally stymied, the Dodgers went on to win the game 8–6. In the seventh game, however, the Yankees ended Brooklyn's hopes and captured the world championship with a commanding 5–2 victory at Yankee Stadium.

The Gionfriddo catch has become a central event in the DiMaggio story, taking on mythological proportions. Despite the availability of television replays, which clearly show that the ball would not have left the park, numerous historians, including several DiMaggio biographers, have claimed that Gionfriddo's catch robbed DiMaggio of a game-tying home run. At most, the ball would have landed for a double, or possibly a triple. As historian Eric Enders notes in his history of the World Series, "Though most newspaper accounts of the game said the hit would have been a homer, this was merely an example of the halo granted DiMaggio by the New York media. Film of the play clearly shows that it would not have left the park. Indeed, Gionfriddo caught the ball two full steps in front of the fence."[13]

DiMaggio's reaction to the play, in which he kicked the dirt around second base in frustration after Gionfriddo caught the ball, has also become an event of central importance to the DiMaggio mystique. According to the oft-repeated story, this public display of disgust marked the only time the normally placid DiMaggio ever exhibited his emotions on the baseball field. "In all the years I played with Joe, I think I only saw him get mad once," Phil Rizzuto told Maury Allen, in a statement that is echoed by many. "That was in the World Series of '47 when he hit that long fly ball in the sixth game with two on and Al Gionfriddo caught it in front of the bullpen. . . . He was really steamed."[14]

Although DiMaggio was indeed one of the most even-tempered players in history, this characterization of Joe's reaction to Gionfriddo's catch as somehow unique and unprecedented is also not accurate. Just six years earlier, in the 1941 World Series, DiMaggio exchanged heated words with the Dodgers pitcher Whit Wyatt, who had thrown some pitches too close to his chin. After DiMaggio flied out, he reportedly yelled to Wyatt, "This Series isn't over yet." Wyatt's response, "If you can't take it why don't you get out of the game?" caused DiMaggio to go after the pitcher, but both benches emptied before any punches were thrown.[15] In addition, teammates also remembered DiMaggio once kicking a bag full of balls in frustration, sending the balls rolling all over the dugout. In other words, DiMaggio was a human being, prone to angry outbursts and displays of frustration like anyone else. "The halo effect" noted by Enders not only exaggerated DiMaggio's exploits, such as erroneously claiming that his fly ball in Game 6 would have been a home run, it also caused his contemporaries to engage in selective memory for a player whose skills and temperament they greatly admired. Though the Gionfriddo play was clearly not the only time DiMaggio displayed any emotion on the baseball field, to believe otherwise was to assert the existence of an imaginary, sanctified DiMaggio.

The sportswriters who voted for the 1947 American League Most Valuable Player engaged in similar wishful thinking when they awarded DiMaggio his third MVP trophy, by just one point over Ted Williams. Judged by the standards of who had the better season, DiMaggio's selection remains one of the most inexplicable in the history of the award. In 1947, DiMaggio had a good year, but Williams, who won baseball's Triple Crown with 32 home runs, 114 RBIs, and a .343 batting average, had a far superior one. Not even the difference in the two players' defense and base running could make up for that gap.

According to Bill James' player evaluation system, Williams collected 44 Win Shares, DiMaggio only 30. In an attempt to justify the unjustifiable, sportswriters such as Red Smith asserted that DiMaggio deserved the award because he was a "real champ," who, "if all other factors were equal save only the question of character . . . never would lose out to any player."

Of course, all things weren't equal: Williams had the better season. In selecting DiMaggio, some of the writers probably rated him ahead of Williams because Joe's team won the pennant while Ted's team did not, but others did it out of spite for the Splendid Splinter. Never on good terms with their city's best player, two members of the Boston media left Williams off their ballot entirely (writers were—and still are—allowed to select up to ten players), thus handing the award to DiMaggio. "It wasn't the first time Williams earned this award with his bat and lost it with his disposition," Red Smith noted.[16] One could argue that just the opposite was true for DiMaggio, that he won the 1947 MVP for his "disposition," rather than his performance. Though it would be the last MVP of his career, the 1947 selection illustrates just how far DiMaggio had come from his early days as an awkward rookie who "lacked color." More than a decade later, DiMaggio was now perceived by the media as embodying all the great American virtues: to the public he was modest, dignified and graceful, a terrific team player who could still excel as an individual. Though his private life contradicted many of these assumptions, this perception would remain the prevailing wisdom about DiMaggio for the rest of his life.

NOTES

1. Leo Durocher, with Ed Linn, *Nice Guys Finish Last* (New York: Simon & Schuster, 1975), 118.

2. Allen, *Where Have You Gone*, 117.

3. Cataneo, *I Remember*, 55.

4. Ibid., 66.

5. Cramer, *Joe DiMaggio*, 217.

6. Allen, *Where Have You Gone*, 62.

7. Henrich, *Five O'Clock Lightning*, 146. DiMaggio's inability to hit the slider is also testified to by teammate Bobby Brown in Cataneo, *I Remember*, 87.

8. Allen, *Where Have You Gone*, 120.

9. Cataneo, *I Remember*, 180.

10. Cramer, *Joe DiMaggio*, 226.

11. Dan Daniel, "Yanks Run Extra Camp for DiMag," *New York World Telegram*, March 28, 1947.

12. Allen, *Where Have You Gone*, 128.

13. Eric Enders, *100 Years of the World Series* (New York: Barnes and Noble Books, 2003), 118.

14. Allen, *Where Have You Gone*, 124–125.

15. Seidel, *Streak*, 213.

16. Red Smith, DiMaggio Clippings File, National Baseball Hall of Fame Library.

"His Bat Spells Bingo"

The baseball star is made out to be a puppet. But he has his sensations and his feelings, he has his ills and his hopes and his fears, he has his stomach aches and his nights of walking the baby, he has his scraps with the Missus or his courting misunderstandings with the Miss. . . . This is an effort to give you a picture of the Joe DiMaggio we of the New York press box know.

—Dan Daniel

Perhaps no player in baseball history enjoyed a better relationship with the reporters who covered him than Joe DiMaggio. In the last half century, the New York sports media has acquired a reputation for being overly-critical and sensationalist, muckraking and sleazy, and the list is long of players who have come to New York high on their horses only to leave with their tail between their legs. Yet despite the numerous daily newspapers who covered him, DiMaggio scarcely ever had any difficulties in his dealings with the press. Reporters did chastise him for his 1938 holdout, but they forgave him far more quickly than the fans. When the fans started booing him again in 1942, the press played dumb, obscuring the possible reasons for the public's displeasure. They covered the details of his divorce from Dorothy Arnold in 1944, but never dwelt on the breakup once the sourness had passed. During his slumps they remained confident that their star player would pull through, during his moments of triumph they often inflated his achievements beyond their actual scale.

How is it that this son of a Sicilian fisherman came to own the media capi-

Brooklyn Dodgers catcher Roy Campanella looks on as DiMaggio is greeted by the Yankees bat boy following Joe's fourth-inning home run in Game 5 of the 1949 World Series. *National Baseball Hall of Fame Library, Cooperstown, N.Y.*

tal of the world? The answer to this perplexing riddle is a complex of three factors: DiMaggio's introverted, unassuming personality, his magnificent performance and professional deportment on the baseball field, and the Yankees unprecedented success during his career.

As Daniel related the story, when DiMaggio arrived for his first spring training with the Yankees in 1936, he came to visit the writer, on the advice of a San Francisco reporter with whom DiMaggio had enjoyed a pleasant relationship. Upon their meeting, the veteran sportswriter provided the rookie with simple advice that would aid him for the rest of his career. "Don't be suspicious of the writers," Daniel told the young DiMaggio. "Don't be too talkative, but don't crawl into a shell and stay there. As I size you up, you have a level noggin and a sense of humor. Those are the two main essentials in relations with the press. Just be yourself."[1] For Joe, the "don't be too talkative" advice was easy enough to follow. And though he initially crawled into a shell, as he matured he slowly came out of it. He answered reporters' questions matter-of-factly, rarely playing up his own achievements and often showering praise on his teammates; in this respect, he had an excellent model in Lou Gehrig. Perhaps more importantly, he got to know many of the team's beat writers off the record, often spending his leisure hours with Lou Effrat, Dan Daniel, and Jimmy Cannon at Toots Shor's restaurant. The writers gradually came to befriend DiMaggio, to like him on a personal level, which naturally led them to submerge any criticism of the star when they went to write their game stories and weekly columns.

Besides which, there wasn't much to criticize. During DiMaggio's first six seasons, the Yankees won five world championships, already more than Babe Ruth had won in his entire career in pinstripes. Most years, DiMaggio was the best player on the team, and some years, the best player in the entire league. His demeanor on the field was unassailable; never once ejected by an umpire during his entire career, DiMaggio rarely showed his displeasure at a bad call or a teammate's mistake. The New York media had hyped DiMaggio to absurd proportions before he ever played a major league game, and though he never possessed the "color" of Ruth, his no-nonsense approach to the game melded perfectly with the more sober times in which he played. DiMaggio's simplistic grace and quiet, unassuming air were the perfect match for a nation that had been virtually torn down and rebuilt again within the span of a decade by the Great Depression and World War II. DiMaggio embodied the ideal manhood for an era characterized by privation and sacrifice; he'd beat your brains in on the baseball field, but he wouldn't gloat over it or boast about it afterward.

In this respect, DiMaggio's Sicilian heritage, his awkward adolescence as the child of illiterate immigrant parents, and his innate shyness, played to his advantage. DiMaggio's personality made manifest a kind of cultural crossroads—between his introverted personality, born of his uneasy connections to the Old World, and confident athleticism, his mastery of the American pastime. Each worked to mitigate the other. Without the confidence, DiMaggio would have been little more than an enigma, his shyness mistaken for diffidence, surliness, or stupidity. Without the shyness, his confidence would have seemed excessive arrogance, a personality trait that only pays dividends with the sports media if you also have the brash sense of humor of a young Dizzy Dean. But when those two qualities—shyness and confidence—came together in DiMaggio, the result was a player whose public deeds and habits were utterly beyond reproach. As a result, the world's most powerful media machine became for Joe a hammer and chisel, carving out a myth, solid as marble, of DiMaggio as the athletic embodiment of perfection, instead of a shovel used to bury his deeds under a mountain of personal castigation. That unkind fate would be reserved for Ted Williams, who was many of the things DiMaggio was not: outspoken, boastful, hot-tempered, and who also had the misfortune of never playing for a championship-winning team.

"Oh, I hated that Boston press," Williams later wrote in his autobiography. "I've outlived the ones who were really vicious, who wrote some of the meanest, most slanderous things you can imagine. I can *still* remember the things they wrote, and they still make me mad. . . ."[2] By contrast, DiMaggio actually dedicated his autobiography, in part, to "the sports writers of all the papers, who have always given me a break. . . ." For Williams, it wasn't difficult to understand why the writers always seemed to be on DiMaggio's side; it was, he noted pointedly, "because the Yankees won."[3]

In the wake of their 1947 World Series victory over the Brooklyn Dodgers, the Yankee's franchise experienced another jolt when MacPhail tendered his resignation. During his short two years with the club, MacPhail had overhauled much of the Yankee's roster, ushering in the franchise's next great era, but he had also antagonized nearly everyone in the organization, from the owners all the way down to the field manager. Considering MacPhail's impulsive nature (during his Brooklyn days, he often "fired" manager Leo Durocher only to re-hire him the following morning), most assumed that he would change his mind and return for another season. However, following a drunken rampage at the team's victory dinner—in which he "fired" George Weiss, the Yankee's farm director, then proceeded to punch the club's traveling secretary in the face for defending the character of Branch Rickey—MacPhail's days with the Yankees, and his career in baseball, were at an end. Weiss was quickly named his replacement as the club's general manager.

One of Weiss' first challenges in his new capacity as GM was to resign Joe DiMaggio. This he did, for the princely sum of $70,000, making Joe the second-highest paid player in Yankee history, behind only Babe Ruth, who had earned $80,000 in 1930 and 1931. Following off-season surgery on bone chips in his elbow, DiMaggio declared himself as physically fit as he had ever been since becoming a major leaguer. The regular-season results would bear that assessment out, as DiMaggio missed only one game all season, and put together his best year since returning from the Army.

After a sluggish start, DiMaggio hit his stride in mid-May, when he homered six times in the span of four games, culminating in a three-home run performance against the Cleveland Indians on May 23, with the first two round-trippers coming against Bob Feller. After connecting for just one more home run in his next twenty-six games, DiMaggio blasted another seven circuit clouts in as many games. By the All Star break, DiMaggio had 19 home runs,

73 RBIs, a .302 batting average, and a .607 slugging percentage. DiMaggio's hot hitting put the Bombers in third place, just 2½ games behind the frontrunning Cleveland Indians. With Tommy Henrich en route to a career high 138 runs scored, and Yogi Berra continuing his development into one of the game's most dangerous hitters, the Yankee offense was carrying its share of the load. The pitching, on the other hand, had fallen on harder times. Between starters Ed Lopat, Vic Raschi and Allie Reynolds, not one of the Yankee's top pitchers sported an ERA below 3.50, and the staff's once-unhittable closer, Joe Page, had become merely average, walking nearly as many batters as he struck out and posting an ERA above 4.00.

DiMaggio's defensive play enjoyed a renaissance that year, as he appeared to be fully recovered from the bone spurs that hampered him in 1947. In contrast to that season, when he posted the fewest put-outs per game of his major league career, in 1948 DiMaggio had arguably his best defensive season, registering a career-high 2.90 putouts per game. Though the 33-year-old DiMaggio no longer possessed the foot speed of his younger days, he more than compensated for it with his superior knowledge of the opposing hitters and uncanny ability to put himself in the right place at the right time.

As Ed Lopat later recalled for John Tullius in *I'd Rather Be a Yankee*:

> It's about the fifth or sixth inning and Boudreau's the hitter. I sorta turned around to center field, trying to make up my mind what I wanted to start Boudreau with, and I noticed Joe was playing Boudreau straight away in dead center.
>
> So I turned around, got the sign, threw my pitch, and it was a ball. So I turned around to center again to think what I was gonna do with the next pitch and DiMag is still in dead center, and I went back to the rubber and got the sign and missed again. Now, I'm 2–0 and really peeved, and this time I don't turn around. On the next pitch Boudreau hits a frozen rope over Rizzuto's head right in the gap and as I turned to follow the ball, I'm thinking, "Oh my God, there goes a triple at least." As I followed the ball out to the outfield, Joe was standing right there. Never moved. I was shocked. So when the inning was over, I went over and sat down next to him. "Joe," I said, "I noticed on the first two pitches to Boudreau you were playing dead center. How the hell did you get over in the hole waiting for the ball?"
>
> He says, "Well, I seen you pitch enough to know if you were even up or ahead of him, you wouldn't let him pull the ball. But when you got behind two balls and no strikes, I just moved over seventy, eighty feet in the hole."

That's when I said to myself, "Now I know what makes that guy great."[4]

With DiMaggio gobbling up fly balls in center field, and defensive standout Phil Rizzuto anchoring the infield, the Yankees defense made their mediocre pitching staff seem acceptable, and helped keep the team in the pennant race.

As the summer months dragged on, the Boston Red Sox, led once again by Williams, pushed themselves into a four-way hunt for the pennant with the Indians, Athletics, and Yankees. After the Yankees dropped five of seven games, slipping into fourth place in mid-August, the four teams still stood within five games of one another. The Yankees recovered to win 20 of their next 23 games, moving to within 1½ games of the first place Red Sox, with the Indians holding steady in third place, 4½ games out, and the over-matched Athletics having fallen out of contention.

Though slowed by a bad charley horse in his left leg and another developing bone spur in his right heel, over the season's final three weeks DiMaggio played brilliantly, posting a .449 batting average, clubbing 6 more home runs, and driving in 28 runs. But it wasn't enough. The Yankee's pitching staff continued to give up too many runs, allowing 6 or more tallies in 10 of the club's final twenty-three games. With 2 games left in the regular season, both the Red Sox and Yankees stood 1½ games behind the red-hot first-place Indians. The season ended for the Yankees in a two-game showdown at Fenway Park. The Red Sox faithful heckled Joe during the series with a clever retouching of the lyrics to *Maryland, My Maryland:* "He's better than his brother Joe—Dom-in-ic Di-Mag-gi-o!"[5]

For his part, DiMaggio thought the razzing rather humorous, and anyway, it didn't affect his performance on the field, as he went 5-for-9 for the Series. But the Yankees lost both games, as the pitching staff yielded a combined 15 runs for the series. The Red Sox victories, coupled with an Indians loss to Detroit on the season's final day, set up a one-game playoff between the two clubs, won by the Indians, 8–3. Cleveland would go on to win the World Series over the Boston Braves in six games. It would be the Indians last world championship of the century, and it would also be the last World Series won by a team not from New York until 1957.

In that year's MVP balloting, DiMaggio finished a distant second to Cleveland's player-manager Lou Boudreau, who in addition to guiding the Indians to their first pennant in 28 years had also batted .355, second in the league to Williams' .369 average. Though his .320 batting average was only seventh best in the league, in other respects DiMaggio's 1948 performance ranks among the best of his career, and certainly better than his MVP-winning 1947 campaign. In addition to his stellar defensive play, DiMaggio led the American League in home runs (39), RBIs (155), and total bases (355), while finishing second in the league with a .598 slugging percentage. It might not have merited the MVP Award, but it was a performance good enough to put him once again on the cover of *Time* magazine, which noted that although "DiMaggio does not hit the ball as hard as the mighty Ruth did, nor as often as Ted Williams does . . . as a clutch hitter he is terrific. With men on bases and the chips down, his bat spells bingo."[6]

The following February, Joe hit the jackpot, signing a $100,000 contract for the 1949 season, the highest salary in baseball history up to that time. The blockbuster deal was a real roll of the dice for the Yankees. Three months prior to signing, DiMaggio had undergone another operation, this time to remove the bone spur in his right heel. Nonetheless, DiMaggio told reporter John Drebinger that he expected to come back strong again in 1949, and most observers felt DiMaggio was worth the money. "Go ahead and look at the averages and you will see that Williams outhit DiMaggio for the season," Chicago sportswriter John C. Hoffman opined. "But you won't see there that indefinable something DiMaggio had and Williams didn't have when the chips were down during the final weeks of the struggle."[7]

What Joe had was an injured foot. Shortly after reporting for spring training on March 1 in St. Petersburg, Florida, DiMaggio began experiencing chronic pain in his right foot. Despite a restricted workout schedule and specially-designed sponge rubber heels that were inserted into his shoes, the pain only intensified when DiMaggio attempted to play in exhibition games that spring. When he tried to compensate for the heel ailment by running on his toes, he developed painful blisters. By the end of March, the *New York Times* reported, DiMaggio's heel was "now so painful as to preclude the possibility of his running on it at all." Conceding the obvious, on April 12 DiMaggio checked himself into Johns Hopkins Hospital for what was considered at the time to be revolutionary treatment: X-ray treatments supplemented by regular injections of novocaine. Diagnosed with a "thickening" of the heel, doctors expressed confidence that DiMaggio eventually would recover and be able to return to baseball, though they could provide neither DiMaggio nor reporters with a timeline for his recuperation. DiMaggio, "grim-visaged" according to the *Times*, admitted that "This just didn't come on me now. It has been bothering me all the time."[8]

Now, some wondered if the $100,000 DiMaggio would ever play baseball again. "It is a pretty solid conviction with those close to the situation that DiMaggio never again will be the DiMaggio of old," James P. Dawson reported in the *Times*. For their part, Yankee officials refused to even speculate on DiMaggio's retirement. "It's embarrassing even to discuss such possibilities when everything is problematical," Weiss said. "I know that Joe is anxious to play and we're anxious to have him do so."[9]

They would have to wait. Joe stayed in the hospital for only a few days, but the constant presence of newspaper reporters and photographers in the lobby caused him to uncharacteristically lash out in anger and frustration. "Don't you think you've gone far enough?" DiMaggio shouted to the assembled newsmen as he made his way through the lobby on crutches. "You guys are driving me batty. Can't you leave me alone? This affects me mentally, too, you know."[10]

For the next several weeks, DiMaggio lived in the posh Hotel Elysee, where his friends Toots Shor and George Solotaire brought him meals. In May, he learned that his father had died in San Francisco. After flying to California for the funeral, DiMaggio quickly returned to New York, and still his heel showed no signs of progress. To visitors, he seemed unusually belligerent and anxious. "What a year," he glumly noted to Dan Daniel. "I have lost close to 10 pounds. On top of all my baseball troubles, I lost my father. . . . Sitting around is wearing me down. I have been out of action in other years. But I never suffered so much."[11] Finally, on May 23 he reported to Yankee Stadium for a workout. The results were not good. After running through just a few exercises, the pain in his heel swelled up to unbearable levels. "Nothing I can do about it," DiMaggio lamented. "All I know is I'm back in civvies for today and tomorrow at least. And probably longer than that the way things are looking. It's terribly discouraging."[12]

When the extent of DiMaggio's injury first became apparent, the *World-Telegram* carried the headline "Yanks Are Futile Without DiMag." As it turned out, they weren't. At the end of May, the Yankees found themselves in first place, with a 25–12 record, 4½ games in front of the second place Boston Red Sox. Though the Yankees were getting solid performances from Berra, Henrich, Rizzuto, outfielder Gene Woodling, and third baseman Bobby Brown, as well as solid pitching from Page, Lopat, and Raschi, many observers credited the Yankees success to their new manager, Charles Dillon "Casey" Stengel.

Stengel's hiring in October, just a few days after the club fired Bucky Harris, shocked reporters, who could not square Stengel's reputation as a clown with the Yankees staid, corporate image. Born in Kansas City, Missouri, (the "Casey" nickname was derived from "K.C."), Stengel enjoyed a prosperous major league career with the Dodgers, Pirates, Phillies, Giants, and Braves. Aside from his excellent foot speed (he won Game 1 of the 1923 World Series with an inside-the-park home run), Stengel was most famous for his antics: in 1919, he responded to some hecklers by placing a live sparrow in his cap. When he returned to the field, he lifted the cap, thus giving all the fans in attendance the bird. After his playing days were over, Stengel managed several mediocre teams for the Dodgers and Braves, never finishing higher than fifth place. In the words of historian Robert Creamer, Stengel was considered a "court jester" to the press, good for a funny quote but little else. Though Stengel did contribute many humorous sayings, or "Stengelese," to the lexicon—"All right everybody," he once instructed his team, "line up alphabetically according to your height"—he also possessed a keen analytical mind. He became one of the first managers to platoon his hitters to maximize their effectiveness, and he also relished using younger, untested players. Nonetheless, Stengel's antics had many in the New York press corps skeptical that he could make the grade in the Big Apple. "I never saw such a bewildered guy in my life," sportswriter Art Daley told DiMaggio during spring training. "He doesn't seem to know what it's all about."[13] Soon, however, Stengel's success with the DiMaggio-less Yankees turned many skeptics into true believers. "Casey did take time out occasionally to tell a joke," Dan Daniel noted after the season. "But he proved himself one of the most astute managers the major leagues have seen."[14] A clown one day, a genius the next, Casey Stengel was on his way to the most successful managerial tenure in baseball history.

While the Yankees battled the Red Sox for first place, DiMaggio continued to wait for his swollen heel to improve. He occasionally tested himself with routine practice—shagging fly balls, playing "pepper" with teammates—but even these simple activities had become for DiMaggio "great adventures." With each passing day, his frustration mounted, and he once again took to guzzling cups of coffee. Up late most nights, DiMaggio paced the floor of his hotel room, wondering if his career was over. Historian David Halberstam thought it "the worst time in his life."

Then, miraculously, one day in mid-June the pain was gone. DiMaggio woke up and no longer experienced the sharp agony when his heel struck the floor. After testing out the foot by walking around the city, DiMaggio started taking batting practice again. Soon, he was no longer shagging fly balls, but running full speed after them. Still erring on the side of caution, DiMaggio decided to play in an exhibition game against the New York Giants before committing himself to regular-season duty. He went hitless in four at-bats, but again, there was no pain. Finally, just before a June 28 game against the Boston Red Sox at Fenway Park, the first in a pivotal three-game series, DiMaggio told Stengel he was ready. At the start of the series, the Red Sox, now managed by DiMaggio's old friend and boss Joe McCarthy, were in third place, a half-game behind the Philadelphia Athletics, and five games behind the front-running Yankees. Of the sixty-five games DiMaggio missed at the start of the season, Stengel and the Yankees had won forty-one of them.

Next to his fifty-six-game hitting streak, DiMaggio's performance in the three games at Fenway Park, from June 28 through June 30, stands as the most memorable achievement of his major league career, perpetuating the belief among many that DiMaggio was perhaps the greatest clutch hitter and team leader in baseball history. For the three games, all won by the Yankees, DiMaggio collected five hits in eleven at-bats, including four home runs, nine RBIs, and five runs scored. "He murdered us," remembered Red Sox pitcher Boo Ferriss. "He came back and, oh man, it was like he'd never been away. We couldn't get him out."[15]

In the first game of the series, DiMaggio singled in his first at-bat, then slammed a two-run home run off Red Sox starter Mickey McDermott, giving the Yankees a 5–0 lead. Behind Reynolds and Page, they would hold on to win the game 5–4. The next day, the Red Sox stormed to a 7–1 lead heading into the fifth inning. With two men on base, DiMaggio smashed an Ellis Kinder delivery over the fence in left center, making the score 7–4. DiMaggio came up again in the eighth inning with the score now tied, 7–7, and Boston relief pitcher Earl Johnson on the mound. Johnson's first offering was a low and inside curveball, which DiMaggio promptly golfed over the Green Monster for a solo home run. The Yankees won the game, 9–7.

By the following day, June 30, DiMaggio's comeback had already become something of a national sensation. *Life* magazine's observation that "it was one of the most heart-warming comebacks in all sports history, and from one end of the country to the other it became the summer's prime topic of conversation,"[16] recalled the summer eight years earlier, when DiMaggio had also dominated the sports world. Though not quite on that level, DiMaggio's stirring performance did compel sportswriter Robert Ruark to proclaim DiMaggio the "first real sports colossus since the Dempsey-Jones-Ruth era."[17]

His performance on June 30 provided a fitting conclusion to his three-day rampage. With the Yankees leading 3–2 in the seventh inning, DiMaggio came to the plate with two men on base and two men out, facing the Red Sox ace left-hander, Mel Parnell, who would go on to win twenty-five games that year. June 30 would not be one of those games. After getting ahead 0–2, Parnell three times tried to coax DiMaggio to chase a pitch out of the strike zone, but Joe wouldn't bite. Finally, with the count 3–2, Parnell threw DiMaggio his best fastball. It was the pitch DiMaggio had been waiting for the entire at-bat, and he pounced on it, sending a towering shot that clanged off the steel towers beyond the left field fence for a three-run home run. That proved to be the difference, as the Yankees won the game, 6–3. With the loss, the Red Sox fell all the way into the second division, eight games out of first. Many assumed that DiMaggio had driven the final nail in their coffin, but they would come back.

In the meantime, everyone marveled at what DiMaggio had accomplished.

"Babe Ruth alone could match Joe's flair for drama, for putting on a show and responding to an occasion," an ebullient Stengel observed after the final game of the Series. "And not even Ruth would have put on the kind of demonstration DiMaggio staged here. Eight workouts, and then socko. Four homers. The answer is this—the man is a pro."[18] After a half-season of pain and heartache, DiMaggio was overjoyed, and relieved, by his performance. On the train heading out of Boston, Jerry Coleman remembered, DiMaggio sat back in the corner of the dining car, his hand clutching a bottle of Pabst Blue Ribbon beer, and quietly said, as the city disappeared from view, "Can't beat this life, kid."[19]

"DiMaggio's spectacular pennant debut served notice on the rest of the American League that the Yankees were very much in the pennant fight," Dan Daniel observed in the *Sporting News*. "They were up there minus Joe; they are going to be so much tougher with DiMaggio in action."[20] Instead of running away with the pennant as they had in years past, however, the Yankees played ordinary ball for the rest of the summer, posting a 33–23 record during the months of July and August; during that same time span, the Red Sox went 42–20, moving to within two games of first place. DiMaggio did his part, posting a .346 batting average and .596 slugging percentage over the remainder of the season, though lingering soreness limited his effectiveness in the outfield, as his put-outs per game declined to 2.56. Stengel, who had a bevy of outfield options with youngsters Cliff Mapes, Gene Woodling, and Hank Bauer, in addition to mainstays Billy Johnson and Johnny Lindell, was concerned. "Have I been watching DiMaggio in center field?" he asked. "Yes, with keen interest. He has told me that his heel bothers him again."[21] DiMaggio was benched for two games in late August because of what the *New York World-Telegram* described as his "obvious inability to cover his center field territory due to recurring heel trouble, plus a slightly sore shoulder."

Though DiMaggio returned to the line-up on August 25, it wasn't long before he was sidelined again. On September 18, with the Yankees still clinging to a 2½ game lead over the Red Sox, DiMaggio came down with an unusually strong case of pneumonia. Weakened by a fever that ran as high as 104 degrees, DiMaggio missed the next 12 games. During that span, the Yankees went 6–6, including a disastrous three-game sweep at the hands of the Red Sox from September 24 to 26. After losing 4–1 to the Athletics on September 30, the Yankees fell into second place, one game behind the Red Sox. All that remained was a two-game series against Boston at Yankee Stadium that would decide the American League pennant.

DiMaggio's illness was severe enough for him to undergo penicillin shots in the hospital, and still, his body hadn't recovered. During his absence, he had lost 18 pounds; simply walking around his apartment for a few minutes caused him to lose his breath. Still, he knew he had to play in the climactic showdown with Boston. Weakened by the persistent pneumonia and hobbled by a bothersome heel, DiMaggio told Stengel he could play three innings of the first game.

As it turned out, he played all nine. The Red Sox jumped out to a 4–0 lead before the Yankees mounted their comeback in the fourth inning. Once again, DiMaggio was the catalyst. After connecting for a double off Mel Parnell, DiMaggio scored the Yankees first run on a Hank Bauer single. The following inning, the Yankees tied the game, aided in part by DiMaggio's infield single. The game remained at a 4–4 deadlock until Johnny Lindell smashed a solo home run in the eighth inning, giving the Yankees a 5–4 victory and a tie for first place with one game left to play.

It was another heroic performance, but in the season's final game, DiMaggio had nothing left in the tank for a suitable encore. Simply trotting out to his position in center field consumed most of what little energy he had left. Still, the Yankees tagged Boston pitchers Ellis Kinder and Mel Parnell for five runs, and carried a 5–0 lead into the top of the ninth inning. After recording the first out, Yankee starter Vic Raschi walked Ted Williams, then surrendered a single to Vern Stephens. The next batter, Bobby Doerr, hit a long fly ball to center field. It was well struck, but it was the type of ball that DiMaggio, when healthy, would catch with ease. But now his weakened legs refused to carry him where he needed to go, and as he stumbled after it the ball landed over his head for a bases-clearing triple. With that, the exhausted DiMaggio signaled to Casey Stengel to take him out of the game. Cliff Mapes replaced him in center field, and after the Red Sox plated one more run, Raschi retired the side to give the Yankees a 5–3 victory and the American League pennant.

That year's World Series, against the Yankee's old rivals, the Brooklyn Dodgers, was dominated by pitching. The Series started in Yankee Stadium on October 5, three days after the Yankees had clinched the pennant, and by then DiMaggio had finally overcome his crippling battle with pneumonia, though he still hadn't returned to full strength. He started every game of the Series, but could only muster a .111 batting average, with one of his two hits coming on a solo home run in the fifth game. In his struggles at the plate, however, he was hardly alone. The Yankees as a team batted just .226; the Dodgers, just .210.

In Game 1 of the Series, Brooklyn's Don Newcombe shut down the Yankee offense for 8 full innings, striking out 11 batters. But his opponent on the mound, Allie Reynolds, was every bit as good, keeping the Dodger bats in check for 9 innings, surrendering just 2 hits and fanning 9 batters. The game remained scoreless until the bottom of the ninth, when Tommy Henrich led off with a game-winning home run off Don Newcombe for a 1–0 New York victory. The next day, the two clubs again found themselves in a pitcher's duel, with Brooklyn's Preacher Roe out-pitching Vic Raschi en route to a 1–0 victory. From there, the Series shifted back to Brooklyn, where the Yankees, led by great pitching from Raschi and Joe Page, and great hitting from Bobby Brown and Johnny Mize—a late-season acquisition that boosted the club's flagging offense—won all three games to take the Series, four games to one.

For his career, DiMaggio had now captured seven world championships under three different managers. And though he had good reason to be disappointed by his own performance in the World Series, he couldn't help but marvel at how far he had come in 1949. From signing the most lucrative contract in the history of the sport, through his persistent heel injury, the loss of his father, his stunning comeback in Boston, the pneumonia that sidelined him during the season's pivotal final weeks, he concluded his performance "wasn't too bad."[22]

To show their appreciation, on the next-to-last day of the regular season, when the Yankees were still fighting the Red Sox and DiMaggio was battling his bad case of pneumonia, the organization held a "Joe DiMaggio Day" at the ballpark. Included among the gifts he received that day were two automobiles, a boat, a deer rifle, new carpeting for his living room, a hand-painted tie, a polished wood elephant for good luck, a sack of walnuts, a case of lemonade and a case of frozen lima beans, an ash tray, an alarm clock (presumably to help him get out of bed before 10 A.M.), a dozen golf balls, and a rosary. Moved by the display of gratitude, the emaciated DiMaggio admitted, "This is one of the few times I have choked up." Delivering perhaps the most eloquent speech of his career, he went on to say, "this day proves that New York is the friendliest town in the world. . . . I'd like to thank the Good Lord for making me a Yankee."[23]

Though he had not announced his intentions for the 1950 season, the spectacle caused some to wonder if they were witnessing the denouement of DiMaggio's brilliant baseball career. In an article headlined "Joe's Day Marks End of An Era," Dan Daniel wrote, "Season after season, a star, the fans' player, the players' player, the writers' and the managers' player—Joseph Paul DiMaggio had certainly earned, over and over again, the paean which resounds throughout baseball for him today."[24]

NOTES

1. Dan Daniel, "DiMaggio . . . Everybody's Ballplayer," *Sporting News*, April 28, 1948.

2. Ted Williams, with John Underwood, *My Turn at Bat: The Story of My Life* (New York: Simon & Schuster, 1988), 9.

3. Ibid., 12.

4. Cataneo, *I Remember*, 75–76.

5. "The Big Guy," *Time,* October 4, 1948.

6. Ibid.

7. John C. Hoffman, "DiMag worth 100 Gs a Year," reprinted in Wittingham, *The DiMaggio Albums*, 570.

8. James P. Dawson, "Joe DiMaggio to Miss Yankee Opener," *New York Times*, April 13, 1949.

9. Ibid.

10. "Reporters Upset Ailing DiMaggio," *New York Times*, April 15, 1949.

11. Dan Daniel, "Joe Tense As Heel Improves," DiMaggio Clippings File, National Baseball Hall of Fame Library.

12. *New York World-Telegram*, May 25, 1949.

13. Robert Creamer, *Stengel: His Life and Times* (New York: Dell Publishing Co., 1985), 221.

14. *New York World-Telegram*, October 3, 1949.

15. Cataneo, *I Remember*, 86.

16. *Life,* August 1, 1949.

17. Robert Ruark, "Hero, Non-Global," DiMaggio Clippings File, National Baseball Hall of Fame Library.

18. Dan Daniel, "Joe's Delayed-Action Bombs Exploding," *Sporting News*, July 6, 1949.

19. Cramer, *Joe DiMaggio*, 270.

20. Daniel, "Joe's Delayed-Action Bombs Exploding."

21. Dan Daniel, "Mize-Flag Clincher or DiMag Insurance?," *New York World-Telegram,* August 23, 1949.

22. DiMaggio, *Lucky to Be a Yankee*, 32.

23. Dan Daniel, "'Thank Lord for Making Me a Yankee,' says Jolter," *Sporting News,* October 12, 1949.

24. Dan Daniel, "Joe's Day Marks End of an Era," *New York World-Telegram*, October 1, 1949.

END OF THE LINE

The last couple of years, you could see there was something wrong. . . . He was in pain. You could tell that. The way he went after a ball. He wouldn't get there. Before, he'd be standing there.
—Philadelphia Athletics shortstop Eddie Joost

Following his injury-plagued 1949 season, DiMaggio returned home to California and for the first time committed himself to an off-season training program. He had belittled the need for off-season conditioning in the past, and would later go so far as to claim that he "never needed" spring training. Yet DiMaggio freely admitted to reporters that 1949 had been "the roughest time of my life," and so he filled his winter months with golfing, hunting, and walking, "and some days I walk 20 miles," he noted. "Proper exercise and the establishment of a routine of living have done a lot for me," he added. "My legs feel better than they have for years [with] not a sign of pain in my heels where those bone spurs were removed."[1] The Yankees once again offered DiMaggio a $100,000 contract, and Joe accepted.

For DiMaggio, it was a spring filled with renewed hope and energy. He was 35 years old, possessed a troubling and lengthy history of injuries, but "nonetheless the way I feel now I can't see any reason why there should not be three or four more good years ahead of me." Indeed, DiMaggio's disposition early in spring training was so ebullient that Stengel felt it necessary to reign in his star outfielder. After observing that DiMaggio was running well, "and looks great at

December 11, 1951: DiMaggio poses for the cameras during the press conference announcing his retirement from baseball. *National Baseball Hall of Fame Library, Cooperstown, N.Y.*

the plate," Stengel cautioned, "I would like him to take it easy right through the training season, but he may have different ideas."[2]

DiMaggio did have other ideas. On March 17 in St. Petersburg, he impressed the sportswriters with his batting performance against the Senators, as he smashed a home run (measured at over 440 feet) and two singles in a lopsided 13–2 exhibition victory for the Yankees. Six days later, however, he was briefly benched with a charley horse. When news of the injury reached the press, DiMaggio cautioned, "don't write that I am washed up as a ball player."[3]

His performance early in the regular season led some to wonder. Shortly before Opening Day, DiMaggio pulled the calf muscle in his left leg, and admitted that his left shoulder was routinely popping out of its socket. That injury wouldn't affect his throwing, but it did affect his hitting. By May 20, his batting average was an anemic .235, and he had connected for just three home runs and driven in only 17 runs. Over the next six weeks, however, DiMaggio went on a power barrage, connecting for 13 home runs and nine doubles, but by the end of June his batting average still stood at only .262. With the Yankees four games behind the first place Detroit Tigers, Stengel decided to make a change. On July 2, he announced to reporters that he was moving DiMaggio to first base, to give the younger Cliff Mapes a shot at center field, and also to allow outfielder Hank Bauer, on his way to a season's batting average of .320, to play against both left-handers and right-handers. Ultimately, the first base experiment lasted only one game, as DiMaggio returned to center field when Bauer went down with an injury. "I was in a cold sweat every minute," DiMaggio later admitted about his one day at first base. "I was never so nervous in my life."[4]

But Stengel didn't stop there. A few days later, he shifted DiMaggio from his accustomed cleanup spot in the batting order, the same position he had occupied since 1938, down to the fifth slot. Stengel tried to explain his decision in baseball terms, by arguing that the move gave him a better platoon advantage, but DiMaggio and many of his allies in the Yankee clubhouse perceived the change as nothing more than an insult, a personal affront. By 1950 DiMaggio had become the organization's sacred cow, not to be moved under any circumstances, for any reason. To play him at first base or bat him anywhere other than cleanup suggested that he was not the flawless ballplayer romanticized by his admirers in the sporting press and the dugout.

But Stengel, his mind constantly fixated on ways to improve his line-up with new platoons, younger players, new batting orders, or playing guys at new positions, was not interested in sacred cows or preserving old traditions. Tinkering with DiMaggio like he was just another player, and not The Great DiMaggio who enchanted the imaginations of his admirers, could help cement his authority with the club. "I really think Casey hated [DiMaggio]," teammate Jerry

JOE DIMAGGIO

Coleman later told Maury Allen. "Casey had a large ego and I don't think he liked the idea of anybody on the team being bigger than Casey. Joe was bigger than Casey, bigger than anybody in baseball and most people out of baseball."[5]

Though DiMaggio was soon restored to his customary position in the cleanup spot, DiMaggio and Stengel developed a healthy dislike for each other. During the season, word of the rift between the manager and his star player reached the press, with one sportswriter criticizing DiMaggio for "sulking like a sophomore." "No one denies this great player his right to his pride," the scribe continued, "but he is carrying things too far when he refuses to talk to his manager, curtly cuts the newspapermen who have been his friends for years and maintains a stony silence toward all but a few of his teammates."[6]

Both DiMaggio and Stengel publicly denied they were feuding. "I've been in baseball a long while and I've known a lot of team players," Stengel said. "DiMaggio is one of the greatest and I'd be a poor sort of manager if I didn't think the world of a guy like that."[7] But behind the scenes, teammates insisted the tensions between the two were very real. "Casey couldn't wait until DiMaggio quit," Rizzuto later asserted. "Casey wanted one leader on the team—him. When he got there, DiMaggio was the leader. Everybody looked up to him. When we had our meetings for splitting up World Series shares, DiMaggio would decide who would get a full share and who wouldn't. One year we kidded about not giving Casey a full share, but it would have caused too much of a furor."[8]

For DiMaggio's part, he nursed his grievances in private. But when later asked about Stengel's phenomenal success with the Yankees—New York would win seven world championships and 10 American League pennants during his tenure—DiMaggio would simply say, "he had the horses." And when asked which manager he preferred, Stengel or Joe McCarthy, DiMaggio's choice was clear: "Stengel has revolutionized the game with his platoons," he said. "McCarthy struck on a line-up and stuck with it. I guess you'd have to say I liked McCarthy best. . . . But I have a soft spot in my heart for Joe. All during my hitting streak he gave me the hit sign even when the count was 3 and 0."[9]

By the summer of 1950, those halcyon days of 1941 seemed like a distant memory for DiMaggio, who was now struggling just to hit better than the league average. As the weeks passed, he slowly pushed his batting average up towards the magic .300 level, but he wasn't getting his hits the way that he used to. Now bothered by sore knees in addition to his other ailments, DiMaggio could no longer get the same torque into his swing, and his reflexes at the plate had noticeably slowed. A consistent pull hitter in his prime, DiMaggio, unable to turn on a good inside fastball anymore, and still bedeviled by those low-and-away sliders, started to take more pitches and push the ball towards the opposite field.

118

For some batters, patience at the plate and hitting to all fields were marks of achievement, but for DiMaggio, it was a sign of retreat. Yet even as everyone, including DiMaggio, bemoaned the decline in his skills, Joe quietly began to put together another outstanding season.

With Phil Rizzuto enjoying a career year and on his way to winning the American League MVP, and with the pitching staff bolstered by the midseason arrival of rookie Whitey Ford, who went 9–1 with a 2.81 ERA down the stretch, the Yankees pushed their way into a tie for first place by the end of July. They were helped by a resurgent DiMaggio, who batted .363 for the month. He went into a brief tailspin at the start of August, collecting only four hits in 35 at-bats and dropping a routine fly ball in Boston, leading the *Sporting News* to characterize his play as "tired and jaded." But after Stengel judiciously rested him for six games (another move that Joe resented), DiMaggio came back stronger than ever, enjoying what would prove to be the last sustained period of excellence in his playing career. From August 17 until the end of the season, Joe batted .373 with 11 home runs, including three four-baggers against the Washington Senators at Griffith Stadium on September 10, the third and final time in his career that he hit that many roundtrippers in a single game. The late-season surge carried DiMaggio to another exemplary year at the plate: for the season he finished with a .301 batting average, 32 home runs, 122 RBIs, and a career-high 80 walks. His .585 slugging percentage led the American League, and the Yankees won the pennant by three games over the Detroit Tigers.

On paper, it looked like a typical DiMaggio year, but when the MVP ballots were distributed to the writers at season's end, Joe pulled only enough votes to finish in ninth place. Despite his statistical success, several sportswriters declared that DiMaggio's 1950 season had been the "worst" of his career. Yet it was actually similar to his MVP-winning 1947 campaign, except that in 1950 DiMaggio actually got on base more often, hit with considerably more power, and drove in more runs. But the press saw only his determined struggle to bat better than .300, the constant pain he experienced in both legs, and interpreted both as a sign of diminished value. "It would not be wise to write DiMaggio off now with finality," Dan Daniel allowed in September. "But the handwriting on the wall becomes increasingly sharper. His repeated disabilities can mean only one thing; he is getting closer and closer to the finish. The fissure is beginning to widen. It has been clearly visible from the press box for some time."[10] Even DiMaggio agreed with his critics, declaring that "there was no excuse, none at all, for my 1950 performance."[11] DiMaggio's 1950 season should have earned him praise for his continued excellence in the face of advancing age and mounting injuries. Instead, both DiMaggio and the press viewed it with dismay. The beauty of his play, so evident early in his career, had been used to overestimate his value in his prime. Now, at the end of his career, the sudden absence of those same aesthetic qualities caused observers to underestimate his still-considerable accomplishments. The DiMaggio myth, it turned out, was always a double-edged sword. "I hope the fellows who write about him will stop trying to deify him and start trying to humanize him," one Yankee told a reporter for *Sport* magazine. "It's guys like you who are making it tough on him. . . . If you ask me, the windup would be a lot easier for Joe if the writers would just try to stress that the guy is only human—just like you and me."[12]

In the 1950 World Series, DiMaggio and the Yankees faced the surprising Philadelphia Phillies, dubbed the "Whiz Kids" by the press for their youth and exuberance. They gave the more experienced Yankees all that they could handle, as three of the Series' games were decided by one run. Unfortunately for the Phillies, all three of those games were won by the Yankees, who took the Series in a four-game sweep. The high point for DiMaggio, who batted .308 in the four games, came in Game 2 at Philadelphia's Shibe Park, when he broke a 1–1 tie in the top of the tenth inning with a solo home run off the Phillies ace righthander, Robin Roberts. Earlier in the game, DiMaggio had even flashed some leather, tracking down a long drive off the bat of Del Ennis to squelch a potential Philadelphia rally in the sixth inning. For DiMaggio, it was a satisfactory conclusion to a long, and (his words) "bad season."

He decided to come back and play for the 1951 season, and initially refused to say whether he would continue to play after that. "Just how many more years I'll be able to give it as a player, I don't know," DiMaggio wrote after the 1950 season. "I do know, however, that I'd rather make up my own mind about it and not have somebody come to me one day and say, 'Joe, maybe you ought to get out of there and give this young fellow we just brought in from our farm club a real good chance.' Nope, I want to find this all out for myself, and when I do I want to be the first guy to go to the manager and tell him I'm through."[13]

In the spring of 1951, DiMaggio came face-to-face with the "young fellow just brought in from the farm" to replace him. His name was Mickey Charles Mantle, a strapping 19-year-old switch-hitter from Commerce, Oklahoma who had decimated the Western Association for Joplin in 1950, leading the league in batting average (.383), runs (141), and hits (199), while blasting 26 home runs and driving in 136 runs. Like the young DiMaggio, Mantle initially played shortstop, though not very well: his strong yet erratic arm convinced the organization that he belonged in the outfield. But he could do everything else. His power at the plate was a revelation: nicknamed "Muscles," Mantle blasted pitches as far as anyone since Babe Ruth, and maybe even farther than that. And one look at him tearing around the base paths or running down fly balls in the outfield immediately clued observers into the origin of his other nickname, "The

Commerce Comet." "My God," Stengel reportedly said when he first saw him run, "the boy runs faster than Cobb."[14] Though he was not a great judge of fly balls, and would never be the fielder that DiMaggio was in his prime, Mantle's speed made up for his fundamental deficiencies, and his arm was as strong as Joe's had been before the injuries, and elicited just as much praise. After Mantle gunned down a runner at home plate, Tommy Henrich could only shake his head in wonder: "That's the best throw I ever saw."[15]

In short, Mantle was the complete package, the best prospect to come into the organization since DiMaggio fifteen years earlier. In fact, the hyperbolic praise his talents elicited from teammates, coaches, and sportswriters was eerily reminiscent of DiMaggio's experiences early in the 1936 season. "He's got to be great," Bill Dickey, now a coach with the team, told the writers. "All that power, a switch-hitter and he runs like a striped ape. If he drags a bunt past the pitcher, he's on base. I think he's the fastest man I ever saw with the Yankees."[16] Infielder Gil McDougald was more succinct in his praise. "Mickey," he noted, "had a spring training like a god."[17]

Though Whitey Ford initially dismissed Mantle as a "hayseed," before long most of the team had embraced the up-and-comer. Stengel practically adopted him, referring to Mantle as "that kid of mine" and predicting great things for his young prodigy. One of the few Yankees who remained cool to Mantle was DiMaggio. Growing up in the Ozarks, Mickey had idolized DiMaggio, but when he finally met him, Joe gave him the cold shoulder. Unlike Lou Gehrig, who had graciously shared the spotlight with the young DiMaggio, old Joe wasn't about to grant any favors to the man who was being groomed to replace him in the outfield.

Publicly, Joe said all the right things about Mantle. "Why should I resent him?" he asked. "If he's good enough to take my job in center, I can always move over to right or left. I haven't helped him much—Henrich takes care of that—but if there is anything I can do to help him, I'm only too willing."[18] In private, however, it was a different story. The young Mantle was too shy to directly ask DiMaggio for help, and the old veteran was disinclined to dispense advice, anyway. As Mantle later related, "I hardly knew [DiMaggio]. He was a loner, always restrained, often secretive. . . . Shy as I was, I never went to him seeking advice. Too scared. It was a simple hello and goodbye. Press me further and I'll admit that DiMaggio never said to me, 'Come on, kid, let's have a beer and talk.'"[19]

Though the Yankees had once again handed him a $100,000 contract for the 1951 season, DiMaggio came to feel that Stengel and Mantle, his would-be successor in center field, were shoving him out the door. In private, he would nurse a grudge against Mantle for the rest of his life. Once, at a baseball memorabilia show, someone informed DiMaggio, "Mickey is here." Without looking up from the ball that he was signing, Joe responded: "Mickey who?"[20]

With the bitterness and isolation exacerbating his persistent injuries, DiMaggio made the sudden and unexpected announcement in early March that 1951 would be his last year as a major leaguer. Though he was coming off a year in which he had led the American League in slugging percentage and had driven in over 120 runs, DiMaggio decided to forego the humiliation of playing through the inevitable decline phase of his career. "He didn't want to embarrass himself or the ball club," Gil McDougald later explained. "He was a man of such incredible pride."[21] At the time of his announcement, DiMaggio, perhaps somewhat disingenuously, insisted that his injuries had nothing to do with his decision. "I'm not a brittle ball player like a lot of writers would have you believe," he declared. "I'm a good strong fellow and always have been." Looking back on his decision after the 1951 season, DiMaggio admitted that "Even if I had batted .350, this would have been the last year for me. When baseball is no longer fun, it's no longer a game." Though Yankee management expressed their shock at DiMaggio's decision, Stengel, no doubt delighted that DiMaggio would soon be out of his way, was philosophical: "Well, what can you do," he noted. "You can't stop a man from doing what he wants. What am I supposed to do, get a gun and make him play?"[22]

That season would be DiMaggio's worst as a Yankee. Limited by persistent injuries to his knees, heels, and back, DiMaggio played in only 116 games, batted just .263, and hit only 12 home runs. "In a way the season was a little sad for Joe," McDougald later told Maury Allen. "You wished he would go out with a really big year."[23] John Drebinger, sportswriter for the *New York Times*, wrote that DiMaggio spent most of the year isolated from his teammates. "He rarely talks to his teammates or manager, let alone anyone remotely associated with the press," Drebinger wrote. "On a recent train ride following a night game in Philadelphia, DiMaggio, in the Yanks special diner, sat by himself at a table for four. It's a queer set-up, but almost everyone traveling with the Bombers is leaving the Clipper severely alone."[24]

That summer DiMaggio had more to mourn over than the loss of his star status. On June 18, DiMaggio's mother, Rosalie, died from cancer at the age of 72. It was a difficult loss for DiMaggio, and it came during a difficult season. Upon his return to the line-up following her funeral, DiMaggio batted just .204 over his next 54 at-bats, uncharacteristically striking out 8 times during that span. By early August, DiMaggio, his batting average still hovering in the .260s, lashed out in anger at reporters who he felt had provided their readers with too much description of one of his strikeouts. "What's the idea of writing that [Senators pitcher Bob] Porterfield purposely threw me three bad ones, then two straight strikes, then a curve to strike me out?" Joe fumed. "Casey Stengel told you that? Then I will have to ask him. I am certainly going to ask him. The plate is only so wide. If the pitcher could put the ball exactly where he wanted to, the batters would just have to go home. You guys call that good reporting. I call it silly stuff."[25]

But when he was in a calmer mood, DiMaggio admitted that his troubles at the plate were not going to go away. "I know what's the matter with me," he told the *Boston Herald*. "I'm not getting the old snap in my swing. I just don't seem to give it that old follow through . . . I'm swinging late. But it's not because I'm biting at bad balls. I'll go for a bad one now and then. But most of the time, they're right down the middle. I see them coming and I set myself. But when I swing, the ball shoots right up at me."[26] After the avalanche of injuries he had suffered throughout his career—the bad heels, the bum knees, the sore shoulders, the neck and back pain that troubled him during that last summer—the raw skills that had carried him to the heights of his profession were now gone.

Still, the Yankees won. On offense, catcher Yogi Berra had matured into one of the game's best players, slamming 27 home runs en route to his first of three career MVP Awards. Mantle, playing part-time in right field while DiMaggio continued to occupy center, showed flashes of brilliance, hitting 13 home runs and driving in 65 runs in 96 games. Though the line-up did not feature any hitters with 30 home runs or 100 runs batted in, and only one player with a better than .300 batting average, the Yankees still nearly led the league in runs scored thanks to Stengel's clever platooning, as 12 different hitters saw significant playing time. For his part, DiMaggio continued to resist Stengel's machinations: Casey gave up a second attempt to move DiMaggio out of the cleanup spot after Joe complained, even though his replacement, Gil McDougald, had done well in his limited tryout in the role. Down the stretch, the unspectacular DiMaggio continued to bat fourth, but the Yankees, thanks to Berra, Stengel and a dominant pitching staff keyed by the starting trio of Vic Raschi, Ed Lopat, and Allie Reynolds, carried away another pennant. They finished the season with a record of 98–56, five games better than the second-place Cleveland Indians. It was DiMaggio's tenth AL pennant since joining the team.

After the Yankees dispatched the cross-town New York Giants in six games, Joe had his ninth career world championship. DiMaggio batted .261 with a single home run and 5 RBIs for the Classic, but also figured in the Series' the most famous play, which would have lasting repercussions for the Yankee franchise. In the fifth inning of Game 2, the Giants star center fielder, Willie Mays, hit a fly ball to short right center field. Mantle, playing right field, went hard after the ball, but had to pull up at the last second when he heard DiMaggio call for it. To avoid a collision, Mantle slammed on the brakes, causing his spikes to catch in the rubber cover of a drain hole buried in the outfield grass. "There was a sound like a tire blowing out, and my right knee collapsed," Mantle remembered. "I fell to the ground and stayed there, motionless." As DiMaggio caught the ball, the awful sound of Mantle's knee blowing out made him briefly think that Mickey had been shot. "I was afraid he was dead," Joe later remembered. A bone grotesquely jutting out of his right leg, Mantle wailed in pain as the trainers prepared a stretcher. DiMaggio leaned in close to him and said, "Don't move. They're bringing a stretcher." According to Mantle, "that was about as close as Joe and I had come to a conversation."

Mantle's career would never be the same. Though he would recover from the injury and go on to have a prolific career for the Yankees, winning six more world championships and three MVPs, the blinding speed that had so impressed observers upon his arrival in spring training that year would never return. Still, Mantle would later say about the play that nearly ruined his career, "I don't know what impressed me more, the injury or the sight of an aging DiMaggio still able to make a difficult catch look easy."[27]

But despite his consummate grace in the field, word had leaked out that Joe DiMaggio was now essentially an ordinary baseball player. For Joe, the final indignity, and the final nail in the coffin that contained his baseball career, came after the Series when *Life* magazine published the Brooklyn Dodgers scouting report on DiMaggio. (The Dodgers had expected to win the National League pennant before their historic collapse down the stretch.) Andy High, the Dodgers veteran scout, wrote of DiMaggio that "He can't stop quickly and throw hard. You can take the extra base on him. . . . He can't run and won't bunt. . . . His reflexes are very slow, and he can't pull a good fastball at all."[28]

It was a devastating, but accurate, assessment of DiMaggio's diminished playing abilities. After the public embarrassment caused by the report's publication, whatever slim chance that remained for DiMaggio to return in 1952 was now extinguished. The Yankees offered him another $100,000 to return, even as a part-time player, but DiMaggio made the official announcement in early December, following his participation in a Japanese tour of "U.S. All-Stars" with his old friend Lefty O'Doul. "I told you fellows last spring I thought this would be my last year. I only wish it could have been a better year," DiMaggio told the assembled throng of reporters at the press conference announcing his retirement. "You all know I have had more than my share of physical injuries and setbacks during my career. In recent years these have been too frequent to laugh off. . . . And so, I've played my last game of ball."[29] Following the announcement, sportswriter Joe Williams, who had covered DiMaggio for his entire career, wrote that it was professional pride that had caused DiMaggio to call it quits. "Every artist must dread the day when his genius begins to grow dim," Williams wrote. "DiMaggio in his field was as authentic an artist as any contemporary leader in music, painting, or literature. Just to see him catch a ball was a memorable experience. Exquisite grace, effortless ease, and brilliant proficiency. But like so many men of extraordinary ability, DiMaggio was exceedingly sensitive, at times apprehensive, as if he had a feeling of troubled insecurity. There was one thing, though, he was most positive of: He was never going to allow the baseball world to see him in tatters."[30]

His brother Tom offered a more succinct explanation for Joe's decision to retire from the game at age 37. "Why did Joe quit when he did? He quit because he wasn't Joe DiMaggio anymore."[31]

NOTES

1. Newspaper clipping reprinted in Wittingham, *The DiMaggio Albums*, 624.
2. "Stengel Has Word for DiMaggio's Training—Caution," *New York World-Telegram*, March 4, 1950.
3. Dan Daniel, "DiMag Starts Regular Play Tomorrow," *New York World-Telegram*, March 24, 1950.
4. Cataneo, *I Remember*, 171.
5. Allen, *Where Have You Gone*, 139.
6. "Yanks Deny DiMaggio Is Feuding with Stengel," Associated Press, August 3, 1950.
7. Ibid.
8. Allen, *Where Have You Gone*, 138.
9. Cataneo, *I Remember*, 179.
10. DiMaggio, Clippings File, National Baseball Hall of Fame Library.
11. DiMaggio, *Lucky to Be a Yankee*, 32.
12. "What about DiMaggio Now?" article reprinted in Wittingham, *The DiMaggio Albums*, 687.
13. DiMaggio, *Lucky to Be a Yankee*, 40.
14. Creamer, *Stengel*, 242.
15. Ibid., 243.
16. Tony Castro, *Mickey Mantle: America's Prodigal Son* (Washington, DC: Brassey's, Inc., 2002), 81.
17. Cramer, *Joe DiMaggio*, 299.
18. Castro, *Mickey Mantle*, 55.
19. Ibid., 108.
20. Engelberg and Schneider, *DiMaggio*, 79.
21. Allen, *Where Have You Gone*, 157.
22. Cramer, *Joe DiMaggio*, 299.

23. Allen, *Where Have You Gone*, 156.

24. Castro, *Mickey Mantle*, 108.

25. Dan Daniel, "DiMag's Voice Booms Over Bat in Slapback at Critical Writers," *Sporting News*, August 22, 1951.

26. Cataneo, *I Remember*, 172.

27. Castro, *Mickey Mantle*, 114–115.

28. Cramer, *Joe DiMaggio*, 313.

29. Dan Daniel, "DiMag Bows Out after 16 Years as Bomber," *New York World-Telegram*, December 12, 1951.

30. DiMaggio Clippings File, National Baseball Hall of Fame Library.

31. Allen, *Where Have You Gone*, 171.

MARILYN

When someone approaches to ask about Marilyn Monroe, the geniality dissolves.
[DiMaggio] rises and says in measured, icy tone, "Stop right there." The words
fall like a black curtain in front of him.

—Roger Kahn

He met her in the spring of 1952, just a few months after his retirement from
baseball. Though his playing career was at an end, DiMaggio had already started
to cash in on the marketability of his name. A few days after he made his retirement official, DiMaggio signed a $50,000 contract to conduct televised in-
terviews before and after Yankee home games for the 1952 season. He
supplemented that income with a fifteen-minute segment, sponsored by the
Buitoni pasta company, which aired every Sunday on NBC. In front of the television cameras, DiMaggio was anything but a natural. He struggled to read his
lines off the cue cards, and appeared wooden and uncomfortable in front of the
camera. Still, his income from doing just a few minutes of television a week
nearly matched his 1951 salary of $100,000. He had his own office, and was
no longer chained to the ballplayer's hectic travel schedule. He could spend his
winters relaxing in California, and his summers enjoying New York. Life was
good. "Do I miss getting into uniform every day?" Joe laughed. "Man, are you
kidding?"[1]

DiMaggio first discovered Marilyn Monroe the same way that millions of
other men around the world did and would—in a photograph. During spring

training, Marilyn had agreed to pose in some publicity shots with Philadelphia Athletics slugger Gus Zernial. DiMaggio saw the photos and was instantly taken with the buxom blonde actress. When he ran into Zernial at a charity baseball game in California a few days later, DiMaggio asked Zernial how he had lucked into such a deal. Zernial gave DiMaggio the name of David March, who had arranged the publicity shoot. DiMaggio then had one of his friends call March, who set up a blind date for two days later at the Villa Nova restaurant on the Sunset Strip in Los Angeles. It would be a double date, with March and his female companion dining with Monroe and DiMaggio.

Reservations had been made for 7 P.M., but Monroe characteristically did not show up at the restaurant for another two hours. She later remembered being impressed by DiMaggio's gravitas and gentlemanly manners. Hearing that DiMaggio was a ballplayer (Marilyn was not a sports fan), she had been worried that he would be loud and obnoxious, "with checked suits, and big muscles, and pink ties." Instead, DiMaggio impressed her as a "reserved gentleman in a gray suit, with a gray tie and a sprinkle of gray in his hair," she later told the writer Ben Hecht. "There were a few blue polka dots on his tie. If I hadn't been told he was some sort of ball player, I would have guessed he was either a steel magnate or a congressman."[2]

During the meal, DiMaggio remained quiet and reserved, speaking only when the topic of conversation briefly turned to baseball. "I could see right away he was not a man to waste words," Monroe recalled. What impressed her more was when the actor Mickey Rooney joined them at the table, and fawned over DiMaggio. Monroe didn't know anything about Joe's career, but the fact that an actor as famous as Rooney was impressed by DiMaggio enhanced his stature in her eyes. For a woman accustomed to grabbing all the attention, spending time in DiMaggio's company was a revelation. "Sitting next to DiMaggio was like sitting next to a peacock with its tail spread—that's how noticeable you were," she said.[3]

It wasn't long before their romance was in full bloom, with the couple spending night after night together while DiMaggio was still living in California, and Monroe traveling east to visit Joe once the baseball season was underway. She enjoyed spending time with him, and appreciated his desire for privacy. As often as not, the couple would spend their evenings together at home, on the couch, watching television. With DiMaggio, Monroe didn't have to put on a show all the time, didn't have to play the role of sex goddess to the world. Soon, rumors began to circulate that the couple (quickly coming to be known as "Mr. and Mrs. America") were secretly married. Marilyn denied it, insisting that "we're just good friends." Nonetheless, the famous couple soon dominated the Hollywood rumor mill and gossip columns. "Marilyn stops at my house after a day at the studio," wrote one Hollywood columnist, "and she sometimes talks about her beau, Joe DiMaggio. I think he's the right man for her. This would be one Hollywood marriage that worked."[4]

Marilyn had been born Norma Jean Baker, on June 1, 1926, in Los Angeles. Her mother, Gladys, suffered from severe mental illness (as did her grandmother, Della), and the identity of Norma's biological father remains unknown. At the time of Norma's birth, Gladys was married to her third husband, Jack Baker, while simultaneously carrying on affairs with several other men. "That baby you're carrying is not mine," Jack told Gladys when she became pregnant with Norma, and with that, he abandoned the family. Young Norma Jean would never develop a relationship with Jack Baker, or with any other father figure.

Eleven days after she was born, and with her mother now committed to a mental institution, Norma Jean was deposited into the home of Ida and Albert Wayne Bolender, Christian evangelists who took in stray children for a fee of twenty-five dollars per month. Norma Jean lived with the Bolenders for eight years, enduring numerous lectures on the sins of smoking, drinking, swearing, dancing, and "play-acting," an activity of which Norma was particularly fond. Whenever Norma broke one of the Bolenders' many rules, the couple dispensed punishment with a leather strap.

When Norma Jean was 9 years old, her mother suffered another mental breakdown, and attempted to kill herself with sleeping pills. One of Gladys Baker's friends, Grace McKee Goddard, took it upon herself to become Norma Jean's legal guardian, but after just a few months, she sent the young girl to the Los Angeles Orphans Society Home, where Norma Jean lived for the next two years. According to the files at the Orphanage, Norma Jean loathed group living, and especially despised the daily chores: Marilyn later claimed that the orphanage paid her five cents a month for washing dishes three times a day. Margaret Ingram, the former superintendent of the orphanage, told the writer Roger Kahn that Norma Jean left because "this particular child had had enough of group living and badly needed some family life."[5] She was handed back over to Grace McKee Goddard and her husband, "Doc" Goddard, a construction worker who struggled to pay the family bills. When it became too expensive for the Goddards to provide for Norma Jean any longer, they sent her into a rapid succession of foster homes. Though the details remain murky, it is clear that at some point, at one or more of these homes, Norma Jean was either molested or raped by one of her caregivers.

Eventually, Norma Jean returned to the Goddards, and attended classes at nearby Van Nuys High School. There she began to date Jim Dougherty, a fellow Van Nuys student who also lived next door to the Goddards. In 1942, when Marilyn was still just sixteen years old, Dougherty proposed marriage, and the

Goddards, who were once again having financial difficulties, urged her to accept. "Grace told me what she wanted in a nice way," Monroe later recalled. "But it came down to the fact that I had to either marry Jim or go back to living in the orphanage."[6] The marriage officially lasted for four years, but really ended after just a few months. In 1943, Dougherty joined the Merchant Marines, and in his absence Norma Jean began, somewhat miraculously, to emerge from the years of abuse and neglect as a confident, beautiful, and ambitious woman.

Living in a town that specialized in the marketing and selling of sex, it didn't take long for Norma Jean Baker to draw the attention of Hollywood. She got her start working as a model for magazines such as *Pageant* and *Family Circle*, and appearing in numerous calendars. "I mostly answered calls for a girl in a bathing suit," Marilyn later remembered.[7] To increase her sex appeal, Norma Jean underwent plastic surgery on her face, and dyed her hair blonde. To put food on the table, she posed naked for a photographer named Tom Kelly. Norma received just fifty dollars for the pictures, which would later appear as the centerfold of the first *Playboy* magazine. Her big break came when Hollywood casting director Ben Lyon of Twentieth Century-Fox spotted her in a magazine photograph, and arranged a test screening. The studio executives liked what they saw, signed her to a seventy-five dollars per week contract, and gave her a new name: Marilyn Monroe.

Fox later dropped her, but after she appeared in a bit part in a 1950 film called *The Asphalt Jungle,* the studio resigned her, this time for $500 a week. Fox cast her as the breathy, beautiful, yet sexually innocent blonde in a series of movies, most notably *All About Eve, We're Not Married,* and *Don't Bother to Knock.* Though often cast in minor or supporting roles, her stunning beauty quickly caused her legend to grow. By 1952, John Crosby, the radio and television columnist, could write: "She is, at the moment, the nation's No. 1 sex thrill. Next to Adlai and Ike, she is the hottest topic of conversation in Hollywood."[8] When the nude photographs of her surfaced (this in an era when none of Hollywood's stars appeared nude before the public), her star grew even brighter, despite, or perhaps because of, the attendant scandal caused by the photographs. Her legendary status was cemented for all time with the 1953 release of *Gentleman Prefer Blondes*, where she starred opposite Jane Russell and stole the show with her performance of the song, "Diamonds are a Girl's Best Friend." The Los Angeles orphan was now a Hollywood idol of the first magnitude.

As Richard Ben Cramer writes in his biography of DiMaggio, this is what the famous couple had most in common. "Both were living inside the vast personages that the hero machine had created for them," Cramer observes. "And inside those personages—those enormous idols for the nation—these two, Marilyn and Joe, were only small and struggling, fearful to be seen. And alone—always. They were like kids, left in a giant house, and they must not be discovered. Or it would all come crashing down. In their loneliness, they might have been brother and sister."[9]

Cramer's analysis describes DiMaggio's disposition towards his fame very well, but it does not explain how eagerly Marilyn pursued the fame she had won for herself. Unlike DiMaggio, whose natural athletic gifts had catapulted him into the national spotlight, Monroe earned her fame the hard way, by suffering through bit parts and the countless indignities that Hollywood thrust upon the myriad of attractive girls looking for stardom. To achieve her fame, Marilyn wore dresses so tight that she had to be sewn into them, studied acting, took singing lessons, endured the unwanted sexual advances of lustful studio executives, did anything she had to do to get ahead. When she finally reached the pinnacle of Hollywood stardom, DiMaggio could not see the value in her achievement. He despised Hollywood, and deep down believed (incorrectly, as it turned out) that Marilyn would gladly give it all up for a life of secluded privacy with him. "She's a plain kid," he insisted to the sportswriter Jimmy Cannon. "She'd give up the business if I asked her. She'd quit the movies in a minute. It means nothing to her."[10]

Though he nursed these delusions, DiMaggio loved Marilyn Monroe. In his biography, Cramer insists that "he never spent an instant of his life to marvel at the beauty of anything. Except maybe a broad. Which wasn't marveling—that was wanting. Wanting he did."[11] But Joe DiMaggio loved Marilyn Monroe. Even when she resisted his attempts to get her to surrender the Hollywood game, he still looked after her, believed that it was his responsibility to take care of her. And she looked up to him, as the father figure she never knew, who would protect her from the worst excesses of the film industry and stand up for her against the callous studio executives. They often got into fights about the direction of her career, and DiMaggio showed little interest in Marilyn's ambition to become a serious actor, but still, his love for her was sincere. As Cramer relates, one Christmas during their courtship, DiMaggio surprised her with a little Christmas tree in her apartment. When she came home from a long day at the studio and saw the tree, she embraced DiMaggio. "Nobody ever gave me a Christmas tree before," she said. "Joe, I love you."[12]

Marilyn also developed a strong relationship with DiMaggio's son, Joe DiMaggio Jr. Following the divorce of his parents, "Joey" DiMaggio struggled to win the attention, much less the approval, of his distracted father, while bearing the weight of the great DiMaggio's accomplishments through their shared name. "Sometimes I cursed the name Joe DiMaggio Jr.," Joey later admitted.[13] Joey could never measure up to his father in athletics, and DiMaggio seemed to pay attention to his son only when he got bad grades in school. Otherwise, Joey spent much of his childhood being shipped back and forth between his mother and father. "He had no one to talk with on a son-to-parent relationship," DiMaggio friend Joe Nacchio said. "At one time, his mother was living in the Waldorf Astoria and his father was in the Elysee Hotel, about a half-mile away. Someone would drop him off at the Elysee and he would stay there for a while, mostly watching TV, and then I would walk him back to the Waldorf Astoria to his mother. It was sad."[14]

With Marilyn Monroe, Joey found a sympathetic friend, and Joey in turn aroused in Marilyn some of the maternal instincts that she would never be able to share with a child of her own. (Her many attempts at bearing a child all ended in frustration and heartbreak.) In the ensuing years, as both Joey and Marilyn struggled through drug abuse and feelings of neglect, they took comfort in their relationship. "I can never be your mother because you already have one," Monroe told Joey, "but I want to be your friend."[15]

For Dorothy Arnold, even that was going too far. When photographs of Joey with a swimsuit-clad Marilyn appeared in the newspapers in 1952, Arnold took DiMaggio to court in an attempt to deny him visitation rights. Her petition was rejected, however, and even worse for Arnold, the judge took the opportunity to lecture her on the mistake she had made in divorcing DiMaggio in the first place. "He's been pretty nice to you, hasn't he?"[16] the judge remarked to Dorothy. One year earlier, Arnold had floated the possibility of a reconciliation with her husband, but DiMaggio now had eyes only for Marilyn.

Their marriage, on January 14, 1954, was supposed to be a secret. But by the time the famous couple arrived at San Francisco City Hall, where they were to be married by Municipal Court Judge Charles Peery, the building was swarming with reporters, who had learned of the planned nuptials earlier in the day. After a brief ceremony, the couple posed for photographs and answered the reporters' questions. "I'm terribly excited," Marilyn told the assembled. "I just couldn't be happier." When a reporter asked if the couple planned on having any children, Joe responded, "Sure, there's going to be a family," and Marilyn chimed in, "Oh, definitely!"[17]

They spent their wedding night at a four-dollar room motel in Paso Robles, a small town located 175 miles south of San Francisco, faking out the crowds of reporters, photographers, and fans who thought they'd be spend their first night in a posh Monterey hotel. After spending the next two weeks relaxing in Palm Springs, they flew to Japan with Lefty O'Doul, where DiMaggio gave baseball clinics to a Japanese public that was now more enthralled with Monroe than DiMaggio. It was, noted Roger Kahn, "the first time Joe saw graphically how big a star she was."[18] Outside the Imperial Hotel in Tokyo where the couple stayed, large crowds gathered, clamoring for a glimpse of Monroe. When she finally appeared on the balcony, the crowd erupted in cheers. According to one person who made the trip with the DiMaggios, all the attention Marilyn received bothered Joe. "He acted a little surly. He gave her orders. 'No shopping today. The crowds will kill us.' She didn't argue but you could tell she didn't like being told what and what not to do."[19]

When an Army officer approached Marilyn at a Tokyo cocktail party and asked her to accompany him to Korea to entertain the troops stationed there, she jumped at the chance. DiMaggio was upset by her decision to leave him in Japan. "Go if you want to," he curtly told Marilyn when she asked his permission. "It's your honeymoon."[20]

After the trip to the Far East, DiMaggio's marriage quickly devolved into a pattern that would have been very familiar to Dorothy Arnold. Monroe pursued her acting career, and DiMaggio stayed at their home on North Palm Drive in Hollywood, watching television and nursing his grievances in a silence punctuated only by the occasional outburst of anger. He suspected Marilyn of cheating on him with several of her male friends and admirers. He showed little or no interest in her ambitions to become a serious actress or to form her own production company, and the books of literature and poetry that she gave him to read went untouched. Joe admitted to Jimmy Cannon that "My life is dull. I never interfere with Marilyn's work. . . . I don't resent her fame. She was working long before she met me. And for what? What has she got after all those years? She works like a dog. She's up at five or six in the morning and doesn't get through until seven at night. We eat dinner, watch a little television, and go to bed."[21]

Ultimately, their marriage fell apart because DiMaggio couldn't understand Monroe's Hollywood ambitions, and he couldn't bear being married to a woman who was a sex object to half the world's population. What he wanted was the world's most beautiful housewife. Once again, the uneasy tensions between his Sicilian heritage, with its emphasis on a male-dominated, family-oriented culture of insulation from the untrustworthy outside world, clashed with his celebrity ego, and its attendant fixation on beautiful, famous women. In selecting a wife for a second time, DiMaggio had made the same mistake again, believing that he could transform his beautiful and ambitious lover into a doting and devoted housewife.

The breaking point came in late summer 1954, when Marilyn began filming for *The Seven Year Itch*, in which she played the role of a beautiful but sexually innocent neighbor to a married man who had begun to harbor delusions of spicing up his dull life with a wild and passionate affair. Filming took place in New York, and DiMaggio, at the insistence of the columnist Walter Winchell, came to the set to watch his wife work. As it just so happened, the day that he decided to start showing an interest in her career was the same day that the crew was set to film the movie's most famous scene—indeed, one of the most famous scenes in movie history—in which Monroe's character, wearing a white summer dress, steps over a subway grating and cools herself with the air from the trains rushing below. During the filming of the scene, as her dress lifted more and more, screaming fans, pushing against police barricades, shouted "Higher! Higher!" At one point, director Billy Wilder had to ask Marilyn to change her underwear because her pubic hair was showing through her sheer panties.

DiMaggio watched the screaming fans, the photographers lying down on the ground, their camera lenses aimed at his wife's crotch, and he became furious. "What the hell is going on here?" he shouted. As DiMaggio stomped off the set, Billy Wilder later recalled, he had "the look of death" written all over his face.[22]

Nearly as famous as that scene was the ensuing fight that evening between DiMaggio and Monroe. There was shouting, pushing, slapping, hitting. As Marilyn later told her hairdresser, Sidney Guilaroff, "Joe slapped me around the hotel room until I screamed, 'That's it!' You know, Sidney, the first time a man beats you up, it makes you angry. When it happens a second time you have to be crazy to stay. So I left him."[23] Apparently, this was not the first time DiMaggio had physically abused Monroe.

Their marriage officially ended a month later. On October 6, 1954, Monroe appeared before the cameras at their North Palm Beach home, tearfully answering reporters' questions with, "I have nothing to say," before collapsing into the arms of her lawyer. A few minutes later, DiMaggio, his things packed, left the property. "I'm going to San Francisco," he told the gathered reporters. "San Francisco's my home. It's always been my home. I'll never be coming back to this house."[24]

On October 27, Marilyn appeared in a Santa Monica court to file her petition for divorce. As with the Arnold breakup, Joe offered no defense. "If she wants the divorce," he said, "she will get it." Monroe told Judge Orlando H. Rhodes that DiMaggio's "coolness and indifference," had ruined their marriage. "My husband would get into moods and wouldn't talk to me for long periods—five to seven days for some times, maybe longer—10 days," Monroe told the judge, clearly echoing Arnold's criticism of DiMaggio years earlier. "And if I tried to approach him, he usually said: 'Leave me alone.' "[25] Monroe's business manager, Inez Melson, testified that DiMaggio had caused Monroe "great unhappiness and mental and physical suffering." After deliberating for a few minutes, Judge Rhodes granted Monroe a divorce. The proceedings lasted just fifteen minutes; their marriage lasted 286 days.

But DiMaggio would continue to love Marilyn Monroe for the rest of her life, and then mourn her loss for the rest of his. Despite his acquiescence to Marilyn's demands for a divorce, Joe remained obsessed with her, and pursued every avenue that could lead to a reconciliation, and, hopefully, remarriage. A few days after the divorce proceedings, an enraged and jealous DiMaggio, believing that Marilyn was in bed with another man, got together with Frank Sinatra and hired a private detective named Martin Ruditsky to break into her apartment. When Ruditsky accidentally wandered into a different woman's apartment, the frightened tenant screamed and screamed until "we all had to head for the hills" according to Ruditsky.[26] Sinatra and DiMaggio would later pay the victim of their wrong-door caper $7,500 in an out-of-court settlement.

With DiMaggio still upset over the breakup, and desperate to see Marilyn, the executives at Twentieth Century Fox instructed the security guards to bar him from the studio, but in short order he and Marilyn were seen together in public again. In January, 1955, just as DiMaggio learned that he had been elected to Baseball's Hall of Fame in Cooperstown, New York, Marilyn told a reporter for the *New York Post* that she might call off the divorce (the judge's ruling had been a one-year interlocutory decree), but that a permanent reconciliation was "not immediate."

Indeed, it wasn't. The divorce was finalized in the fall of 1955, and in the summer of 1956 Marilyn married the playwright Arthur Miller. Wedded to a man who was more sympathetic to her artistic ambitions, Marilyn enjoyed the greatest success of her film career with the comedy *Some Like It Hot*. But emotional and mental breakdowns, and her chronic abuse of sleeping pills and other narcotics soon took their toll, leading Monroe to attempt suicide. Her marriage to Miller ended in 1961, after her unprofessional behavior on the set of Miller's film *The Misfits* angered her husband and rankled her co-stars. Soon after the divorce, Marilyn underwent treatment as a "highly disturbed" patient at the Payne Whitney Clinic in New York. Locked in her cell and kept on a twenty-four-hour suicide watch, Monroe phoned DiMaggio and begged him to come get her. He arrived the next day, and demanded that the hospital staff transfer her to Columbia Presbyterian, where she stayed for a few weeks, with DiMaggio visiting her regularly and filling her room with roses.

Upon her release, DiMaggio had her fly down to St. Petersburg, Florida, where he was serving as a spring training instructional coach for the Yankees. After Marilyn was hospitalized again in June, this time for surgery on her gall bladder, DiMaggio was the only one of her ex-spouses to visit her during her recovery, fueling speculation that the couple was contemplating another marriage. When reporters asked DiMaggio if he and Monroe were going to remarry, DiMaggio only grinned. "What can I say?" he obliquely responded.

But Monroe continued to resist DiMaggio's marital overtures, although she relied heavily on him for emotional support. In February 1962, she told a reporter that she was "keeping my eyes open" for a potential mate. When asked about the persistent rumors that she and DiMaggio were going to remarry, she shook her head and said, "We tried that once."[27]

That summer she started work on her last film, *Something's Got to Give*, but production was canceled after Monroe failed to show up on the set for several days in a row. Her life was falling apart, descending into an endless cycle of drug use and sleepless nights. As her circle of intimates gradually withered away, DiMaggio remained steadfast, pledging his constant love for her, his wish that they would remarry. According to Richard Ben Cramer, DiMaggio once again proposed marriage in July 1962, and this time, Monroe said yes.

Rather than a new start, however, Monroe's acceptance augured a desperate final attempt to hold onto the last remnants of her ruined life. Her physical beauty beginning to crumble from the years of drug abuse and neglect, Monroe spent the last days of her life unable to sleep or eat, and seeing her psychiatrist every day. While DiMaggio made plans for their new life together, Monroe's state of mind hovered over the grave. In a poem that she wrote near the end of her life, Monroe reflects on her rootless childhood through an imaginary conversation between a little girl and her doll. "Don't cry," the child comforts her doll, "I hold you and rock you to sleep." But the poem ends on a sour note, as the child feels "life coming closer / When all I want is to die."[28] She passed away in the morning hours of August 5, 1962, after swallowing between forty and fifty Nembutal pills. A telephone receiver found in her lifeless hand deepened the mystery of her final hours, but it also echoed the closing lines of an Anne Sexton poem, "Wanting to Die," written a few years after Monroe's death, and a few years before Sexton took her own life. The poem speaks of "leaving the page of a book carelessly open . . . the phone off the hook."

DiMaggio was devastated. He assumed complete control over the funeral arrangements, and immediately excluded nearly everyone in Hollywood from attending the ceremony. "Tell them," he fumed, "if it wasn't for them, she'd still be here." Joe blamed them all for her death—agents, directors, producers, studio executives, and actors. He also blamed the Kennedys—Bobby and President John F. Kennedy, who, rumor had it, had both been Marilyn's lovers near the end of her life.[29] They were all barred from the funeral, which was only attended by twenty-three people: Marilyn's closest friends and family, Joe, and his son Joey, now 20 years old and serving as a private in the Marines.

The funeral service, at Hollywood's Westwood Memorial Park, was brief. After Marilyn's acting teacher, Lee Strasberg, delivered a five-minute eulogy, the mourners began to disperse. But DiMaggio lingered over the open coffin, unable to leave. Finally, he kissed Marilyn one last time, and, weeping softly, murmured, "I love you. I love you. I love you."[30]

NOTES

1. Dan Daniel, "Jolter Learning How to Play New Field as TV Commentator," *New York World-Telegram*, April 23, 1952.

2. Cramer, *Joe DiMaggio*, 321.

3. Ibid., 322.

4. Kahn, *Joe and Marilyn*, 244.

5. Ibid., 78.

6. Ibid., 83.

7. Ibid., 84.

8. Ibid., 247.

9. Cramer, *Joe DiMaggio*, 351.

10. Ibid., 327.

11. Ibid., xi.

12. Ibid., 336–337.

13. Engelberg and Schneider, *DiMaggio*, 196.

14. Ibid., 194.

15. Ibid., 196.

16. Cramer, *Joe DiMaggio*, 339.

17. "Marilyn, Joe Wed on Coast in Civil Rights," *New York Daily Mirror*, January 15, 1954.

18. Kahn, *Joe and Marilyn*, 255.

19. Ibid.

20. Cramer, *Joe DiMaggio*, 358.

21. Ibid., 366–367.

22. Ibid., 367.

23. Ibid., 368.

24. Ibid., 369.

25. "Marilyn Sheds Joe, He Wouldn't Talk," *New York World-Telegram*, October 27, 1954.

26. Kahn, *Joe and Marilyn*, 265.

27. Associated Press, "Marilyn Says She's Still Looking," *New York World-Telegram*, February 23, 1962.

28. Carl E. Rollyson Jr., *Marilyn Monroe: A Life of the Actress* (Ann Arbor, MI: UMI Research Press, 1986), 199.

29. Cramer, *Joe DiMaggio*, 418.

30. Ibid., 419.

LEGACIES

He who plays alone never loses, and also, never wins.

—Sicilian Proverb

In the nearly thirty-seven years that elapsed between the death of Marilyn Monroe and the passing of her most famous lover, Joe DiMaggio, eight different presidents served in the White House. The nation suffered through the Cuban Missile Crisis, the Vietnam War, the assassinations of John F. Kennedy, Malcolm X, Bobby Kennedy, and Martin Luther King Jr., the Watergate scandal, the Challenger disaster, and the Oklahoma City bombing. Those who could afford it abandoned urban living for the suburbs, leaving the nation's cities to crumble under the weight of crime, poverty, and corruption. Color televisions became a staple of every living room, and the Internet revolution was born.

Against this backdrop of revolution and retrenchment, Joe DiMaggio remained for the public an enduring icon of consistency, grace, and class. In 1969, when Paul Simon sang about Joe DiMaggio in his song "Mrs. Robinson," he articulated what many Americans felt: a sense of uneasiness over the future, and a wish for a return to the stability of the past. In a national landscape marked by chaos and greed, materialism and lust, the public wanted the aging Joe DiMaggio to embody the purer ideals of 1941, and Joe, after surveying the ruins of his personal life, would oblige them.

What other choice did he have? Following Marilyn's death, all DiMaggio had left was the DiMaggio Myth. The fairy tale of the perfect ballplayer who was also the perfect gentleman, "the last American knight," as the writer Bob Considine put it. "DiMaggio looms above it all," sportswriter Terry Pluto observed. "He is the hero of heroes, the eternal legend. . . . He remains the Yankee Clipper, the man who always made everything look so smooth and so easy."[1] Beneath the smooth surface, however, lay a prideful man tormented by the loss of Monroe, and shadowed by the failures in his personal life, which were considerable.

As he aged, DiMaggio increasingly disconnected himself from his family. He had always held his siblings at arm's length, and as the 1960s progressed, his relationship with his only son, Joey, would shift from uneasiness to estrangement. When Joey had been born in the winter of 1941, the caption accompanying one Associated Press photo of him read: "Presenting the 1963 Batting Champ." In fact, by 1963 Joey had become—at least in the eyes of his father—a failure. One marriage had already ended in divorce. His father's connections had landed him at Yale University, but the young man struggled with his classes and started using drugs. He left Yale for the Marines, but when he completed his training, DiMaggio didn't even want to attend the ceremony. It was Marilyn who finally convinced him he had to go. "You have let that boy down too many times," she said. "This time, either you go or I will."[2]

After Marilyn's death, Joey left the Marines, and was married again, this time to a widow with two daughters. DiMaggio loved spending time with the kids, but disapproved of the marriage and continued to distance himself from his son, who didn't live up to his expectations. Joey got a job working for his uncle Dominic, who had started a polyurethane business following his retirement from baseball. To help run the factory, Joey moved his family to Northern California, but was fired after he got in with the wrong crowd and started abusing drugs again. "Speed. He loved speed," Sue Adams, his wife at the time, later remembered.[3] He took another job running a trucking company, but continued drug abuse made him a frequent tenant of the local jail, and before long, he took to beating his wife. She filed for divorce, and later blamed many of her ex-husband's problems on his troubled childhood. "They [Joey's parents] threw the man away!" she later told Esquire magazine. "[During his childhood] his only entertainment was riding up and down in the elevator."[4] To his most trusted friends, DiMaggio admitted he thought his son was "a bum." But, he hastened to add, "I love him." If DiMaggio loved his son, he showed it not by fostering a nurturing father-son relationship, but rather by sending him money, which Joey then used to buy drugs. "I tried to reach out to him, but I was rejected," DiMaggio later insisted to his doctor. "He was a pothead."[5]

During his life, DiMaggio worked hard to ensure that these details of his personal life never saw the light of day. Among his closest friends there existed an unwritten but inviolable rule: don't talk about Joe to reporters, writers, or would-be biographers. "His friends know," Gay Talese wrote for *Esquire* magazine, "that should they inadvertently betray a confidence he will never speak to them again. . . . They are endlessly awed by him, moved by the mystique."[6] As he grew older, DiMaggio became possessed by a paranoid belief that his friends were only interested in him because it furthered their own interests. If a friend tried to take advantage of the relationship by boasting of his friendship with DiMaggio to a writer, or by trying to show off DiMaggio to his other friends, Joe would cut off the relationship, permanently. The same distrust of outsiders that his father had brought to the United States from Sicily, Joe carried into his old age. "There is one trait about him that I always found tough to take," Joe Reichler, former assistant to the commissioner of baseball, told Maury Allen. "Joe harbors a grudge. He'll cut you off dead, and that will be the end of it. He's done that to a lot of guys through the years. He doesn't care how close he may have been with you at one time—if he thinks you did him dirty, that's it."[7] Just like the old Sicilians, DiMaggio in his retirement viewed outsiders as potential threats, rather than potential friends. By DiMaggio's worldview, people developed friendships not out of genuine fondness or shared interests, but rather because they had ulterior motives, be it fame, money, or both. "He would tell me that everybody wanted something from him," fellow baseball legend Henry Aaron later said, "and he was right."[8]

Ironically, DiMaggio's suspicions gradually chipped away at his circle of friends until the only ones remaining were the sycophants—the lawyers, baseball card dealers, and memorabilia collectors who were willing to flatter his ego, pander to his every whim, and reap a handsome profit on the side. In his last years, Joe's closest friends included his attorney, Morris Engelberg, who would attempt to auction off his personal stash of DiMaggio memorabilia after Joe's death, and the baseball memorabilia king Barry Halper, who helped to found the Score trading cards company. In 1990, Score signed DiMaggio to an exclusive deal to autograph cards which were then randomly inserted into Score trading packs. Halper also used his friendship with DiMaggio to enhance his treasure trove of baseball memorabilia. "Halper had a modus operandi," Engelberg later wrote. "He would get Joe in a good mood by taking him to dinner, and then, almost casually, he would produce something for DiMaggio to autograph. Usually, Joe would do it as a favor."[9] With Joe's help, Halper built up an immensely valuable baseball memorabilia collection, a portion of which Major League Baseball purchased for $7 million, and later donated to the Baseball Hall of Fame.

But Joe made his money, too. The deal with Score netted DiMaggio $125 for each signed baseball card, which came out to more than $300,000 for the deal. An earlier agreement with the Score Board memorabilia company, in which DiMaggio agreed to sign 1,000 baseballs and 1,000 photos a month for two years, netted Joe another $7.5 million. According to Engelberg, DiMaggio made another $1 million in a deal with the Bradford plate company, which packaged baseball cards in tin boxes graced with a painting of DiMaggio's swing by the artist Steven Gardner.

Joe's steadiest source of income in his later years, however, were the memorabilia shows, from which he earned, on average, approximately $500,000 a year. For the biggest shows, DiMaggio charged fans between $125 and $150 for his signature, and often walked away with as much as $250,000 for a single day's work. His card show appearances, however, came with a lengthy list of stipulations. "Joe will not sign the following," a typical notice posted near DiMaggio's table at an autograph show read, "Bats, jerseys, Perez-Steele cards, baseball cards, plates, multi-signature balls, original art, statues, lithos, gloves, albums, caps, cloth or wood items, flats over 16 × 20, books, items not related to baseball . . . NL balls, equipment or personalizations. Joe has the right to refuse to sign any item that in his opinion fits into these categories."[10] While writers and fans bemoaned the escalated player salaries of the free agent era, DiMaggio earned a fortune on his reputation as the living link to an allegedly simpler, nobler past.

For the most part, DiMaggio steered clear of organized baseball. "I've never had any managerial ambitions," he had told a reporter two years after his retirement. "After all, if you are a manager, then you have to be able to get along with the newspapermen, know how to handle them as far as giving out good stories, keeping 'em posted, etc."[11] Such diplomatic functions were not DiMaggio's forte. Nonetheless, he was hurt that no one ever interviewed him for a managing job, even though he undoubtedly would have turned down any offers.

In 1968 he did accept a job as executive vice president and coach for the Oakland Athletics, then managed by former major leaguer Bob Kennedy. The sight of the dignified DiMaggio in the A's garish green, white, and gold uniforms was sacrilege to those accustomed to seeing Joe in pinstripes. DiMaggio in an A's uniform, the sportswriter Bob Broeg wrote, "was about as shocking as having Santa Clause appear in a purple bikini."[12] Nonetheless, DiMaggio enjoyed sitting on the bench again and talking about baseball with the A's younger players, including outfielder Reggie Jackson. But the coaching job also meant a return to the ballplayer's chaotic travel schedule, and DiMaggio left the organization at the end of his two-year contract. In the ensuing years, rumors would surface that DiMaggio was going to work for the Commissioner of Baseball, or assume some executive position with the Yankees, but nothing ever came of them.

Joe still regularly visited the ballpark for Old-Timers Days and other special events at Yankee Stadium. As the years passed, DiMaggio became baseball's foremost elder statesman, and his visits to the Stadium were accompanied by all the pomp and circumstance normally reserved for visiting heads of state. If DiMaggio was going to make an appearance at the park, he demanded two concessions from his hosts. First, Joe had to be announced last, even if the ceremony was for another player. Second, he had to be introduced as "Baseball's Greatest Living Player."

That tag was the result of a special vote by the baseball writers, held in 1969 to commemorate the 100th anniversary of the 1869 Cincinnati Red Stockings, baseball's first openly professional team. The writers voted on an All-Time team, the Greatest Player Ever, and the Greatest Living Player. Ruth won the Greatest Player Ever honors, but DiMaggio grabbed most of the attention for being named to the All-Time outfield, and also for his selection as the Greatest Living Player. "Joe DiMaggio was all ball player," the press release announcing his selection stated. "Fast in the field, speedy on the bases and until he hurt his arm, he could throw with all the throwers baseball has ever seen. There is one word for Joe DiMaggio—perfection."[13]

Aside from such hyperbole, the writers' selection had little to recommend it. At least four players still living in 1969 boasted statistical resumes superior to DiMaggio's, and all of them were outfielders: Ted Williams, Stan Musial, Willie Mays, and Mickey Mantle. A fifth outfielder, Henry Aaron, was on his way to surpassing DiMaggio, if he hadn't already.

DiMaggio was a better fielder than Musial and Mantle, and a much better fielder than Williams, but all three players surpassed the Yankee Clipper in offensive production, at least when measured by the two most important offensive indicators, on-base percentage and slugging percentage. According to OPS+, a metric which combines a player's slugging percentage and on-base percentage, adjusts for park effects, and then compares the player to the league average, DiMaggio was 55 percent better than the league during his thirteen-year career. Musial, playing in 1,290 more games, was 59 percent better; Mantle, playing in 665 more games, was 72 percent better, and Williams, playing in 556 more games, was 90 percent better. All three hitters, despite playing in a significantly higher number of games than DiMaggio, were more productive offensive players during their respective careers. No difference in defensive ability could possibly make up for such a large gap.

Though Mays and Aaron were both still active when the writers cast their ballots in 1969, both players were nearing the ends of magnificent careers. Through the 1968 season, Mays had already played in 2,446 games, 710 more than DiMaggio, and was on his way to a career OPS+ that was 56 percent better than the league average. Mays, a better defensive player than even DiMaggio, with comparable offensive credentials, would conclude his career with 2,992 games played, 660 home runs, and 1,903 RBIs. Even through the end of the 1968 season, however, Mays already had hit far more home runs (587 to 361), and driven in more runs (1,654 to 1,537) than DiMaggio. This discrepancy was not lost on at least one observer, sportswriter Jim Graham, who noted after the writers' vote that "Joe DiMaggio was one of our favorite ballplayers, but to choose him over Willie Mays, who has more runs, doubles, triples, homers, hits, run batted in, and a higher fielding average, not to mention stolen bases, makes you wonder."[14] Graham could have made much the same argument for Aaron, who by 1968 had already played in 2,279 games, collected 510 home runs, and driven in 1,627 runs. For his career, Aaron would post an OPS+ of 155, identical to DiMaggio's, only he accomplished it in a staggering 1,562 more games.

Traditionally, DiMaggio's supporters have pointed to three factors that make up for DiMaggio's statistical deficiencies: the unparalleled postseason success the Yankees enjoyed during his career (ten American League pennants, nine World Series championships), DiMaggio's ability to perform well in the clutch, and the fact that he lost three years of his prime while serving in the Army in World War II.

In citing DiMaggio's postseason laurels, his backers do a disservice to the greatness of the Yankees, as a team, from 1936 to 1942, and 1946 to 1951. For instance, of the ten American League pennants captured by the Bombers, half of them were won by ten or more games, and only two of them, 1949 and 1950, were won by less than five games. In other words, most years the Yankees were blowing away the rest of the competition in the American League, so much so that it probably would not have mattered who their center fielder was. The same holds true for the World Series. Of New York's nine World Series championships during DiMaggio's career, six of them were won in four or five games, and only one of them, the 1947 World Series, went the full seven games. Additionally, DiMaggio's overall performance in the Fall Classics was less than spectacular, giving the lie to the claim that he was a hitter with a unique ability to perform in the clutch. In 199 career World Series at bats, DiMaggio batted .271, with a .338 on-base percentage and .422 slugging percentage, figures far below his regular-season performance.

But perhaps the best indication of how good DiMaggio's Yankees were comes from an examination of their performance when DiMaggio was not in the line-up, a fairly frequent occurrence given DiMaggio's history of injuries. During DiMaggio's thirteen-year-career, the Yankees won 1,272 games and lost 724, for a winning percentage of .637. When DiMaggio was not in the line-up, the team went 173–104, good for a .625 winning percentage. When the Yankee Clipper was in the line-up, the club's record was 1,099–620, for a .639 winning percentage. Clearly, the Yankees were a better team with DiMaggio playing, but their astounding success, even when he wasn't playing, demonstrates just how good the Yankees were during the DiMaggio era. Therefore, much of the credit for those ten pennants and nine world championships must go not just to DiMaggio, but to all the great players who played with him: Bill Dickey, Lou Gehrig, Yogi Berra, Lefty Gomez, Charlie Keller, Tommy Henrich, Joe Gordon, and Phil Rizzuto, as well as Hall-of-Fame managers Joe McCarthy and Casey Stengel.

It is interesting to speculate how DiMaggio would have done from 1943 to 1945 if he hadn't been busy playing baseball for the Army. Clearly, his career numbers would have benefited from the extra years, and it is possible that he would have put together another one or two MVP-caliber seasons, thus boosting his overall statistical record. But it is also important to remember that DiMaggio's contemporary, Ted Williams, also lost playing time due to World War II, and again during the Korean War. In addition, even assuming that DiMaggio would have been healthy during those three years (a risky assumption, given DiMaggio's penchant for injuries, as well as the ulcers that did hospitalize him and prevent him from playing baseball for much of the war), his career would still be much shorter than Williams, Mays, and Aaron's, and of comparable length to Mantle's. Thus, even taking the lost war years into consideration, DiMaggio's selection as the Greatest Living Player remains problematic.

All of this is not to deny DiMaggio's important place in baseball history, or his greatness as a player, which is beyond question. In his *New Historical Baseball Abstract*, Bill James ranked DiMaggio as the thirteenth greatest player, including pitchers, in baseball history. Considering that more than 15,000 men have played in the major leagues since 1876, that is a considerable accomplishment, to say the least. However, James also rates Mays, Mantle, Williams, Musial, and Aaron ahead of DiMaggio. Statistically speaking, DiMaggio was never the game's "Greatest Living Player," not during his career, not upon his retirement in 1951, and certainly not in 1969.

When DiMaggio received the award at a special ceremony in Washington, D.C. in July 1969, he said all the right things. "When I heard my name announced at the dinner in Washington I was stunned," he told the *New York Sunday News*. "When you consider all the outstanding, really great players eligible for the award you don't think you have a chance." For the next thirty years, however, DiMaggio would wear the title "Greatest Living Player," as if it were a rank of nobility, with all the rules of etiquette that normally accompany such distinctions. For many, DiMaggio in his last years did approach something like

American royalty. He was, according to first baseman Steve Garvey, "the last true American hero."[15] Though the country speculated about what the private DiMaggio was really like, it also complimented him for his insistent protection of his personal life. In an age of celebrity excess, DiMaggio stood out as the celebrity who didn't really want to be a celebrity.

Even his forays into television, through his commercials for Mr. Coffee and the Bowery Savings Bank, supported this impression. DiMaggio appeared wooden and a little uncomfortable in front of the cameras, as if, Richard Ben Cramer notes, he was "a bit aloof even from the commerce that landed him on the screen."[16] In the eyes of the public, DiMaggio aged gracefully, with dignity and class, and the nation rewarded him for it. In 1977, he received the Presidential Medal of Freedom, and later he was awarded honorary doctorates from both Columbia and New York University.

Meanwhile, the fallout from DiMaggio's wrecked personal life continued. After narrowly escaping death in a car crash in 1976, Joey joined a motorcycle gang near San Francisco. He started living in hobo camps, spending the money his father sent him on drugs and alcohol. Sam Spear, a friend of the elder DiMaggio's who worked in the area as a horseracing announcer, remembered accompanying DiMaggio on trips through the San Francisco area, as the father went in search of his son. On one occasion, Spear and DiMaggio spotted Joey, looking emaciated in jeans and a t-shirt, walking in the gutter. As Spear later related to Morris Engelberg, when DiMaggio tried to talk to Joey, his son shouted, "You don't know me. You don't know who I am. Leave me alone."

"It was a poignant moment, and in a way, Joey was telling the truth," Spear said. "I feel they didn't know each other. Joe got back in the car. He was hurt and embarrassed. He said nothing, and neither did I. I didn't want to invade his privacy. We just went on."[17]

DiMaggio also struggled to bury his love for Marilyn Monroe. He never again seriously considered marriage, and his devotion to her was so intense that for years, he sent flowers to her grave every week, and even the mention of her name caused him pain. A proposed autobiography, which would have been written with Joe Durso and would have paid DiMaggio $2 million, was scuttled when the publisher insisted that the book had to include some mention of Monroe. "The overriding fact was that he cherished, preserved, and sheltered the memories of Marilyn Monroe," Durso later wrote, "and he didn't know if he could unfurl them even in a shallow way without a sense of betrayal. Not even for two million dollars."[18] DiMaggio was willing to do many things for money, from selling his image to charging exorbitant prices for his autograph, but he would not betray his love for his beloved Marilyn. In the end, Durso wrote the book without DiMaggio's help, and ever after, Joe regarded the book with contempt, and refused to autograph it, even for his closest friends. Those same friends also knew that, as a topic of conversation, Marilyn Monroe was strictly off-limits. Even if his beloved grandchildren tried to ask him a question about Monroe, DiMaggio would cut them off and say, "Those are my memories." According to Morris Engelberg, DiMaggio refused to visit Monroe's grave, because he believed photographers anxious to get a picture of him at the site would then make money off the image. Instead, he would send someone else to the grave and have them report back on how Monroe's tombstone looked.

As he entered his eighth, and then ninth, decades, DiMaggio continued to engender the public's good will through his occasional appearances at the ballpark, and his connections with philanthropic causes. He donated his image and name to the Joe DiMaggio Children's Hospital in Hollywood, Florida, where he purchased a home and spent much of his retirement. Billboards all around Hollywood showed a picture of DiMaggio with a smiling baby and the caption "DiMaggio and the Babe." Many observers, and even some reporters, made the mistake of assuming that DiMaggio donated his money to the hospital as well. In fact, Joe DiMaggio didn't give money to the Joe DiMaggio Children's Hospital, except for one donation of a few hundred dollars, made at the behest of one of his grandkids. Nonetheless, on the strength of his name alone, the Hospital was able to solicit upwards of $2.5 million a year in donations, eventually making it one of the best-renowned children's hospitals in the world. According to Morris Engelberg, DiMaggio's connection to the hospital became his greatest source of pride, greater even than his induction into the Baseball Hall of Fame. "Not too many ballplayers have hospitals named after them," DiMaggio noted.[19]

Though he was raking in millions of dollars a year in endorsements and autograph shows, DiMaggio guarded his money closely in his old age, and grew paranoid over outsiders potentially making a buck off of him. As Cramer writes, when it came to making business deals, "Joe wanted to know the whole deal, from the cost of the item he was going to sign, down to the final price the retail buyer was going to pay. . . . Who else would make money in the deal? How much? Why should those guys make a buck off my life?"[20] This fear was encouraged by Engelberg, a Florida attorney who began representing DiMaggio in the 1980s, and who, by the 1990s, had made his most famous client millions of dollars, launching an entire operation, Yankee Clipper Enterprises, to promote his interests. Engelberg, who advertised himself as DiMaggio's "long-time personal attorney, confidant, and closest friend," drove up the value of DiMaggio's autograph to between $150 and $175 a signature. If DiMaggio stopped in a hotel lobby to sign a piece of paper for a little kid, Engelberg would whisper into his ear, "You know what you just did? You just gave away a hundred dollars—might as well just pull out a hundred and throw it away."[21] Engelberg played into DiMaggio's fears that he was being exploited, while flattering his ego by telling him he was interested in representing Joe only because he loved him, and because he admired his achievements. As Engelberg liked to say, "Although I negotiated millions upon millions of dollars in deals for DiMaggio, I never took a nickel from him. No amount of money could have bought what I gained through my association with him. I was transported from the mundane life of a probate, estate and tax lawyer to an exciting new world."[22]

In his 2000 biography of DiMaggio, Richard Ben Cramer alleged that as the 1990s progressed, and Engelberg kept churning out multi-million dollar deals for his client, the lawyer began planning for a financial windfall of his own. In taped conversations with a New Jersey memorabilia dealer named Scott DiStefano, later reported on by the Associated Press, Engelberg revealed that he was stashing away signed balls, that he later hoped to sell, splitting the profits with DiStefano. In one taped conversation, from September 4, 1998, Engelberg told DiStefano: "I'm having [Joe] sign three, four thousand balls. He loses track. Five thousand balls. That's how I dribble mine in." Engelberg then added, "There's millions of dollars in this thing here if you don't blow it."

After DiMaggio's death, Engelberg refuted the allegations, and produced a notarized statement from DiMaggio, dated October 9, 1998, in which DiMaggio states that he "listened in [Engelberg's] presence to numerous telephone calls between Scott DiStefano and yourself in connection with the . . . baseballs, sale of jerseys, your personal memorabilia collection including my jersey which I gifted to you over the years, the sale of other items of my memorabilia collection, as well as future memorabilia ventures."[23]

The deal between Engelberg and DiStefano never took place, but in April 2000, Engelberg attempted to auction off dozens of DiMaggio items from his personal collection. According to *Vanity Fair*, however, "the prices [were] so stratospheric there were virtually no bidders."[24] As the representative of the DiMaggio estate, Engelberg also sold a large cache of signed DiMaggio memorabilia to a Charlotte, North Carolina, collector for an estimated $3 million. Among the items sold were baseballs signed by DiMaggio on his deathbed. "It's really sad to see that scrawled, weak signature," a prominent memorabilia dealer told the *New York Daily News*. "Joe was always so proud of his autograph."[25] Many of DiMaggio's associates also believed that Engelberg unduly influenced DiMaggio, ostracizing him from friends and family. "Joe suffered from a Stockholm syndrome at the end of his life," an associate of DiMaggio's said. "The older Joe got, the less he was able to extricate himself from the relationship."[26] Bernie Esser, a longtime friend who used to get Joe to autograph books and baseballs for his grandkids, remembered that during their last meeting, Joe refused to sign anything, saying only, "I've got to call my attorney."

"Engelberg had convinced Joe that anyone who wanted something from him was trying to use him," Esser concluded.[27] But if Engelberg exploited DiMaggio's latent paranoia, his fear of being exploited, DiMaggio's anger toward the outside world could also be reflected back onto himself. When a writer once tried to approach DiMaggio for an interview, saying, "I think you're a great man, and . . ." DiMaggio cut him off. "I'm not great," he responded. "I'm not great." For all his accomplishments on the baseball field, DiMaggio never overcame his sense of isolation, his guilt at having succeeded so admirably at his profession while failing so miserably as a husband and father. In the end, the world Joe DiMaggio constructed for himself was a world dominated by loneliness, isolation, and heartbreak.

It was in the summer of 1998, which ended with the last Joe DiMaggio Day at Yankee Stadium, that DiMaggio started coughing up blood. At first, doctors couldn't detect the cause of the problem, but after the illness lingered into September, DiMaggio underwent additional tests at Memorial Regional Hospital in Hollywood, Florida. The diagnosis, lung cancer, was kept secret from the press and from Joe's family for several weeks. The same week that newspapers reported DiMaggio was suffering from a "major pneumonia infection," he went into the hospital for surgery to remove the tumor in his right lung. According to Engelberg, the operating surgeon told DiMaggio that he'd be "on the golf course in ten days" after the surgery. Instead, he would remain hospitalized for more than three months, as his right lung became infected following the operation and pneumonia settled in his left lung. For a time, DiMaggio slipped into a coma, and then the full extent of his health problems came out. Dr. Earl Barron, DiMaggio's chief physician told reporters on December 7 that "Joe has had a significant and serious turn for the worse. The outlook has dimmed over the past 72 hours. He's not in good shape."[28] DiMaggio emerged from the coma however, and the doctors removed the respirator long enough for him to rasp to his doctors, "No more news." That brought an end to the press releases.

DiMaggio's condition improved enough that he was able to leave the hospital on January 19, and return to his Hollywood, Florida home. But though the news was greeted warmly by the baseball world, with George Steinbrenner, owner of the Yankees, going so far as to predict that "Joe DiMaggio will throw out the baseball to open the season," in reality his condition remained so severe that he could hardly get out of bed, and required constant, round-the-clock medical attention. On January 24, the *New York Daily News* reported that "DiMaggio remains too weak to undergo chemotherapy for his lung cancer or to breathe on his own for any sustained period of time." Over the next two months, DiMaggio continued to receive visits: from Engelberg, Steinbrenner, his friend Joe Nacchio, and his brother Dominic. He saw his son for the last time as well, but on television, when Joey did an interview with *Inside Edition* for $15,000. Describing himself as a "free spirit," Joey refused to blame his personal troubles on his father, adding, "You know, I never got the words 'come now,' or I would've been there in a flash."[29]

In early March, DiMaggio took another turn for the worse, and stopped eating. "It's no good," he told a personal assistant, "I wanna die."[30] Engelberg, acting as Joe's medical surrogate, made the decision to "let Joe go." A hospice nurse was brought in, who took Joe off the respirator and gave him morphine to ease the pain. At a few minutes past midnight, on March 8, 1999, Joe DiMaggio passed away in his sleep.

DiMaggio's body was flown to San Francisco, where a funeral service was held at Sts. Peter and Paul Church, the same church where he had married Dorothy Arnold sixty years earlier. Following the funeral, Joe's body was taken by black hearse to Holy Cross Cemetery in nearby Colma, California. He was laid to rest in an unmarked crypt in the mausoleum where his parents, Giuseppe and Rosalie, were also interred. "For several generations of baseball fans, Joe was the personification of grace, class, and dignity on the baseball diamond," Bud Selig, the commissioner of baseball, said upon DiMaggio's passing. "His persona extended beyond the playing field and touched all our hearts. In many respects, as an immigrant's son, he represented the hopes and ideals of our great country. Joe DiMaggio was a hero in the truest sense of the word."[31]

Five months after his father passed away, Joe DiMaggio Jr., following decades of substance abuse, died of an apparent heart attack at the age of 57. At the time of his death, Joey had been living in a junkyard in Martinez, the same small fishing village where his famous father had entered the world eighty-four years before, and countless lifetimes away.

NOTES

1. Terry Pluto, "DiMaggio Still Loved," *Cleveland Plain Dealer*, February 7, 1980.

2. Engelberg and Schneider, *DiMaggio*, 197.

3. Ibid., 199.

4. Luke Cyphers, "DiMaggio's Son Given the Brush-off—Mag," *New York Daily News*, May 14, 1999.

5. Engelberg and Schneider, *DiMaggio*, 197.

6. Gay Talese, "The Silent Season of a Hero," *Esquire*, July, 1966.

7. Allen, *Where Have You Gone*, 215.

8. Engelberg and Schneider, *DiMaggio*, 72.

9. Ibid., 116.

10. Cramer, *Joe DiMaggio*, 469.

11. Cataneo, *I Remember,* 180.

12. Bob Broeg, "Even in Finley Garb, DiMaggio is a Welcome Sight," *St. Louis Post-Dispatch*, April 15, 1968.

13. DiMaggio Clippings File, National Baseball Hall of Fame Library.

14. *Denver Post*, July 28, 1969.

15. Harry Jupiter, "DiMaggio: The Name is Still Magic," *San Francisco Chronicle*, March 24, 1978.

16. Cramer, *Joe DiMaggio*, 433.

17. Engelberg and Schneider, *DiMaggio*, 203.

18. Durso, *DiMaggio,* xii–xiii.

19. Engelberg and Schneider, *DiMaggio*, 305.

20. Cramer, *Joe DiMaggio*, 450–451.

21. Ibid., 463.

22. Engelberg and Schneider, *DiMaggio*, 108.

23. Associated Press, August 26, 2001.

24. Buzz Bissinger, "For Love of DiMaggio," *Vanity Fair,* September, 2000.

25. Bill Madden and Luke Cyphers, "Joe D Selloff draws fire," *New York Daily News,* June 20, 1999.

26. Bissinger, "For Love of DiMaggio."

27. Cataneo, *I Remember*, 144–147.

28. Bill Gallo and Richard T. Pienciak, "Joe D Takes Major Turn For Worse," *New York Daily News*, December 8, 1998.

29. Cathy Burke, "Jottin' Joe Jr. Breaks Silence on Dad," *New York Post*, February 11, 1999.

30. Cramer, *Joe DiMaggio*, 507.

31. "What They're Saying," *Albany Times-Union*, March 9, 1999.

EPILOGUE:
MAKING OF A LEGEND

With the possible exception of Babe Ruth, no baseball player has had more books written about him than Joe DiMaggio. Writer Joe Durso remembered how DiMaggio "used to say that thirty-three books had been written *about* him and he didn't like *any* of them." For that, Joe had nobody but himself to blame. During his long retirement, he made it nearly impossible for would-be biographers to write about him; he refused to speak or cooperate with them and he often instructed his closest friends and advisors to do the same. The impact of this closed-door policy on the DiMaggio literature was severe, yet predictable. The vast majority of books published on the Yankee Clipper contained little more than excessive flattery, syrupy nostalgia, and superficial insights into the life of the reclusive star.

Then along came Richard Ben Cramer. A determined researcher and reporter, Cramer spent five years working on his biography of DiMaggio, tracking down anyone and everyone who could provide insight, on or off the record, into DiMaggio's private self. When his 548-page book, *Joe DiMaggio: The Hero's Life* (New York: Simon & Schuster), was finally published in the fall of 2000, it rocketed to the top of the best-seller lists. The book portrayed DiMaggio as a jealous, greedy, and callous man who physically and verbally abused his two wives and ostracized his only child. Despite its many revelations, Cramer's book has its shortcomings, the most serious of which is the lack of footnotes, an omission made even more significant by the many new, yet undocumented, allegations contained within the book. Cramer contends that DiMaggio committed tax fraud on his considerable earnings from his baseball memorabilia contracts, and also alleges that DiMaggio had intimate connections with the Mafia. While such charges are sensational, readers are left wondering where Cramer got his information. He does not divulge his sources for any specific allegations, and DiMaggio refused to speak with him while he was working on the book. With those reservations, however, Cramer's work still stands as a notable achievement; it is arguably the first serious attempt to present a comprehensive and balanced view of DiMaggio, blemishes and all.

While Cramer's book is the most thorough biography of DiMaggio published to date, many of its predecessors also offer unique insights. Foremost among them is Maury Allen's *Where Have You Gone, Joe DiMaggio? The Story of America's Last Hero* (New York: E. P. Dutton and Co., 1975; 222 pages). For the book, Allen interviewed scores of DiMaggio's teammates, managers, family members, friends, and admirers, weaving a narrative of the ballplayer's life around their anecdotes. Although DiMaggio was still living when this book was published, the mosaic of impressions contained within its pages contains both flattering and not-so-flattering portraits of the Yankees star. Nearly thirty years after its publication, this book remains a valuable resource for DiMaggio scholars, and also an enjoyable read for baseball fans.

Eleven years after Allen's book was published, an even more balanced critique of DiMaggio's life and career emerged with the publication of Roger Kahn's *Joe and Marilyn: A Memory of Love* (New York: William Morrow and Company, 1986; 269 pages). The book's title is misleading because only the last chapter actually deals with DiMaggio and Monroe's stormy relationship. Nonetheless, this superbly written book is really two biographies, Monroe's and DiMaggio's, contrasted against each other. Kahn is primarily interested in how Joe and Marilyn each came to win their fame, and then how they responded to their celebrity status. In examining these questions, Kahn provides the reader with a portrait of the centripetal forces that brought DiMaggio and Monroe together, as well as the centrifugal forces that ultimately tore them apart.

In addition to the above books, scholars and fans interested in learning more about DiMaggio's personal life, particularly after his retirement from baseball, should consult Gay Talese's article in the July 1966 issue of *Esquire*, "The Silent Season of a Hero," which documents the loneliness that defined DiMaggio's life following the death of Marilyn Monroe.

Despite the continued public fascination with DiMaggio's persona, his signature achievement remains his baseball career. Cramer, Kahn, and Allen all discuss his exploits on the baseball diamond at length, but there are also other works worth looking into. Three of these books were published with DiMaggio's consent. The first two, *Lucky to Be a Yankee* (New York: Grosset and Dunlap, 1951; originally published in 1947) and *Baseball for Everyone* (New York:

McGraw-Hill, 2002; originally published in 1948) list DiMaggio as the author, but were actually ghost-written by sportswriter Tom Meany. *Lucky to Be a Yankee* is the only ostensibly autobiographical work on DiMaggio. Written in the bland style of most sports autobiographies published before Jim Bouton's ground-breaking *Ball Four*, *Lucky to Be a Yankee* focuses primarily on DiMaggio's playing career up through the conclusion of the 1950 season. The book's most interesting moments occur when DiMaggio talks about his childhood and early baseball career. The book also includes DiMaggio's thoughts on Lou Gehrig, Joe McCarthy, Lefty Gomez, and his fifty-six-game hitting streak. By contrast, *Baseball for Everyone* is an instructional book about how to play baseball. When it came to fielding, DiMaggio was truly a student of the game, and so the passages on how to play the outfield sparkle most. This book is recommended for anyone interested in learning more about how DiMaggio approached his craft.

In 1989, DiMaggio agreed to publish *The DiMaggio Albums: Selections From Public and Private Collections Celebrating the Baseball Career of Joe DiMaggio* (New York: G. P. Putnam's Sons, 1989), a two-volume set edited by Richard Wittingham that reprints hundreds of newspaper clippings, photographs, and magazine advertisements from DiMaggio's baseball career. DiMaggio provides an introduction to the set and short commentary for each season. Because DiMaggio himself approved the project, the selection of clippings, although voluminous, is predictably biased, with some glaring omissions. There is, for example, no mention of either Dorothy Arnold or Marilyn Monroe in the set. As long as the reader bears in mind that the selections in the albums reflect only what DiMaggio wished to see published, the two volumes combined offer a fascinating tour through DiMaggio's baseball career.

DiMaggio also figures as a significant character in a number of books that cover only specific seasons. In this genre, the most significant work is Michael Seidel's *Streak: Joe DiMaggio and the Summer of '41* (New York: Penguin, 1989; 260 pages). Perhaps the best-written book that takes DiMaggio as its subject, Seidel offers readers an insightful and evocative history of America during the summer of 1941, the central focus of which is the "streak journal," Seidel's day-by-day, at-bat-by-at-bat examination of DiMaggio's batting exploits during the fifty-six-game hitting streak. No other book comes close to capturing the drama and zeitgeist of DiMaggio's signature season. For a look at the statistical significance of DiMaggio's hitting streak, see Stephen Jay Gould's essay "The Streak of Streaks," which was originally published as a review of Seidel's book in *The New York Review of Books*, but later reprinted in Gould's 1991 anthology, *Bully for Brontosaurus: Reflections In Natural History* (New York: W.W. Norton and Company). Two other notable books featuring DiMaggio are Robert Creamer's

Baseball in '41: A Celebration of the Best Baseball Season Ever—In the Year America Went to War (New York: Viking Books, 1991; 330 pages), and David Halberstam's *Summer of '49* (New York: Avon Books, 1989; 336 pages).

Since the publication of Cramer's watershed book in 2000, two other significant books about DiMaggio have been written. The first, David Cataneo's *I Remember Joe DiMaggio: Personal Memories of the Yankee Clipper by the People Who Knew Him Best* (Nashville, TN: Cumberland House, 2001; 224 pages), is written along the same lines as Maury Allen's book, published twenty-six years earlier. Cataneo's collection of DiMaggio anecdotes contains less narrative, but more balance and perspective because it was published two years after the Yankee Clipper's death. The book contains an index and endnotes. Like Allen's book, Cataneo's volume is an invaluable resource and an easy read. The author has pieced together previously published statements made about DiMaggio by the ballplayer's friends, teammates, opponents, and family members, while also including some new interviews, as well as a collection of statements from DiMaggio himself.

In 2003, Morris Engelberg, the controversial Florida attorney who represented DiMaggio for the last two decades of his life, published *DiMaggio: Setting the Record Straight* (St. Paul, MN: MBI Publishing Company; 418 pages), with co-author Marv Schneider. Although the book advertises itself as "setting the record straight," much of it confirms what Cramer and others had already discovered: that DiMaggio was alienated from his son, obsessive about his privacy and about money, and that Engelberg made DiMaggio millions in the memorabilia industry. Engelberg considers DiMaggio his best friend, so much of the book paints a highly flattering, but not quite believable, portrait of DiMaggio's character. Nonetheless, this book is a valuable addition to the available literature because Engelberg enjoyed far greater access to DiMaggio's private sphere than any of his previous biographers.

APPENDIX: JOE DIMAGGIO'S CAREER AND WORLD SERIES STATISTICS

CAREER STATISTICS

Year	Club	League	G	AB	R	H	2B	3B	HR	RBI	BA	PO	A	E	FA
1936	N.Y. Yankees	AL	138	637	132	206	44	15	29	125	.323	339	22	8	.978
1937	N.Y. Yankees	AL	151	621	151	215	35	15	46	167	.346	413	21	17	.962
1938	N.Y. Yankees	AL	145	599	129	194	32	13	32	140	.324	366	20	15	.963
1939	N.Y. Yankees	AL	120	462	108	176	32	6	30	126	.381	328	13	5	.986
1940	N.Y. Yankees	AL	132	508	93	179	28	9	31	133	.352	359	5	8	.978
1941	N.Y. Yankees	AL	139	541	122	193	43	11	30	125	.357	385	16	9	.978
1942	N.Y. Yankees	AL	154	610	123	186	29	13	21	114	.305	409	10	8	.981
1943	In Military Service														
1944	In Military Service														
1945	In Military Service														
1946	N.Y. Yankees	AL	132	503	81	146	20	8	25	95	.290	314	15	6	.982
1947	N.Y. Yankees	AL	141	534	97	168	31	10	20	97	.315	316	2	1	.997
1948	N.Y. Yankees	AL	153	594	110	190	26	11	39	155	.320	441	8	13	.972
1949	N.Y. Yankees	AL	76	272	58	94	14	6	14	67	.346	195	1	3	.985
1950	N.Y. Yankees	AL	139	525	114	158	33	10	32	122	.301	376	9	9	.976
1951	N.Y. Yankees	AL	116	415	72	109	22	4	12	71	.263	288	11	3	.990
Major League Totals (13 Seasons)			1736	6821	1390	2214	389	131	361	1537	.325	4529	153	105	.978

WORLD SERIES RECORD

Year	Club	G	AB	R	H	2B	3B	HR	RBI	BA
1936	N.Y. Yankees	6	26	3	9	3	0	0	3	.346
1937	N.Y. Yankees	5	22	2	6	0	0	1	4	.273
1938	N.Y. Yankees	4	15	4	4	0	0	1	2	.267
1939	N.Y. Yankees	4	16	3	5	0	0	1	3	.312
1941	N.Y. Yankees	5	19	1	5	0	0	0	1	.263
1942	N.Y. Yankees	5	21	3	7	0	0	0	3	.333
1947	N.Y. Yankees	7	26	4	6	0	0	2	5	.231
1949	N.Y. Yankees	5	18	2	2	0	0	1	2	.111
1950	N.Y. Yankees	4	13	2	4	1	0	1	2	.308
1951	N.Y. Yankees	6	23	3	6	2	0	1	5	.261
World Series Totals		51	199	27	54	6	0	8	30	.271

A = assists; AB = at-bats; BA = batting average; E = errors; FA = fielding average; G = games; H = hits; HR = home runs; PO = put-outs; R = runs; RBI = runs batted in; 2B = doubles; 3B = triples

SELECTED BIBLIOGRAPHY

BIOGRAPHIES AND AUTOBIOGRAPHIES OF JOE DIMAGGIO

Allen, Maury. *Where Have You Gone, Joe DiMaggio?: The Story of America's Last Hero*. New York: E. P. Dutton and Co., 1975.

Cataneo, David. *I Remember Joe DiMaggio: Personal Memories of the Yankee Clipper by the People Who Knew Him Best*. Nashville, TN: Cumberland House, 2001.

Cramer, Richard Ben. *Joe DiMaggio: The Hero's Life*. New York: Simon & Schuster, 2000.

DiMaggio, Joe. *Baseball for Everyone: A Treasury of Baseball Lore and Instruction for Fans and Players*. New York: McGraw-Hill, 2002.

———. *Lucky to Be a Yankee*. New York: Grosset and Dunlap, 1951.

Durso, Joe. *DiMaggio: The Last American Knight*. Boston: Little, Brown, and Company, 1995.

Engelberg, Morris, and Marv Schneider. *DiMaggio: Setting the Record Straight*. St. Paul, MN: MBI, 2003.

Kahn, Roger. *Joe and Marilyn: A Memory of Love*. New York: William Morrow and Company, 1986.

BOOKS AND ARTICLES

Alexander, Charles. *Breaking the Slump: Baseball In the Depression Era*. New York: Columbia University Press, 2002.

Castro, Tony. *Mickey Mantle: America's Prodigal Son*. Washington, DC: Brassey's, Inc., 2002.

Creamer, Robert. *Baseball In '41: A Celebration of the Best Baseball Season Ever—In the Year America Went to War*. New York: Viking, 1991.

————. *Stengel: His Life and Times.* New York: Dell Publishing Co., 1985.

Durocher, Leo, with Ed. Linn. *Nice Guys Finish Last.* New York: Simon & Schuster, 1975.

Enders, Eric. *Ballparks: Then and Now.* San Diego: Thunder Bay Press, 2002.

————. *100 Years of the World Series.* New York: Barnes and Noble Books, 2003.

Gould, Stephen Jay. "The Streak of Streaks." In *Bully for Brontosaurus: Reflections In Natural History.* New York: W.W. Norton and Company, 1991.

Gregory, Robert. *Diz: Dizzy Dean and Baseball During the Great Depression.* New York: Viking, 1992.

Halberstam, David. *Summer of '49.* New York: Avon Books, 1989.

Henrich, Tommy. *Five O'Clock Lightning: Ruth, Gehrig, DiMaggio, Mantle, and the Glory Years of the NY Yankees.* New York: Carol Publishing Group, 1992.

Linn, Ed. *Hitter: The Life and Turmoils of Ted Williams.* New York: Harcourt Brace and Co., 1993.

Mangione, Jerre, and Ben Morreale. *La Storia: Five Centuries of the Italian American Experience.* New York: HarperPerennial, 1992.

Rollyson, Carl E., Jr. *Marilyn Monroe: A Life of the Actress.* Ann Arbor, MI: UMI Research Press, 1986.

Seidel, Michael. *Streak: Joe DiMaggio and the Summer of '41.* New York: Penguin, 1989.

Talese, Gay. "The Silent Season of a Hero." *Esquire*, July 1966.

Williams, Ted, with John Underwood. *My Turn at Bat: The Story of My Life.* New York: Simon & Schuster, 1988.

Wittingham, Richard, ed. *The DiMaggio Albums: Selections From Public and Private Collections Celebrating the Baseball Career of Joe DiMaggio.* New York: G. P. Putnam's Sons, 1989.

NEWSPAPERS AND MAGAZINES

Cleveland Plain Dealer
October 28, 1937
February 7, 1980

Denver Post
July 28, 1969

Life
April 30, 1939
August 1, 1949

New York Daily News
December 8, 1998
May 14, 1999
June 20, 1999

New York Herald-Tribune
October 10, 1936

New York Journal American
April 6, 1938
August 31, 1939

New York Mirror
April 19, 1938
January 15, 1954

New York Post
February 11, 1999

New York Sun
March 20, 1936
May 4, 1936
May 22, 1936
June 6, 1936

April 14, 1938
May 1, 1944

New York Times
April 15, 1938
April 13, 1949
April 15, 1949

New York World-Telegram
March 9, 1936
March 11, 1936
March 18, 1936
July 7, 1936
July 9, 1936
October 8, 1936
February 12, 1937
March 20, 1937
April 15, 1938
April 28, 1938
November 8, 1938
March 7, 1940
May 15, 1941
June 26, 1941
June 30, 1941
November 12, 1941
May 9, 1942
May 12, 1944
May 25, 1949
October 1, 1949
October 3, 1949
March 4, 1950

March 24, 1950
August 10, 1951
December 12, 1951
April 23, 1952
October 27, 1954
February 23, 1962

Riverdale Free Press
January 14, 1932

St. Louis Post-Dispatch
April 15, 1968

San Francisco Chronicle
March 24, 1978

*San Francisco Sunday Examiner
and Chronicle*
December 21, 1980

Sporting News
October 6, 1938
December 21, 1939
November 30, 1944
April 28, 1948
July 6, 1949
October 12, 1949

Time
October 4, 1948

Vanity Fair
September 2000

ARCHIVAL SOURCES

DiMaggio Clippings File, National Baseball Hall of Fame Library, Cooperstown, New York.

INDEX

Aaron, Hank, 141, 143–144

Adams, Sue, 140

Adler, Polly, 37–38

Allen, Maury, 5, 90–91

Anderson, Red, 67

Appling, Luke, 63

Arnold, Dorothy: childhood of, 53–54; death of, 83; divorce from DiMaggio, 79–82; film credits of, 54, 82–83; marriage to DiMaggio, 54–55, 73–74, 76; motherhood and, 74, 79–80, 82, 131–132

Auker, Eldon, 65

Averill, Earl, 50–51

Babich, Johnny, 66–67

Bagby, Jim Jr., 70–71

Baker, Gladys, 129

Baker, Jack, 129

Baker, Norma Jean. See Monroe, Marilyn

Barath, Steve, 15

Barrow, Ed, 17, 19, 41, 45, 89

Berardino, Johnny, 65

Berra, Yogi, 93, 96, 105, 108, 123

Bevens, Bill, 93, 97

Blaeholder, George, 92–93

Boldender, Ida and Albert Wayne, 129

Bonds, Barry, 72

Boudreau, Lou, 70–71, 105–106

Brands, E. G., 42

Broeg, Bob, 142

Brown, Bobby, 99, 108, 113

California, lure of, 4, 11

Campanella, Roy, 102

Cannon, Jimmy, 5, 103, 133

Casey, Hugh, 73

Caveney, Ike, 9

Chandler, Spud, 81, 93, 96

Chapman, Ben, 25, 29

Chase, Hal, 64

Churchill, Winston, 64

Cobb, Ty, 19, 61

Cobbledick, Gordon, 39

Coleman, Jerry, 37, 91, 111, 117–118

Combs, Earle, 17, 64

Considine, Bob, 140

Courtney, Alan, 68

Cramer, Richard Ben, 3, 8, 16, 37, 80, 130–131, 148

Creamer, Robert, 61–62, 109
Cronin, Bob, 18
Cronin, Joe, 48
Crosby, John, 130
Crosetti, Frank, 12, 19, 27, 30, 43, 53, 56, 63, 65, 90
Cuomo, Mario, 26

Dahlen, Bill, 61
Dahlgren, Babe, 48
Daley, Art, 109
Daniel, Dan, 21, 24, 45, 48, 62, 65, 68, 75, 80, 83–84, 101–103, 108–109, 111, 113, 119
Dawson, James P., 107
Dean, Dizzy, 43
Delahanty, Ed, 24
Densmore, James, 17
Dickey, Bill, 30, 38, 48, 56, 90, 93, 121
DiMaggio, Dominic, 5, 39, 55, 92, 106, 149
DiMaggio, Giuseppe, 3–5, 7–8, 15, 108
DiMaggio, Joseph: Army service of, 80–84; base-running exploits of, 48–49, 52–53; batting stance of, 13, 35; birth of, 4; business ventures of, 39, 141–142, 147; celebrity and, 130–131, 133, 149; childhood poverty and, 5; clutch hitting of, 106–107, 109–112; comparisons with Ted Williams, 72–74, 94, 98–99, 107; confidence of, 28–29, 42, 103; contract disputes of, 19, 33–35, 39–41; courtship of Marilyn Monroe, 128–129, 131, 135–136; death of, 150; demand for privacy of, 141, 146–147; early employment of, 8; earnings of, 31, 141–142; endorsements and, 37, 69–70, 127, 146; fatherhood and, 74, 79–80, 82, 131–132, 140, 146, 149–150; fielding of, 9, 12–13, 18–19, 24–25, 29, 35, 37, 49–52, 63, 96, 105–106, 117, 120, 124; fishing and, 5; habits of, 15, 31, 40, 56, 66, 115; hitting approach of, 13, 24, 26, 35–37, 92–94, 118–119, 124; hitting streaks and, 14, 35, 61–72; honors of, 19, 38–39, 53, 68, 74, 80, 98, 113, 135, 143, 146; iconic status of, 72, 75, 117–118, 120, 139–140, 145–146; illnesses of, 83–84, 111–112, 149–150; injuries of, 16–17, 24–25, 35, 41, 47–48, 51–52, 55–56, 72, 92, 94–96, 106–109, 111, 117–118, 122–123; as Italian American hero, 26; leadership of, 47–48, 62, 71, 89–91, 118; marital difficulties of, 55, 73–74, 79–82, 133–134; marriage to Dorothy Arnold, 54–55; marriage to Marilyn Monroe, 132–134; memorabilia business and, 141–142, 147–148; mourning over Monroe's death, 136–137, 146–147; myths concerning, 36, 50, 97–99, 103, 140, 144–145; nicknames of, 15, 24, 51, 91, 140; as Oakland Athletics coach, 142; physical development of, 6, 8, 13–14; popularity of, 14–15, 26, 31, 37, 39–42, 65–69, 72, 75–76, 79, 103; press relations and, 24, 40–41, 53, 74, 91, 99, 101–104, 108, 122–123; pride of, 92–93, 103, 118, 121–122, 124–125, 134; professional debut of, 9; retirement from baseball of, 122, 124–125; salary of, 9, 12, 16, 19, 35, 41, 43, 55, 62, 75, 85, 104, 107, 115, 121; sandlot exploits of, 6, 8–9; schooling of, 5–8; scouting report on, 124; selfishness of, 85, 118, 145–146; shyness of, 6, 15, 24–28, 30–31, 37, 91, 103, 122; Sicilian heritage of, 103, 133, 141; work ethic of, 23, 103; World Series performance of, 30, 38, 43, 52–53, 73, 97, 102, 112, 120, 123–124, 144
DiMaggio, Joseph Jr.: birth of, 73; childhood of, 82, 131–132, 140; death of,

150; drug addiction and, 140, 146,
150; Marilyn Monroe and, 131–132
DiMaggio, Michael, 5
DiMaggio, Rosalie Mercurio, 3, 8, 122
DiMaggio, Thomas, 5, 15–16, 85, 125
DiMaggio, Vincent, 5, 7, 9, 12–13, 39,
55
DiStefano, Scott, 148
Doerr, Bobby, 112
Dougherty, Jim, 129–130
Drebinger, John, 122
Durocher, Leo, 90, 104
Durso, Joe, 146–147

Effrat, Lou, 103
Enders, Eric, 12, 97–98
Engelberg, Morris, 141, 147–150
Ennis, Del, 120
Esquire magazine, 140
Esser, Bernie, 148–149
Essick, Bill, 17
Estalella, Bobby, 47

Farrell, Eddie, 17
Fay, Bernard, 21
Feller, Bob, 36, 64, 75, 80, 86, 93,
104
Ferriss, Boo, 110
Ford, Whitey, 93, 119, 121
Fox, Pete, 51, 63
Foxx, Jimmie, 53

Galan, Augie, 9, 12
Galehouse, Denny, 65
Gambino, Richard, 7
Garbark, Mike, 84
Gardner, Steven, 142
Garvey, Steve, 146
Gaynor, Sidney, 95
Gehrig, Lou, 17, 23–24, 28–30, 35, 38–
39, 42, 45–47, 63–64, 69, 103
Gehringer, Charlie, 38–39
George, Steve, 14

Gionfriddo, Al, 97–98
Goddard, Grace McKee and "Doc,"
129–130
Gomez, Vernon "Lefty," 12, 27, 38–39,
47, 56, 90
Goodman, Ival, 53
Gordon, Joe, 42, 48, 65, 83, 93
Gould, Stephen Jay, 59, 61, 66, 72
Graham, Charlie, 12, 14–16, 18
Graham, Frank, 40, 51
Graham, Jim, 144
Gray, Pete, 84
Great Depression, 8, 11, 19–21, 40
Greenberg, Hank, 51, 57, 62, 85
Grimes, Oscar, 71

Halberstam, David, 109
Halper, Barry, 141
Harris, Bucky, 93, 95
Harrison, Cliff, 18
Hartnett, Gabby, 39, 42
Hatten, Joe, 97
Henrich, Tommy, 48, 64–67, 73, 92–93,
96, 105, 108, 112, 121
Hildebrand, Oral, 47
Hitler, Adolf, 64, 68
Hoffman, John C., 107
Holmes, Oliver Wendell, 33–34
Homer, Ben, 68
Howard, Elston, 86
Hubbell, Carl, 39
Hudson, Sid, 67
Hughes, Ed R., 15

Immigration, 1
Isola Delle Femmine, 3
Italian Americans: success in baseball, 7;
prejudice against, 26

Jackson, Joe, 13, 24
Jackson, Reggie, 142
James, Bill, 74, 99, 145
Joe DiMaggio Children's Hospital, 147

Johnson, Billy, 96, 111
Johnson, Earl, 110
Johnson, Roy, 23
Joost, Eddie, 115

Kahn, James, 24–25, 30
Kahn, Roger, 127, 132
Keeler, Willie, 61, 68–69
Keller, Charlie, 48, 53, 64–65, 73, 84
Kelly, Tom, 130
Keltner, Ken, 70–71
Kemp, Abe, 19, 73, 91
Kinder, Ellis, 110, 112
Kofoed, Jack, 14–15
Kramer, Jack, 69

Landis, Kenesaw Mountain, 79
Lang, Jack, 36
Lavagetto, Cookie, 97
Lazzeri, Tony, 19, 27, 30
Lee, Bill, 48
Lee, Thornton, 64, 69
Leonard, Dutch, 67
Lindbergh, Charles, 68
Lindell, Johnny, 81, 111
Lodigiani, Dario, 14, 49, 63, 81, 85
Lombardi, Ernie, 52–53
Lopat, Ed, 105–106, 108, 123
Lyon, Ben, 130

Mack, Gene, 63
Mack, Ray, 71
MacPhail, Larry, 89–90, 93, 104
Mangione, Jerre, 3
Mantle, Mickey, 120–124, 143
Mapes, Cliff, 111–112
March, David, 128
Markham, Edwin, 11
Martin, Hersh, 84
Martinez, California, 4
Mays, Willie, 123, 143–44
McCarthy, Joe, 23–26, 40–42, 45, 49–50, 52, 55, 65–66, 69, 89–90, 109, 118

McCormick, Mike, 81
McDermott, Mickey, 110
McDougald, Gil, 121–123
McQuinn, George, 96
Medwick, Joe, 39
Melson, Inez, 134
Metheny, Bud, 84
Miley, Jack, 37
Miller, Arthur, 135
Mize, Johnny, 113
Monroe, Marilyn: childhood of, 129; death of, 136–137; divorce from DiMaggio, 134; first marriage of, 129–130; introduction to DiMaggio, 127–128; marriage to DiMaggio of, 132–134; modeling career of, 130; movie career of, 130, 133–136
Morreale, Ben, 3
Most, Stanley, 82
Murphy, Edward T., 50
Musial, Stan, 143
Myers, Billy, 52

Nacchio, Joe, 132, 149
Ness, Jack, 14
Neun, Johnny, 93
Newcombe, Don, 112
Newhouser, Hal, 64
Newkirk, Floyd, 17
Newsom, Bobo, 96
Newsome, Dick, 68
New York City, 21
New York Yankees: attendance, 23, 34–35; home run hitting of, 64; as pennant winners, 30, 38, 42, 51–52, 72, 75, 81, 95–96, 112, 119, 123; scouting and purchase of DiMaggio, 17; in World Series, 30, 38, 42–43, 52–53, 73, 76, 81, 96–98, 112–113, 120, 123–124
Niarhos, Gus, 93
Norbert, Ted, 17
Nuxhall, Joe, 84

O'Doul, Lefty, 18, 25, 29
Owen, Mickey, 73

Page, Joe, 90–91, 96, 105, 108, 110, 113
Painter, Doc, 25
Parnell, Mel, 110, 112
Passeau, Claude, 69
Pearson, Monte, 30, 47
Peckinpaugh, Roger, 64
Pluto, Terry, 140
Povich, Shirley, 37
Powell, Jake, 29–30
Powers, Leslie, 17
Purcell, Ed, 61

Quinn, Johnny, 67

Raschi, Vic, 93, 105, 108, 112–113, 123
Reichler, Joe, 141
Reserve clause, 33–35, 40
Reynolds, Allie, 93, 96, 105, 110, 112,
    123
Rhodes, Orlando H., 134
Rickey, Branch, 86, 96, 104
Rizzuto, Phil, 65, 71, 89, 91, 98, 105–
    106, 108, 118–119
Roberts, Robin, 120
Robinson, Jackie, 86, 96–97
Roe, Preacher, 113
Rolfe, Red, 30
Rooney, Mickey, 128
Roosevelt, Franklin D., 19–20, 64, 79
Rose, Pete, 61
Rossi, John, 8
Ruark, Robert, 110
Ruditsky, Martin, 135
Ruffing, Red, 30, 35, 47, 56, 81
Ruppert, Jacob, 17, 31, 33–35, 39–41, 45
Ruth, Babe, 17, 21, 23–25, 30, 36, 38,
    40, 72, 104

St. Paul, 4–5
San Francisco: earthquake of 1906, 4; ef-

fects of Great Depression on, 11–12;
    North Beach section, 4–5
San Francisco Examiner, 16
San Francisco Mission, 9
San Francisco Seals, 9, 12
Scott, Frank, 95
Seeger, Pete, 80
Selig, Bud, 150
Selkirk, George, 30
Sexton, Anne, 136
Shea, Spec, 93, 96–97
Sheehy, Pete, 66
Shor, Toots, 27–28, 56, 73, 92, 103,
    108
Sicilians: character of, 3, 74; emigration
    of, 3–4; prejudice toward, 3–4
Sicily: conditions in, 3; history of, 1–3
Simon, Paul, 139
Sinatra, Frank, 135
Sisler, George, 61, 65, 67
Smith, Al, 70–71
Smith, Edgar, 62
Smith, Red, 99
Snodgrass, Fred, 63
Solotaire, George, 108
Spahn, Warren, 81
Speaker, Tris, 13, 24, 50
Spear, Sam, 146
Sporting News, 14
Stainback, Tuck, 84
Stalin, Joseph, 64, 68
Steinbrenner, George, 149
Stengel, Casey, 108–109, 111, 115, 117–
    118, 122
Stephens, Vern, 112
Stevens, Mal, 94–95
Stirnweiss, George Henry "Snuffy," 84
Strasberg, Lee, 136
Sturm, Johnny, 63
Suplizio, Sam, 49

Talbot, Gayle, 53
Talese, Gay, 141

Terry, Bill, 30, 51
Time Magazine, 31, 107
Topping, Dan, 89, 94
Travis, Cecil, 80–81
Trevelyan, Raleigh, 3
Tullius, John, 105

Venezia, Frank, 6

Walsh, Ed Jr., 14
Washington, Booker T., 1
Web, Del, 89
Weiss, George, 104, 107–108
Werber, Billy, 52
Wilder, Billy, 134

Wilhoit, Joe, 14, 69
Williams, Joe, 33, 41–43
Williams, Ted, 13, 52, 69, 72, 74–75,
    94, 98–99, 104, 112, 143, 145
Wilson, Jack, 68
Woodling, Gene, 108
World War II, 57, 64, 68, 75–76, 83–85
Wyatt, Whit, 98

Yankee Stadium: changes to, 90; dimen-
    sions of, 36
Yawkey, Tom, 94
York, Rudy, 63

Zernial, Gus, 128

About the Author

DAVID JONES is a writer and historian, and the author of numerous articles in official Major League Baseball publications. He is the editor of the forthcoming *Deadball Stars of the American League*, which is slated for publication in 2005. Jones lives in Scotia, New York and is currently pursuing his Masters degree in history at the University at Albany.